WHEN YOUR KIDS PUSH YOUR BUTTONS

"I loved this book! Finally, a parent expert that speaks to parents like a best friend."

—Karen B. Walant, Ph.D., psychotherapist
and author of *Creating the Capacity for Attachment*,
Advisory Board, attachment Parent International

"I wish Harris had written this book twenty years ago, when my child was little. It presents everyday situations with solutions that are laced with wisdom, humanity, and uncommon sense."

—Cherie Carter Scott, Ph.D.,
bestselling author of *If Life Is a Game, These Are the Rules*
and *The Gift of Motherhood*

"A valuable resource....In a highly readable format, Harris presents vignettes that illustrate the frustrations that all parents face and an approach that can help resolve these issues. I recommend this book for all parents, including pediatricians!"

—Elvin Kaplan, M.D., assistant professor of pediatrics,
Dartmouth Medical School

WHEN YOUR KIDS PUSH YOUR BUTTONS

and

What You Can Do About It

BONNIE HARRIS

WARNER BOOKS

NEW YORK   BOSTON

Text copyright © 2003 by Bonnie Harris
Illustrations copyright © 2003 by Marty Kelley
All rights reserved.

Warner Books

Time Warner Book Group, 1271 Avenue of the Americas, New York, NY 10020
Visit our Web site at www.twbookmark.com.

Printed in the United States of America
Originally published in hardcover by Warner Books

First Trade Printing: July 2004
10 9 8 7 6 5 4 3 2

The Library of Congress has cataloged the hardcover edition as follows:

Harris, Bonnie.
When your kids push your buttons : and what
you can do about it / Bonnie Harris.
p. cm.
ISBN 0-446-53015-8
1. Parent and child.   2. Parenting.   3. Children—Family relationships.
I. Title.
HQ755.8 .H365 2003
649'.1—dc21   2002031132

Book design by Fearn Cutler de Vicq
Cover design by FLAG
Cover photograph by Getty Images/Nicki Pardo

ISBN: 0-446-69285-9 (pbk.)

This book is dedicated to Casey and Molly,
without whom I never would have found my path.

ACKNOWLEDGMENTS

This book emerged from several years of teaching these concepts in a parent education course originally called "Defusing Your Buttons" through The Parent Guidance Center. All of the parents in these groups have guided me and helped me clarify the material with each of their struggles and triumphs. Some of their stories are included in the book. Many previous courses with many more parents led to the creation of the "Buttons" course. I could not have developed the course or written the book without the commitment and willingness of all of these parents. To each and every one of you who has ever taken a course with me, I am truly grateful. Your desire to learn has helped me learn. I honor your courage, your willingness, and your determination to be the best parents you can be. I only wish I could list you all.

One's whole life and experiences are cumulative players in a project like this. My gratitude must go way back. But for the sake of space, I will thank the more immediate players.

To Liz Broderick, Lee Burwell, Nancy Gorr and to every parent educator, staff member and board member of The Parent Guidance Center, I bless you for the dedication, wisdom, time, and guidance you have each given to The PGC, which has enabled me to be the teacher I needed to be instead of the administrator I never was meant to be.

To Mary MacDowell, I thank you for giving me the jump start I needed, the opportunity to know that I could indeed do this, and the faith that it was worth publishing—along with some good ideas that are included in the book.

I am filled with awe and gratitude at the incredible chain of events that so quickly led to the publication of this book. When I felt the need to get some professional help with my first draft, Polly Bannister led me to Susan Peery, who gave me editing guidance, strongly needed encouragement, and support, and a call in to Writer's House. There I found my miraculous agent, Al Zuckerman, via Fay Greenfield, his assistant extraordinaire. A mere few days after sending the proposal to publishers, my editor, Amy Einhorn, read it, saw her daughter in a new light, and convinced Warner Books that it worked. Throughout the editing process, as Amy helped me get clearer with the book, the book helped Amy get clearer with her daughter. Amy's guidance has been exactly what I needed. To all of you, I feel blessed by your attention and belief in me. Thank you for helping spread the message and for your conviction that yet another parenting book could make it.

To Frances Jalet-Miller, for your second pair of eyes, reassurance, and praise. Thanks for the reality check.

To Emi Battaglia and Chris Dao, for carrying the message on to greater heights.

To Cynthia West, Laura Scott, Pam Erdman, Jane LaRoche, Cleary Donovan, Kristin Miller, Amy Franzen, Chris Daisy, and Raye Lankeford for reading versions of the manuscript. Thank you for your time, support, and insightful suggestions.

To so many friends who have been supportive, helpful, and right there throughout the writing process including Annie Graves, Kin Schilling, and my wonderful women's group: Susan Knight, Polly Bannister, Chasey Usher, and Judy Orme. To Dennis Ferrill for helping me get the proposal off the ground. To Jan Miller for your guidance over the years, your good suggestions, and your love and support. To Sally "Bones" Jackson for refining and buffing my rough edges and lending her contacts. To Tricia Jalbert for believing in my work and connecting me with so many professionals in the field. To Irv Richardson for providing a critical piece of information. To Kraig Schwartz for giving me the right direction for the cartoons. And to Marty Kelley for making the cartoons a reality. And most especially to Libby Comeau and Jeri Robertson-Hanson for having faith in my voice and helping me to go as far as I can go.

To my wonderful children, Casey and Molly, I give you my undying love and gratitude for opening me up, teaching me the most valuable lessons of my life, and leading me in the direction I needed to go. Thank you for your encouragement, support, pride, and love. I admire you both so much.

But most of all, to my husband, Baxter Harris, who should strongly consider a career in editing. I give you my love and gratitude for bearing with me through each and every word, time after time. From the beginning, you have been my sounding board, my clarity gauge, my thesaurus, my diagram designer, and the gentle wielder of the ax. You helped me turn my concepts into understandable words. Thank you for your wholehearted belief in my work and for sustaining me with your love and support. I owe you one.

CONTENTS

The stories in this book are true stories from the parents in my parent education classes. With their permission, I share them with you. Their names and some of the circumstances have been changed to protect their privacy.

Your children are not your children.
They are the sons and daughters of Life's longing for itself.
They come through you but not from you,
And though they are with you yet they belong not to you.

You may give them your love but not your thoughts,
For they have their own thoughts.
You may house their bodies but not their souls,
For their souls dwell in the house of tomorrow, which you cannot
    visit, not even in your dreams.
You may strive to be like them, but seek not to make them like you.
For life goes not backward nor tarries with yesterday.

—KAHLIL GIBRAN, *The Prophet*

But then, Ellie threw the sweater I had made for her across the kitchen, aimed right at me. It landed in the garbage can on top of a freshly discarded, sticky pancake. In less than a second, I found myself wishing I could tear her arms off. I grabbed her by the arm and dragged her to the garbage can. "You'll wash that sweater yourself before you set foot out of this house, young lady," I shrieked an inch or two from her startled little face. Who was I, and—my god—what had happened to me?

—a normally well-balanced, loving mother
who has just had her button pushed

INTRODUCTION

No! You do it," yelled not-yet three-year-old Jacob when his mother told him to clean up the milk she was sure he had deliberately spilled on the floor. Louise could feel her temperature rising.

"You spilled it; you clean it up," she said with as much patience as she could muster.

"No, it's your job," Jacob jeered with that look that insinuated "so what are you going to do now?"

Louise felt a familiar rage rising up from her toes. She could not believe her little boy could taunt her like this. *What a brat he is,* she thought. *How dare he disobey me.* Everything in her background told her he should be punished. She automatically raised her hand, but caught herself. She saw Jacob flinch.

Separate the child from the problem. Don't blame the child, she remembered from her parenting class. She took a deep breath, then several more. *I'll try it,* she thought, convinced it would never work.

"Okay, the milk has spilled," she said as if she were reading from *Dick and Jane.* "You don't want to clean it up, and I don't want to clean it up. What should we do about it?"

Jacob's whole body brightened. "I know!" he said as if he had the answer to win the prize. "Let's call Sophie. She can lick it up, and I'll clean up the rest."

Louise was speechless. A stunned, "Okay," escaped from her mouth.

Jacob climbed down from his stool, ran to the door, and called the dog. Sophie was more than happy to oblige when Jacob showed her the puddle of milk on the floor. He grabbed the stool, climbed up to rip off a paper towel, and happily wiped up the slobber and milk that Sophie had left behind.

Louise is an average, middle-class mother, trying to get through breakfast, get her son to day care, and herself to work—on time, for once. Jacob pushed her button, and she almost lost control. But she didn't. Instead, she defused her button and was able to use a parenting skill that worked—not only for her but for her son, too.

"But shouldn't he be punished for talking to her that way? He can't get away with that!" is the reply of so many parents to this scene. Why? What would Jacob learn from being punished? Louise held him accountable for his spilled milk and gave him an opportunity to solve the problem. And he did, indeed, solve the problem—creatively and cheerfully. But somewhere deep down inside us, we want our children to suffer when they "make us" suffer. Retaliation comes automatically—it's what we know.

All parents get their buttons pushed by their children. Too many are provoked to react harmfully. Parents often hate the way they react but don't know how to stop themselves.

Our children push our buttons more skillfully than anyone else. They can bring out the worst in us and instantly turn us into the parents we swore we would never be. And the most infuriating part is that the angrier we get, the more our children push those buttons! "I don't mean to, but I open my mouth to tell my child to stop, and out come the words I swore I would never say!"

When Your Kids Push Your Buttons is about taking responsibility for your part in the conflict and then learning to neutralize your reactions so they stop interfering with your parenting. It puts a magnifying glass on your buttons. Authority is lost when you lose control in rage or withdrawal. Your child ultimately loses when he can push your buttons and watch the fireworks go off. Authority is regained when you can respond with clarity and neutrality, and your child regains a sense of security. This book can help you do that.

We punish our children in an attempt to keep them from pushing our buttons, often escalating the original problem into a cycle of anger and blame. *When Your Kids Push Your Buttons* is not about what to do to your kids to get them to stop pushing your buttons. This book is about how to be the parent you wish you could be—the parent that only you are holding yourself back from.

After teaching parenting classes for more than ten years, I realized that many parents returned to class more discouraged than ever. These parents were excited to try out their new skills, convinced they would work. But then something would interfere and they couldn't do it. It was because their buttons were getting pushed. **No skill can come to the rescue of a parent whose button has been pushed.** I realized a critical step was missing in parent education—how to get that button defused so the skills could work.

This book is the result of many more years of teaching a parenting course called "When Your Kids Push Your Buttons." As is the course, the book is meant to be interactive so that you can apply it to your own situations. The exercises are meant to help you do that.

It must be acknowledged that the expectations and values that parents hold for their children's behavior vary from culture to culture. The behavioral examples I use in this book may not fit all readers—they may not be your button-pushers. What I intend is for you to translate these examples into whatever behavioral difficulties may be creating the dramas that play out in your own parent/child relationship. The exercises will help you do that.

When Your Kids Push Your Buttons is based on four fundamental principles:

Principle #1. There is nothing more important in parenting than connecting with your child. When we are connected, we can pass on our values and influence their decisions.

Principle #2. Every child is born perfect no matter what its physical or neurological condition. Each one comes to us, whether by birth or

xxii   Introduction

adoption, for the benefit of our mutual learning and brings us an opportunity for our personal growth.

Principle #3. Children want to be successful. No child is happy being manipulative or out of control.

Principle #4. Children's behavior is symptomatic of their internal emotional, physical, or neurological state. To affect their behavior, their internal state must first be understood, then accepted, then addressed.

Button-pushing behavior is a clue to an unattended need in the child, and in the parent as well. Becoming conscious of those needs is the first and most important step. Without consciousness, we will continue to focus on preventing our children from pushing our buttons and hence tapping into a very uncomfortable place.

I often hear in my classes, "Why can't they just do what I want for once? Why do I always have to be the one to be considerate of their needs?"

Because it's our job.

It's our job to reach across to our children; step into their shoes; consider their developmental stage, their individual temperament, their level of normal egotism; and know what we can appropriately expect of them. Asking children of any age to be responsible for how we are feeling and to behave in a way that is convenient for us or will make us happy is wrong.

The good news about getting our buttons pushed by our vociferous children is that, in the pushing, they present us with an opportunity for personal growth and healing. The question is, will we use that opportunity? Or will we reprimand our children for being unruly and ourselves for being incompetent?

We can fool ourselves into believing that we are behaving in our children's best interest when we force them to do and be what we want. In doing so, we risk their needs for the sake of putting an end to our frustration, impatience, or rage. We work hard at training our children to be who we want them to be. Some children acquiesce and some don't.

The ones who don't are our teachers.

A Note about the Exercises

The exercises at the end of each chapter are intended to build on one another and tap different areas of your thinking and memory. Take the time to do them as you go. If you wait until you finish reading the book, go back and do them in order.

You may be surprised by the awareness they bring you. "I never thought of it that way before," "I didn't realize I did that," "Now I see the connection" are all comments from parents who have done them in my groups. You may want to make copies prior to filling them in so you can use them more than once. You can either concentrate on the same button-pushing behavior in order to look at different aspects of it or change the behavior with each exercise and look for patterns.

The complete-the-sentence exercises have an example with each to give you an idea of how they work. Use the examples as a guide only. There is no right and wrong way to do them. If some of my words don't quite work, change them. Each complete-the-sentence exercise is followed by a question format for you to write in paragraph form. I found in my classes that parents prefer one or the other, so I offer you both. Choose which works best for you or do them both.

Do them quickly. Don't analyze or think too hard. Make things up if your memory is fuzzy. What you make up is probably what is lying in your subconscious and, as irrational as it may seem, may be just what you need to make the connection. Allow yourself to be brutally honest. You are not alone in having monstrous thoughts about yourself or your child. This book would not exist if you were the only parent who ever felt the way you do.

PART ONE

SOMETHING OLD

CHAPTER ONE

THE ROAD RAGE OF PARENTING

If the doors of perception were cleansed,
everything would appear to man as infinite.
—WILLIAM BLAKE

Molly is my teacher. She is also my daughter. She is a delightful young woman of twenty. We have a mutually nurturing relationship. But it wasn't always this way.

When Molly started walking at eleven months, she began pushing my buttons. Compared to her easygoing older brother, her demands seemed unrealistic, her needs insatiable, her moods dark and unpredictable. She usually woke crying. Her face seemed to wear a permanent pout. Power struggles were daily occurrences for the first five years of our relationship.

And I was a parent educator! I had a master's degree in early childhood education. I designed and taught parent education classes to help parents understand their children's behavior and respond respectfully. But I wasn't doing a very good job myself.

When Molly was four she started a new preschool. Each morning she trudged into our bathroom after being dragged from her bed, her lower lip protruding as far as it would go, whining that she didn't want to go to school, that she hated school, and that I was mean to make her go. I thought she was an unreasonable slowpoke, bound and determined to ruin my day. I had fears that I had to find a new school, and that somehow this was all my fault. My daily reaction was various themes of angry impatience: "Stop whining and complaining. Hurry up. You'll be late. You've got to get dressed. Why can't you ever just be pleasant and put your clothes on? Why do we have to fight about this every morning?" You know the litany. By eight each morning, I felt like a resentful, nagging mother who should just go back to bed and start over. If only I could!

I clearly remember the morning when something switched in my head. I had been studying innate, individual temperaments of children and had begun teaching that in my classes. I knew that Molly, now age five, had a hard time with transitions in her life (moving from New York City to rural New Hampshire had already been a two-year struggle for her and wasn't over yet), but it had never occurred to me that merely waking, getting out of bed, and starting the day was a tough transition for her as well. Perhaps this was why she had always cried as a baby upon waking. School days only made it worse.

This particular morning, my learning and her struggle came together. My focus shifted from myself—my reactions, my fears, my inconvenience, my agenda—to her and her problem. Instead of thinking, "What's wrong with her? Why does she always have to do this to me? What have I done wrong?" My thinking changed to, "This is how she is. How can I help her?"

I sat down on the floor, invited her onto my lap, and said, "You really don't want to get dressed, do you?"

"No," she said.

"And you really don't want to go to school and leave me."

"No," she said, much more fervently.

"I don't blame you," I said soothingly. "You know what? I hate getting up in the morning too."

"You do?" She looked up at me incredulously. It had never occurred to her that anyone else suffered her plague. And it had never occurred to me to tell her.

"Yep," I continued. "My least favorite part of the day is when my alarm goes off, and I have to pull back the covers and put my feet on the floor."

Suddenly, we connected. She was glued. Our conversation continued as I acknowledged her frustrations and her point of view. She began to melt into my body as we sat cuddled on the hard floor in the bathroom. Shortly, we got dressed together, continuing to talk about our mutual dislike of early mornings, and started our day pleasantly.

So what happened? **I changed my perception of her behavior.** I became more detached from her pain and discomfort. I didn't take it so personally. From this new place, I was able to support and listen to her rather than my own inconvenience. I could then create all kinds of strategies to motivate her. I could set limits on her behavior without yelling and putting her down. In short, I had defused my button and could be the parent she needed.

Now I won't tell you that from then on life with Molly was a breeze and that she never pushed another button; but mornings were much easier, our power struggles ended, and our relationship took a turn that never reversed. Most importantly, she was no longer left in a world where she felt misunderstood and unaccepted.

If it weren't for my struggles with Molly, I would never have been able to understand the struggles of the parents I teach and counsel. Molly has provided me with many opportunities. I had the choice of learning to understand her or fighting her for the rest of my life. Our battles became opportunities for *my* personal growth. As I grew, I could not help but see her needs and parent her in a more connected way.

Our Children Get the Worst of Us

No one pushes our buttons like our children. No one knows our buttons as intimately as they do. No one can make us soar to our heights or bring us to our knees more quickly than they can. But when we are in a state of anger, hopelessness, or resentment, we are not effective parents. We can't or won't understand their feelings, see their point of view, or respond objectively. We want them to know how angry they are making us, so we revert to retaliation, yelling, and punishment, and we end up in power struggles.

Road Rage

We all know what it feels like to have our buttons pushed. Something physical happens: a particular energy takes over, and we "see red." Adrenaline rushes; muscles tighten; palms sweat; voices change register. Your face looks really ugly, and you turn into somebody no one wants to be around. It happens to the best of us.

"Road rage" is a good example. You're in a rush to get where you're going and some guy pulls in front of you with only inches to spare. In the privacy of your car, you feel at liberty to scream every expletive in the book, honk, flash your lights, and fantasize pushing a button to release four missile-like spears aimed directly at each of his tires.

In this state of mind, it would never occur to you that the other driver does not have a personal vendetta against you. He may have just received a call that his wife is in labor, his son was in a car accident, or he just drives recklessly. Regardless of the reason, the smart thing to do is slow down and back off. But no, when that button is pushed, you in fact speed up, get as close to him as possible, so that he will at least know how mad he has made you and that he can't get away with pushing you out of your rightful place in the line of traffic. You honk your horn, pass him in a no-passing zone, throw daggerlike looks his way as you pass, and endanger the lives of both of you.

The same thing happens when your own darling child does something that catapults you directly and instantly into your out-of-control zone. There's an excellent chance that your child's behavior has tapped into something deeper in you than mere annoyance. You react in ways that are irrational, horrifying, and all too familiar. You open your mouth intending to teach your child something and out comes your mother. You may even have learned all the "right" parenting skills and know just what you should be doing, yet you lose it anyway. Not only are you *not* the parent you want to be, but you *are* the parent you swore you would never become.

Button-Pushing Behavior

Many times our children cause us annoyance and anger, prompting us to curtail their behavior with limits and strong expectations of better behavior. Sometimes it pushes our buttons, and sometimes it doesn't.

If your child is hitting, she needs to stop. You may feel angry that she is hitting, but when you can control that anger without blaming your child for it, your button has not been pushed. It is when you cannot respond effectively, when you lose it and instantly react, that your button has been pushed. You become a big part of the problem, emotions escalate, and chances are you will not be able to stop the hitting.

Getting your button pushed results in many degrees of emotional reactions. Button-pushing behaviors can be relatively insignificant or quite serious. But to the parent whose button has been pushed, it is always serious—in that moment, anyway.

Whatever the behavior, it may be helpful to know where on the **Button Meter,** between mere annoyance and vindictive rage, you find yourself.

No matter what your reaction, when your button has been pushed you lose authority, break connection, and leave both you and your child feeling angry, defensive, frightened, and inadequate. Nothing productive can be taught no matter how hard you try. Attempts to control the situation only push your child farther from your intentions

ZONE 1   ZONE 2   ZONE 3   ZONE 4

SIMMER   BOIL   BOIL OVER   EXPLODE

BUTTON METER

or teach her to obey you out of fear—neither of which is a desirable outcome.

"How do I know if my button has been pushed?"

In many cases it is all too clear. But sometimes you may be too focused on your child's behavior to see the button. You know your button has been pushed when one or more of the following happens:

- An all-too-familiar emotion (rage, hopelessness) floods your body, and you react in a way you regret.
- Your spouse says, "Why do you always get so upset about that? Just let it go." Or, "She never does that with me." Or, "What's the big deal? He's just being a boy!"
- Visions of your grown child unable to accomplish anything, alone and friendless or behind bars, loom vividly.
- Rational behavior seems suddenly and completely out of reach.
- Your child reminds you of a relative you have judgments about.
- You know you could never have gotten away with what your child is saying or doing.
- You see fear on your child's face.
- You are at the end of your rope, swear you have tried everything, and nothing works.

Going on Automatic

When we snap at behaviors we don't like, say and do things we regret—get our buttons pushed—we go on automatic. Daniel Goleman, author of *Emotional Intelligence*, refers to **automatics** as "emotional hijacking." He describes one's normally rational mind being "swamped" by emotions.

In a raging argument over curfews, Howard and fifteen-year-old Adam shouted words at each other that shocked them both. The pinnacle was Howard's unintended banishment of his son when he proclaimed, "This is my house. You will obey my rules or you know where the door is!" Throwing his baseball glove on the table, the angry teen said, with a foreboding calm, "Fine," then slammed the door as he left. Howard intended to get his son to mind his curfew. He never intended to say what he did. His automatic spun the argument out of control. The result was the last thing in the world Howard wanted. And he didn't even know how it had happened.

Our automatics happen spontaneously and derail our best intentions. They are rarely effective, and never do they take into consideration the needs of our individual child. They are the angry reactions we

have when we wish we could calm down but can't even remember
what that feels like. They are the route for passing on harmful patterns
to the next generation.

Automatics Are Familiar

Automatics pop up uncontrollably from our subconscious mind
where we have sequestered old habits, beliefs, and emotions that we
don't like. Many of these habits and emotions construct our relationships and determine how strongly we protect and defend ourselves.

But many others lie dormant in our subconscious, the attic of our
mind, until we have children. When they push our buttons, our children unabashedly bang on that attic door for the first time. When the
door is opened, we feel pain. We react by either denying it with defensive behavior or blaming our children for causing the pain. The actual
problem that provoked the automatic is lost.

Automatics can take many different forms. But they are all in reaction to behavior that taps an old wound. They are often verbalized with
eerily familiar tones and phrases. A few examples:

Angry retribution: "You're grounded for the next two weeks!"
Threat: "You say that once more, and you'll wish you hadn't."
Criticism: "Why can't you ever just do what I tell you?"
Fear tactic: "Your teeth are going to rot, and then you'll be sorry."
Sarcasm: "Fine, you want to ruin your life? Far be it from me to
    stop you."
Guilt trip: "After all I've done for you, this is the thanks I get?"

Automatics Are Our Responsibility

Automatics are our attempt to control our child's behavior in order
for us to feel better and for them to react differently. In doing that, we
place responsibility on our child for turning the situation around. This
does not mean the child's behavior should be accepted. **It does mean
that in order to stop the reactive cycle from spinning, the parent
must be the first to stop reacting.** It never works to expect our child
to act like the grown-up first.

> If there is anything that we wish to change in our children, we should first examine it and see whether it is not something that could better be changed in ourselves.
>
> —Carl G. Jung,
> *The Development*
> *of Personality*

If we are reacting automatically and irrationally, we cannot expect our children to behave rationally and cooperatively. It is our choice whether we react to potentially escalating situations with tones and attitudes that either slow them down or speed them up. We cannot leave the job up to our children to set the tone of a situation and determine what direction it takes, no matter what age they are.

It is our choice to react automatically or respond consciously. Most of us were never taught how to make that distinction. But we can learn. We can let our children show us how.

What Now?

"Am I too late?" is a question I am asked from parents of two-year-olds through teens. The resistance children present to us—from their first "no" to the cold shoulder of adolescence—represents their growing drive toward independence. How we perceive their resistance and what we do about it is our responsibility, not our child's. It starts before age two and continues right through their separation from home and beyond. At any point, children will be thrilled with a parent who is willing to see that resistance through clearer eyes and take responsibility for their own emotions and reactions.

The younger the child, the sooner you are likely to see results with a new approach. But I have seen relationships with older teens turn around too. It may just take a little longer for a teenager to trust the change in your approach than a four-year-old. But it is never too late to connect with your child.

● EXERCISE 1: **Identifying Your Buttons**

How do you know when your button has been pushed?

List your child's behaviors that push your button.

What are your typical automatic reactions?

Where do your automatics tend to put you on the Button Meter?

Do different times of the day change your Button Meter? Is there a pattern?

What typically causes you to hit the boiling-over or explosion zone?

What are your reactions to your child when you are in each zone?

CHAPTER TWO

WHAT'S YOUR AGENDA?

There cannot be a crisis next week. My schedule is already full.
—Henry Kissinger

ey, wait a minute. This isn't about my child, is it? This is about me!" is an inevitable remark from a parent in one of my classes. It may appear that I am placing the blame for a child's behavior on the parent. Not at all. In fact, I am saying that the parent *is not* responsible for the child's behavior. The parent *is* responsible for her reaction to the behavior. It's what is going on in our own heads that is the culprit when our buttons get pushed.

The mother of a child who is hitting is not responsible for the hitting. She is responsible for how she reacts to the hitting, which in turn impacts her child's subsequent behavior. If she were to take responsibility for the hitting, she would not be effective in handling the situation, because she would be focused on feeling responsible. She might feel embarrassed in front of others, angry that her daughter made her look bad, and fearful that the child is becoming a bully—all of which are the mother's agenda and can interfere with helping her daughter stop. What time of day it is, what has just happened, what she has to do next, and how she is feeling will all play into how this mother handles the hitting. All this she *is* responsible for.

The Agenda Puzzle

We function every minute of every day with an agenda. Our agenda is made up of our thoughts and perceptions, the standards of behavior we hold, the beliefs we have about ourselves and others, as well as our circumstances and physical and emotional state. Our agenda determines how we are going to react to a situation in the present moment—how sensitive our buttons are.

YOUR AGENDA CONSISTS OF

Present circumstances—what's going on that is demanding my attention

Experiences—what I anticipate happening based on past experience. I know what this is leading to. If I say that, he'll have a tantrum.

Expectations—what do I/you have to do, what should I/you be doing, what do I/you wish had happened

Standards of behavior—the bar by which I set my expectations

Emotions—what I'm feeling about past, present, or future experiences

Assumptions, perceptions, fears

Hormonal balance/imbalance

Stress level

Attitude

Beliefs about self and others from past experience

Imagine your agenda as a puzzle. Each piece is a picture, even though incomplete by itself. Each piece is a part of the whole. The whole picture is a sum of its pieces. Some pieces give more clues to the whole picture than others. Some pieces give clues to other pieces.

What I need to buy at the grocery store, how little time I have to get there, my frustration with my son over not getting his coat on, the hopelessness I feel about the argument I had with my husband this morning, how resentful I am about missing dinner with my friends, what a mess my house is, my guilt over not having called my sick aunt for over a month and how awful my hair looks are only a fraction of the thoughts that occupy my mind at any given moment—and these only concern the present.

We want our children's behavior to change so that our agenda is not disrupted or inconvenienced. After all, what thoughts *we* have on our minds, what *we* have to do, what *we're* worried about is what matters.

If I have a report due at work tomorrow, my house is a disorganized mess, and my child is being defiant, my agenda is loaded. So if I am tired, have not started the report, have no time to clean, have an empty refrigerator, know how my husband feels about disorganization, and my four-year-old has left his toys all over the living room, guess who I will take it out on when he says, "I can't pick up my toys; I'm too tired"? In this state of mind—with this agenda—it is highly unlikely that I will be considerate of my son, handle the situation effectively, or understand *his* agenda.

Your Child's Agenda

Usually if we are conscious of our child's agenda at all, it is only in relation to how it affects us. Seldom do we spend the energy to step out of our own agenda to see what is going on with our child.

But children experience stress, fear, and exhaustion just like we do. They put expectations on themselves just like we do. They sometimes have difficulty trying to figure out how to make friends, how to be like their big brother, how to get their parents to accept them the way they are. But they don't have the words or the complex understanding of feelings to tell us what is going on. All they have is their behavior.

They worry and wonder about what we are going to say when they want something, when they explore new territory, when they make a mistake, when they become independent. Their well-being is critically dependent on our approval, but their desire to follow their impulses is often stronger.

Young children are affected by temperament, hunger, and tiredness; they often feel out of control, scared, and powerless when the big people in their lives tell them what to do. Older children desperately want their independence but are scared of the responsibility that it brings.

Children of any age have agendas.

Your child's agenda is as important to her as yours is to you.

When we acknowledge the importance of their agendas, we are parenting respectfully—our best bet at earning their respect in return. Even when their impulses are getting the best of them, we need to understand and accept them, if not their behavior. If a child's agenda has been acknowledged, even a two-year-old building a block tower will feel the respect and thus be more likely to cooperate with a parent who needs to get to work on time. "I know how much you want to finish your tower. You must feel mad when I say it's time to stop playing and get ready for day care. You can put two more blocks on and then set them up so they are ready to work on as soon as we get home." This is not a guarantee of happy cooperation, but the likelihood of getting out the door on time is far greater than when you think your agenda is the only one.

Thomas was alone for the weekend with Amanda, eight, and Jared, twelve, while his wife was away on business. Thomas wanted to do something that would be fun for all three of them, and so he decided to take them skiing. Early Saturday morning they left to spend the day on the slopes.

No sooner had they arrived, bought lift tickets, and got themselves on the chairlift when Amanda started whining and complaining—a familiar button for Thomas. "Every time we get out in public or off on an adventure, she starts her griping," Thomas complained to his "Buttons" class. "Nothing is ever good enough for her. 'Daddy, I don't want to go on that trail. It's too hard for me. You're making me do it, and I don't want to.' She was driving me nuts!"

Having seen Amanda zip down the trail with ease in the past, Thomas was puzzled, but more than that, he was angry. "Can we go to the lodge? I'm cold." "My boots hurt." "How come we always have to go on the trails Jared wants to go on?" Jared called her a baby and suggested that she just get lost. Amanda screamed.

Thomas was trying hard to contain his anger, but soon he blew. "Why can't you ever be happy with what we do? You always whine and complain, and you're ruining things for everybody else. Do you realize how lucky you are to get to spend a day skiing? What is the matter with you anyway? I have a good mind to take you home right now!"

Amanda started crying and yelled, "It's no fair. Jared always gets his way. You never do what I want."

Jared fueled the fire with, "That is so not true, and you know it. If anything, you always get your way 'cause you crab and moan so damn much. You're a pain in the butt."

Everything spun out of control, and Thomas' plans for a great time crumbled. Now he was furious at both kids and took them to the lodge for a break. After a change of atmosphere, warm toes, and a little food, Thomas was able to see the scene from a better perspective.

"While the kids were eating, I started thinking about the class when we were talking about agendas and realized how strong mine had been for this day," he said. "I knew I couldn't stand to be home alone with the two kids for the whole weekend. It had been weeks since I'd been skiing, and I thought I'd be giving them a treat. But my agenda was to go skiing and to make them think I was the best dad in the world for taking them. When Amanda complained, my buttons got pushed."

After this realization hit, Thomas said to the kids, "What do you think we need to do to make the rest of the day enjoyable?"

Jared said, "I want to ski the hard slopes without Amanda."

Amanda said, "I just want to be with you, Daddy."

Thomas suggested that they look into a private lesson for Jared, something he had promised a long time ago. Jared was thrilled. Amanda got to spend an hour alone with her dad and ended up choosing the trail she hadn't wanted initially. After the hour lesson, the three of them skied peacefully together for the rest of the day and went home happy and tired.

Thomas said to the class, "I realized on the way home how easy it would have been to avoid the first hour of anger and frustration, if only I had been more aware of everyone's agendas. If I had taken this into consideration on the first chairlift ride, or even asked before we left home what they wanted to do once we got to the mountain, I could have defused the situation before it escalated. I could have acknowledged Amanda's need to slow down and let Jared take a run or two on his own while Amanda and I took our time on an easy trail until she got her ski legs."

When Thomas was able to step back, he could see that Amanda's whining and complaining wasn't out of ingratitude or intent to make them all miserable. It was because she was feeling rushed and pressured. Her temperament demanded slower transition time. Thomas realized that he often forgets this. He expects her to respond quickly and easily the way Jared does. Two separate children. Two separate temperaments. Three separate agendas.

Our Past Is an Important Piece of the Puzzle

Aside from present-time agendas, what and who we have brought with us from our past are permanent aspects of the agenda puzzle affecting our emotional state and thus our reactions.

When your child exhibits a strong will and persistent nature by resisting your requests, you may hear your own mother's or father's voice calling out from the attic. "How dare you. Don't you ever talk back to me again, or you'll wish you hadn't" might be a familiar refrain that subconsciously loads your agenda, provoking you to explode with anger and dump the same words onto your child. It might have been just a look or the knowledge that your wishes were never considered. Naturally, it feels fundamentally wrong when your child does what you never could.

These patterns of behavior and parental expectations that we were brought up with form the undercurrent of our agendas. Anything present-day rests on top. Our buttons get pushed when that undercurrent is activated.

As we go farther, we will explore these fundamental aspects of our agendas that get in our way of effective parenting, causing our buttons to get pushed. Specifically we will focus on our perceptions and assumptions, the standards of behavior we hold for ourselves and our children, and the beliefs we continue to have about ourselves from our experiences as children. But first, we'll look at how our best intentions get lost in the gap.

● EXERCISE 2: **Agendas (example)**

Recently, when my agenda was to __*get to the supermarket before my older child was*__
(get somewhere or do something)

__*due home from school*__ , my child pushed my button by __*having a tantrum*__

__*when I was trying to get him to put his coat on*__ .

I reacted by __*getting really angry and yelling at him*__ , because I thought __*he*__

__*should realize that I had to do this and should be considerate of me for once*__ .
(what you expected your child to do)

My reaction may have had a lot to do with my agenda because, __*I was in a hurry be-*__

__*cause I had been on the phone and now I didn't have much time*__ .

Some other things that were loading my agenda might have been __*the fact that my*__

__*husband criticized the dinner I made the night before, saying we have the same*__

__*thing all the time. I wanted to tell him to make dinner from now on. Also I had*__

__*just found out that my cousin was diagnosed with cancer*__ .

When my child pushed my button the voices I heard my parent/s say was __*you will*__

__*put on that coat and get in the car now*__ .
(what you were told or not allowed to do)

My child's agenda at the time was to __*stay home because his favorite show was com-*__

__*ing on TV. And he hates going to the supermarket. The last time we were there*__

__*he had a tantrum and I got angry at him*__ .

If I had acknowledged my child's agenda, I could have said __*I know you don't want*__

__*to go. Let's tape your show and you can watch it as soon as we get home*__ .

● EXERCISE 2: Agendas

Please complete either or both of the exercises that follow.
A:

Recently, when my agenda was to _____
(get somewhere or do something)

_____ , my child pushed my button by _____

_____ .

I reacted by _____ , because I thought ____

_____ .
(what you expected your child to do)

My reaction may have had a lot to do with my agenda because _____

_____ .

Some other things that were loading my agenda might have been _____

_____

_____

_____ .

When my child pushed my button the voices I heard my parent/s say was _____

_____ .
(what you were told or not allowed to do)

My child's agenda at the time was to _____

_____

_____ .

If I had acknowledged my child's agenda, I could have said _____

_____ .

● EXERCISE 2: **Agendas (continued)**

B:

Describe a situation when you had a strong agenda and your child pushed your button.

What was your agenda? Describe all the different parts of it that made it loaded.

Describe your child's agenda. What was your child wanting, feeling, thinking to the best of your knowledge?

How did that impact on what you wanted/had to do?

How could you have acknowledged your child's agenda? Would it have made a difference?

CHAPTER THREE

WHY KIDS ARE PARENT-DEAF

*If you are not conscious of each part of yourself, you will
have the experience of wanting to say, or to intend, one thing,
and finding yourself saying or intending something else.*
—GARY ZUKAV, *The Seat of the Soul*

You're talking on the telephone to your mother. Your four-year-old interrupts. You intend to teach her proper behavior when you're on the phone. You say, "Don't interrupt. I'm on the phone. Now leave me alone and go play by yourself till I'm through." She begins to cry, demanding you even more. Nothing you try gets her to stop. If she does leave, she goes in the other room to bop her brother over the head to ensure your arrival. On the other end of the line, your mother tells you what she needs is a good spanking. You yell at your daughter to stop crying, stop hitting . . . just stop! She covers her ears and will not listen. You end up making excuses to your mother, hanging up the phone, and dragging your daughter off to her room, both of you locked in a power struggle.

What happened to your intentions? Not to mention your child's intentions? Neither of you planned on screaming at each other and feeling miserable. Your child's agenda may have been to make sure you were there for her, to avoid feeling alone and ignored. She doesn't like knowing that when the phone rings, you are instantly unavailable. She may feel scared or angry. She needs reassurance. Her agenda is loaded. Her intention is to get that reassurance.

Your initial agenda was to talk to your mother. Your intention was to

22

teach your daughter not to interrupt. You think her demands were just for attention and that she was being rude and manipulative. Your agenda got loaded, and your button got pushed. Your intention was lost altogether. It didn't make it easier hearing your mother's admonitions on the other end of the line.

Parent-Deafness

After all is said and done, you end up in a puddle of guilt, locked in a struggle between your mother's voice, your daughter's needs, and your best intentions. Your daughter feels unheard, blamed, and angry. You feel resentful and out of control, and while you know you should not be saying or doing what you said and did, you say and do it anyway.

Your child becomes parent-deaf when she does not want to hear what you have to say. Your intention has turned to anger and punishment, and your daughter has learned nothing about interrupting. Depending on her temperament, she will either fight harder to be heard or withdraw silently to stay out of trouble.

Our best intentions get lost in the gap.

The Gap

The gap is the space between the message the parent intends and the message the child receives. A *seemingly* clear statement of direction is often ignored, disputed, or rejected by a parent-deaf child when that message turns into something the child does not want to hear.

It works the other way as well. The child's button-pushing behavior is intended to send a message to the parent. It is a cue to the parent that something is wrong. But when the behavior pushes a button, the parent is unable to understand the intention, takes the behavior at face value, and reacts to it. The child's message to the parent gets lost in the gap as well.

We cannot expect our children to look for and understand the intention behind our reactions. But **it is our job to look beneath our**

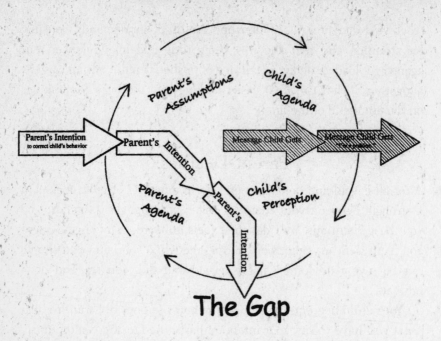

children's behavior for their intentions, rather than taking the behavior literally.

Our Best Intentions Can Plant Seeds of Hurt

While waiting for a bus, I witnessed an interesting, yet ordinary, occurrence between a mother and child. The mother was waiting for the bus with her toddler, who was sitting in a stroller in front of her facing out to the street. At the time I started paying attention, the little girl was getting fussy and frustrated, making whining sounds and straining her body to look behind at her mother, trying to get her attention. Her mother chose to ignore her. As if a veil had descended, she removed all expression from her face and focused on the direction from which the bus would eventually come. As soon as her attention disappeared, the child began to cry louder and strain harder in her seat belt. She grabbed one of her mother's fingers resting on the back of the stroller. The mother briefly glanced at her and, in what I thought would be a compassionate gesture, took the little girl's hand in hers, pressed it away as if it were distasteful, removed both of her hands, and put them in her lap out of her daughter's reach. Unmoved, she continued to watch for the bus.

I recall vividly a conversation I had with a friend of mine about why he always had a hard time loving or physically responding to his mother. He told me that he was convinced that she didn't love him. Since to me it seemed as though she had given him so much, I asked why he had that impression. He said, "All my life I have lived with a very clear memory of reaching my hand up to her and her pulling her hand away."

I find sadness in how ordinary these stories are. I don't know the circumstance of my friend's memory. Surely there was more contributing to his resentment. But I'm sure the mother at the bus stop was intending to teach her child that she couldn't get what she wanted by crying, whining, and banging on the stroller. She might have purposefully ignored her daughter assuming that she would learn to act more sociably in the future. Or perhaps her mind was on other things, and she just didn't want to be bothered. If the bus had not come when it did, I might have seen her child turn back in her seat, maybe cry for a while longer but eventually stop. To this mother, to many mothers, this would have seemed a small victory. She would have believed that her tactic had worked.

It is likely that my friend misunderstood the withdrawal of his mother's hand as a withdrawal of her love. The gesture may have had a similar intention to the bus-stop mother's—to stop the child from being disruptive. The message my friend received, however, was quite different.

What would have happened had the bus-stop mother chosen to comfort her child and pick her up? Would the child have learned that she could easily manipulate her mother into getting what she wanted? Would the mother have spoiled her by giving in to her demands? Would she be trapped from then on into always giving her child whatever she wanted? I don't think so, but it feels like a risk to many.

I think the child would have felt understood. In her preverbal stage of development, she would have gotten the message that her signals of distress to her mother had been heard and attended to. She would have had faith in her ability to communicate her needs, and she would have felt cared for and important—that her agenda mattered too. Is this bad for her developing social skills? How many of us have memories of, or more likely cannot remember, similar instances in the throes of which we too decided in our childish analysis that we were not loved or accepted?

In that moment, connection was broken for this little girl. The gap widened. There was no abuse—none that we would have labeled as such. But the subtlety of such a small gesture can be damaging when repeated again and again. It is highly unlikely that her mother's intention taught her that next time she should sit quietly in order to get the attention she desired. It is more likely that her mother's gesture led her to think that she was bad for wanting her mother and that her wishes were unimportant—at least in that moment. But moments add up.

Digging the Gap

With all best intentions we dig the gap ourselves. Our intentions filter through our agendas, get lost in the gap, and come out the other end to our child as a different message than we intended. Our child

doesn't like the message he hears and turns parent-deaf. We can turn it around by becoming conscious of all the steps creating the gap and send the message we intended in the first place.

"How many times do I have to tell you not to take food into the den? Pick up your plate and take it to the kitchen," Margaret says to sixteen-year-old Ethan. It is anyone's guess whether or not Ethan will comply. The answer lies in the message Ethan receives. If Margaret is relatively undisturbed by anything else in her life right now—has a rather calm agenda—and is just mildly annoyed by the fact that Ethan has food where he shouldn't, and if Ethan is feeling relaxed and holds no grudges against his mother at this time, chances are good that the food will be taken to the kitchen.

However, if Margaret has had a bad day at work following an early-morning argument with her husband, if she is feeling frustrated with Ethan over a recent rebuke, if this is the umpteenth time she has asked him not to take food into the den, if she had to work too late to make it to the grocery store—if her agenda is loaded—then her tone of voice and body language will add a great deal to her message. Her emotions will color her request as well. If she is feeling angry, used, and taken for granted, the same words will carry a different meaning across the gap to Ethan.

Ethan could feel guilty and a little chagrined that once again he forgot about having food in the den and take his plate to the kitchen without a fuss. Maybe even wash the dishes he left in the sink. But if Ethan is upset about something that happened in school, is sick of his mom nagging him, has just had a fight with his sister, who "never gets in trouble for anything," plus he's hungry and has a temperament that requires quiet after a day filled with noise and stimulation—if his agenda is loaded—we can be pretty sure he will become deaf to his mother's request.

A gap develops between these two people. Words and intentions get convoluted and warped, miscommunicated and misunderstood. A direction from Margaret might be heard as a request, a reprimand, or an attack by Ethan. How it is sent depends on Margaret's agenda. How it is heard depends on Ethan's agenda. Their agendas affect each of their perceptions and determine the width of the gap between them.

It's All in the Interpretation

Even though the intention is lost in the gap, the sender still expects the receiver to understand the original intention and respond cooperatively. In Ethan's case, if his mother tells him to keep his food in the kitchen, but it gets distorted by her agenda, Ethan might hear, "You're a slob; you never listen; you are incapable of doing anything worthwhile." Ethan will react to his *interpretation* rather than to his mother's *intention*. He will likely block what he does not want to hear, become parent-deaf, and continue to eat in the den. However, Margaret still expects Ethan to do as she has requested. She reacts further when he does not comply. The vicious cycle spins. The gap widens. Connection is impossible.

"Well, isn't it their job to listen to us? Who's in charge here, anyway?" is the lament of the frustrated parent of a parent-deaf child. Think about it. Are you motivated to listen to someone who you think is putting you down, blaming, or judging you? When little children cover their ears and walk away, when older children act as if they have not heard, when we complain that "They never listen," it's because they don't like what's being said. They are trying to uphold their integrity. No one wants to cooperate with a tyrant. **We do not have to change what we are asking—just the way in which we are asking it.**

Clearing Your Agenda and Narrowing the Gap

The more you are able to put aside your personal agenda for the moment of interaction—and thus be more objective, calm, and focused—the better you will be able to see your child's need and point of view. Clearing your agenda does not mean changing your plans, canceling your appointments, and letting your child have her way. **It means giving your undivided attention and making your child your priority in that moment.** Putting your agenda aside for the moment is possible when you are aware that you actually have one, are conscious and honest about what it includes, and are willing to take responsibility for it rather than denying it and blaming someone else for how it's affecting you.

When you can step into your child's shoes, you are more able to hear how your words are landing. Think what you would sound like if you were your child. Would you want to listen to you?

Margaret's agenda could include wanting the den to stay clean for a dinner party that night, insisting that Ethan obey her regardless of the request, or wanting to get him in the kitchen away from the TV. Ethan's agenda might be his desire to see a video he has been thinking about all day, feeling cocky over winning a battle with his sister, or feeding his hunger and vegging after a tough exam.

If Margaret is able to clear her agenda, at least for the moment, she will be better equipped to empathize with Ethan. Her message will be clear and nonjudgmental, and her expectation of his behavior will be more flexible, if she takes his agenda into consideration as well. In turn, Ethan will be able to hear his mother because he will not feel blamed, and parent-deafness will turn to parent-awareness. Connection can happen, and cooperation is much more likely.

If Margaret can genuinely say, "Ethan, I know you just got home and are probably hungry and tired," so that he does not expect a "but" on the end, her empathy narrows the gap. She can then make a clear request and set the limit she wants without laying guilt or blame. "The rule is no food in the den. You can either eat first, then watch the video, or vice versa." Ethan is more likely to hear the request as it is intended, rather than as a judgment or reprimand.

Still, Ethan might have a loaded agenda and answer with a, "Yeah, yeah, in a minute," with no intention of moving. Or a more combative, "Mom, lighten up. What's the big deal? It's a stupid rule." There is no guarantee he will respond cooperatively. But if he resists, Margaret can take her next step from her cleared agenda, consider where he is coming from, and set her limit neutrally. "Ethan, I have just cleaned for the dinner party tonight. I need your cooperation. Please bring your food into the kitchen now." If he says, "Mom, I'm zonked and starved. If I get food anywhere, I promise to clean it up," her willingness to negotiate does not mean she is backing down. She is being as respectful of him as she expects him to be of her. Cooperation is more likely. She then needs to make sure he keeps his word with a gentle reminder if he forgets. "Ethan, there are crumbs on the floor. Please clean them up before you leave."

Behavior Is Our Barometer: Recognizing Your Child's Agenda

It is often hard to uncover our children's intentions and understand their agendas, because their development inhibits their ability to tell us clearly what they mean. "Mom, I feel really put down when you yell

at me like that. I would like you to tell me what you want me to do and then give me a few minutes before expecting me to do it," is not something we are likely to hear from a four-year-old, a fourteen-year-old, or many adults for that matter.

Children tell us with their behavior what they need. It is our job to understand what that behavior is telling us. When we can't because our button has been pushed, the cause of the behavior disappears into the gap, and we misinterpret our child's intention, losing the opportunity to help.

Behavior is the clue to our child's well-being. If the behavior is normal and age-appropriate, we know our child is doing fine. When behavior is inappropriate or out of control, that is our clue that something is not right. **Behavior is always an accurate barometer of a child's internal emotional state.** When we react to the behavior at face value by punishing or reprimanding it, we are ignoring the deeper emotional state that caused the behavior. It's like pulling up weeds without getting the roots. The behavior will come back.

When behavior continues to get worse, that is the child's way of saying, "You're not attending to what I need, so I guess I have to scream louder or hit harder to get you to see me." We may be giving plenty of attention, but if it's not the right kind of attention and the cause of the behavior is still not addressed, the behavior will continue.

Children do not scream, punch, or call names because they like to. They do it to tell us something. The cues they send us, from their first cries before language to their defiant behavior as teenagers, should be interpreted as calls for help, not as manipulative devices to get us. How would it serve them? They need us to take charge, to care for them, to be there. Why on earth would they want to get us?

It is in their best interest to please us and cooperate. When they don't, it means they can't, and they need our help to get back on track. When we react, we are not listening. But when we acknowledge that their agendas might be loaded and take the time to find out what is going on emotionally, we can help them not only understand themselves but know that we understand them. When they feel accepted—emotions, agendas, and all—behavior normalizes.

When your button is pushed by your child's behavior, think about his intention beneath the behavior. See if you can get past the *He's doing that just to get me* perception to *What does the behavior mean, and how can I help him?* Consider that your child has a problem instead of making him the problem.

The Opportunity for Connection

If Ethan comes home with a loaded agenda—his girlfriend just broke up with him, he got a D on a paper, or he was not chosen for the basketball team—Margaret could say quite neutrally, "Ethan, the rule is no food in the den. Eat in the kitchen or wait to eat later, please," and Ethan might still blow. "Get off my back, will you! What's up with some stupid food in the stupid den? Leave me alone." Margaret then has a choice. She can either react to his behavior with anger and punishment for his disrespectful attitude, or she can try to respond to the emotions *beneath* his behavior with understanding and support and consider what his agenda might be.

This is the point at which most well-intended parents would call for a punishment or a consequence. Margaret has clearly requested the rule to be followed. Ethan has reacted rudely. Margaret's response, "I will not be spoken to like that. Either change the tone of your voice and eat in the kitchen, or I will not allow television after school for the rest of the week. You decide," would be a perfectly appropriate consequence for the situation. If Margaret is able to remain calm, chances are that Ethan will audibly grumble, loudly drop his plate on the kitchen table, and probably leave it there when he is done—but the rule would be followed.

Another option for a clear-minded parent is to acknowledge a window of opportunity and go for connection. Margaret would ignore his words and, for the moment, ignore the rule. She might say, "Ethan, this doesn't sound like you. Is something going on? I'd like to hear about it." He might open up and share what is on his mind. Or he might say, "It's nothing," but his words will less likely be accompanied by a rude tone of voice. Whether or not Ethan wants to talk to his mother, he will hear the compassion in her voice. She will be far more likely to eventually hear about the girlfriend or the D if she is sensitive to his agenda instead of thinking only of her own and doling out a consequence.

Consistency

All parents know they are supposed to be consistent. But most parents misunderstand what that means and judge themselves harshly when they think they are being inconsistent. Rather than look to the need of their child, they will stand on principle if a rule has been made or a "no" has been said, thinking they are being consistent.

Children need to have a sense of predictability from a parent in order for them to behave in a way that can be expected. If one day Margaret doesn't pay any attention to food in the den, because she is self-absorbed or too fragile to deal with Ethan's complaining and possible confrontation, and yet another day is furious about something that happened at work and takes it out on Ethan by reacting with rage at his defiance of house rules, he will feel like he is walking on eggshells. He will not know what to expect of his mother and thus will have a hard time learning what is expected of him.

Margaret either needs to be in a calm place herself or have the ability to clear her agenda by temporarily putting aside her own "stuff" in order to be consistent from day to day. Her ability to communicate effectively no matter how loaded her agenda is at the moment is the consistency that she needs for Ethan to be able to hear and act on her intention.

Consistency does not mean responding the same way to every misbehavior and never being flexible with a rule or changing a "no" to a "yes." Consistency means that your expectations—ones that are conscious, realistic, and appropriate for each child as well as oneself— remain the same whether you are stressed or calm. **Consistency means coming from the same reference point, an inner set of principles about parenting, regardless of what your agenda is at the moment.** This takes time, knowledge, and practice. It requires the strength of one's convictions to handle problem after problem as they continue to arise and to remain strong, yet flexible.

● EXERCISE 3: My Best Intentions

When I tell my child to ___*clean his room*_____ ,
<small>(what you want child to do or learn)</small>

    I am intending to ___*teach him to be neat and orderly*_____ .

    But I think what my child hears is ___*a nagging, crabby chain of commands*___ .

When s/he hears that, s/he reacts by ___*not doing what I want him to do and yelling,*___

*"you're not the boss of me!"*_____ .

And then I tend to ___*yell back and send him to his room*_____ .

I have focused only on my agenda and created a gap between us by ___*telling him only*___

*what I want him to do and not acknowledging his agenda too*_____ .

In order to get my message across effectively, I need to change how I send the message

    by ___*setting up a time with him that he agrees to*_____

    instead of ___*blaming him with my tone for never listening*_____ .

    When I can do that, my child will hear ___*that I can be reasonable and help him*___

*make a plan*_____

    instead of ___*criticizing and judging what he is doing wrong*_____ ,

    so s/he will feel ___*listened to*_____

instead of ___*blamed*_____

_____

_____

_____ .

● EXERCISE 3: My Best Intentions

Please complete either or both of the exercises that follow.
A.

When I tell my child to _____ ,

    I am intending to _____ .
                          (what you want child to do or learn)
    But I think what my child hears is _____

    _____ .

When s/he hears that, s/he reacts by _____

_____ .

And then I tend to _____ .

I have focused only on my agenda and created a gap between us by _____

_____ .

In order to get my message across effectively, I need to change how I send the message

    by   _____

    instead of _____ .

    When I can do that, my child will hear _____

    instead of _____ ,

    so s/he will feel _____

    instead of _____

    _____

    _____ .

● EXERCISE 3: **My Best Intentions (continued)**

B.

When you get resistance from your child, what was your intention and what was the message you think your child received?

What was your agenda, and what was your child's at the time?

Write down how you could have restated what you said, considering your child's agenda, so the message would be received as you intended it.

If you had said that, how do you think your child would have responded?

CHAPTER FOUR

WHY DO I KEEP DOING THAT?

Nothing is either good or bad, but thinking makes it so.
—WILLIAM SHAKESPEARE

Here we go again," Joan thought when five-year-old Karen stuck out her lower lip as she seated herself at the counter and peered at the plate of food her mother had prepared.

"Yuck, this makes me gag-choke," declared Karen.

Joan could feel her stomach tighten. She knew what was coming. Mealtimes had always been a battleground for Joan and her daughter.

"Ick, that's touching that. I can't eat that! I hate this stuff. I want macaroni and cheese." Joan imagined Karen's body soon looking as thin as that macaroni.

"You can too eat it. It all comes together in your stomach anyway. It won't kill you to try it at least. You can't live on macaroni and cheese." Joan's palms were getting moist.

"I can too. I don't have to eat it if I don't want to, and you can't make me." Karen pouted as she crossed her body with her little arms and pushed her feet against the counter. Her lower lip protruded another inch.

Joan wanted in the worst way to smack that lip. Instead, she roared, "Don't you speak to me that way, young lady. Who do you think I am, anyway? I'm not your short-order cook. You will eat what is put in front of you, and you will like it!"

Karen jumped down from the stool and ran up the stairs to her room, slamming the door behind her and yelling, "Make me!"

Joan slumped in the chair. She feared these battles would never end and her daughter would grow up hating her—if she didn't die of malnutrition first. She felt spent, angry, guilty, and rejected. She sat with her head in her hands. She knew she had blown it once again. But what could she do? She had to get her daughter to eat. What is a mother's job anyway if not first and foremost to make sure her children are fed properly?

Joan's husband infuriates her. He keeps saying, "What's the big deal? She's growing, isn't she?" Joan has stopped telling him about her mealtime struggles. Joan's stomach tightens when she hears Karen's teacher say, "It's not an issue here; she eats fine." The doctor has said that Karen's weight is low but definitely on the chart.

When Joan brought this story to class, she was at her wit's end. "What have I done wrong?" she pleaded. "Why won't she eat? She won't listen to me. She makes wisecracks about her food and about me. I've had enough. I won't stand for it! If I had ever talked to my mother the way she talks to me . . . !" Joan stopped herself and shook her head.

"What are you most afraid of?" I asked her.

"That she's going to die, and it's going to be my fault," she muttered quietly. Joan's automatic reactions fluctuate between fearful indictments, sarcastic remarks, guilt trips, and angry retributions:

"You're going to die if you don't eat."

"Okay, fine. Starve to death, see if I care."

"Why do you always do this to me? You don't appreciate anything."

"There will be no dessert for you! Get to your room."

After Joan wrote down some of the things she has heard herself say to Karen, she realized what her daughter was fighting against. "She must hate me. I hate it when I say these things. But I can't help it. She makes me so mad that I just react. What does she expect? If only I didn't get so mad."

The Emotional Chain Reaction:
When Sparks Fly

We often think that if we could change the way we feel, we could change the way we react. Try as we may, our emotions just happen. We can tell ourselves we shouldn't feel what we feel, but then we just feel guilty. We often cannot control our emotions, even though at times, it seems as if they control us. Joan wishes she wouldn't get so enraged. She knows if she didn't, she wouldn't react the way she does. But her rage comes automatically.

If we don't like how we feel, we blame the other person. With road rage, we say, "If it weren't for that jerk's insane driving, I wouldn't be so stressed out." At home, we blame our children:

Look what you made me do!
You make me so mad!
If it weren't for you . . . !

Joan feels justified in blaming Karen and dispensing punishment and criticism, because she thinks Karen's behavior is responsible for making her so mad. Therefore, Joan releases herself from any responsibility in the battle.

But if Karen's behavior is the reason for Joan's reaction, why doesn't Karen's behavior affect her father in a similar way? If the careless driver is the cause of your screaming, why are other drivers he is recklessly skirting slowing down and remaining calm?

There are other issues to consider than the child's behavior alone.

The Step We Always Forget

It is our **assumptions** about our children that push our buttons and make us nuts. It is what we *think* about what our child is saying or doing, who we *fear* our child is and will become. It is what we *perceive* about what we are doing or not doing about it. We generate the whole thing! Our assumptions flood us in that distraught moment and convince us of "the truth." It is the power of these **assumptions** that generate our **emotions** and then our **reactions**.

The assumptions that pop into our minds so instantly that we are not even aware of their role in the conflict are individual, subjective, and grandiose. They stem from many sources: what we learned about ourselves, our parents, and our siblings growing up; what society has taught us; the expectations we have of ourselves and others; and the standards and beliefs we hold. (We will go into this in more detail in future chapters.)

Karen's behavior of refusing to eat what her mother has prepared instantly triggers Joan's **assumptions**: *Karen is undermining my authority* ("Don't you speak to me that way, young lady"), *She could die of malnutrition* ("You can't live on macaroni and cheese"), *It is my responsibility to make Karen eat* ("You will eat what's put in front of you"), and *I have failed as a mother* ("I must be doing something wrong"). These **assumptions** stimulate Joan's **emotions** of incompetence, powerlessness, fear, and anger, which in turn elicit her **reactions** of criticism, sarcastic remarks, and punishment.

"Why don't you think your husband has an issue with the way Karen eats?" I asked.

"I don't know," Joan said. "He thinks Karen's eating is just fine. He says she doesn't eat a lot with him, but they never fight about it. He thinks it's all me. He's probably right. But it makes me so mad. It's like he sees a different child than I do."

"I don't think he sees a different child," I said. "But I do think he has different **assumptions** about her than you do. Whether or not they're right or wrong, they are his, and they generate different **emotions** and **reactions** from him."

The Chain Reaction Model

There is a chain reaction that happens each time we are part of an event. Between the **event** and our **reaction** to the event, there are two important steps—our **assumptions** or perceptions of the event and the **emotions** those assumptions provoke—before we actually react.

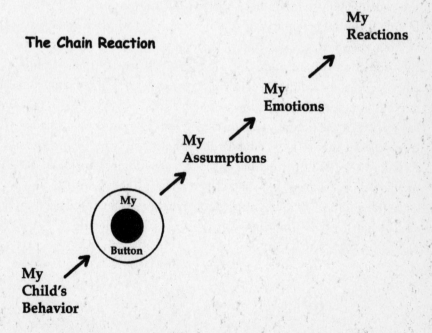

Your child's **behavior** pushes your button. Your button instantly ignites your **assumptions**, which provoke your **emotions**. When emotions are volatile, **reactions** spiral out of control.

A FEW CLASSIC ASSUMPTIONS

She's ruining my life.

He's doing this just to get me.

She's sucking the life out of me.

He's running the family.

I don't have enough to give her.

He can't be trusted.

She thinks the whole world should stop for her.

What will other people think?

I never know what to do.

You're embarrassing me.

You always fight everything I say.

He should know better.

I'm a failure at parenting.

She's doing that on purpose.

If I give him an inch, he'll take a mile.

For instance, you and a friend are walking down the street. Several teenage boys are walking together coming toward you. They are dressed in punk-style clothes, and two of them are carrying skateboards. They are laughing loudly, and a few swear words are audible.

Your friend says, "Oh, God. I hate these kinds of kids. Listen to their mouths! They're nothing but trouble. Where are their parents, anyway? Skateboarding is illegal in town, you know. Let's cross the street. You never know what they're going to do."

You say, "Hey, they're just kids having fun. They're not causing any trouble. And they're not skateboarding; they're carrying their boards. Kids have to be different from the older generation, you know. Remember us?!" You pass them and offer a cheerful, "Hi, kids!"

Same event, same kids, two different reactions. The difference is in the thoughts and **assumptions** you each have about them.

CHAIN REACTION EXAMPLES

Child's Behavior	Parent's Assumptions	Parent's Emotions	Parent's Reactions
Arguing/Power Struggle	• If he gets his way, he wins; then I lose and have no control. • The little brat, she's going to be a monster when she's fourteen. • I can't do this.	• fear of losing control • anger/worry • powerless	• yelling, negating child's voice • ignoring/isolating • giving in/up
Hitting/Pushing	• She is mean and inconsiderate. • He's too young to know any better. I'll fix it for him. • He's going to be in jail by the age of fifteen.	• embarrassment • sympathy/guilt • fear	• criticism, belittling • fix it • hitting back to teach a lesson
Demanding/Persistent	• He can't talk to me like that. I never talked to my parents that way. • She's sucking me dry. • I'm not enough to meet his needs.	• rage • exhaustion • guilt	• banishment, yelling, hitting • giving over power • inconsistent with limits
Poor grades	• He'll never amount to anything. • I've screwed up once again. • She's not as smart as her sister.	• fear • guilt • disappointment	• nagging, yelling • grounding • labeling, comparing

The Self-Fulfilling Prophecy

Changing our assumptions is not always easy to do, especially when we have a stake in their truth. It is possible for us to create the experiences we least want. For example, a mother who is so afraid her son can't take care of himself hovers, protects, and rescues until he flunks out of school. Her fears cause her reactive overprotection, leaving her son believing in his own incompetence. He ends up not being able to take care of himself—a self-fulfilling prophecy.

Karen most likely feels the blame and fear coming from her mother, and even though she fights against that blame with her angry remarks, she is developing an unhealthy belief about herself. She is learning from her mother that she is a poor eater, ungrateful of her mother's attention and someone to be disapproved of and worried about. The self-fulfilling prophecy in this case is that Joan's worry, anger, and blame lead to what she is attempting to prevent with that worry, anger, and blame—a daughter who is refusing to eat.

Albert Ellis, one of the founders of cognitive therapy, explains how we take in only the evidence that confirms our assumptions and beliefs, denying any evidence to the contrary. For example, a young girl who is convinced she is fat, even though her friends and parents tell her otherwise, sees only what she wants to see in her mirror. Her belief about herself is stronger than anything else—even her mirror. Ellis calls this confirmation bias.

We all develop personal and subjective assumptions about any given issue or event. Most of us, especially in our parenting role, believe our point of view to be the correct one and confer only with others who agree with us. We hear what we want to hear, even when that point of view may be harmful.

When I asked her about what other people had to say about Karen's eating, Joan was clear. "I don't care what my husband says. Karen is being highly disrespectful toward me. What does he know, anyway? He hardly ever spends much time with her."

"What about her teacher?" another member of the group asked.

"Oh, Karen probably just wants to do what the other kids are doing. And what does her teacher care, anyway? Karen's not her child."

Fears Can Spin out of Control

The ideas and perceptions we have of our children's behavior can instantly escalate to the realm of fantasy and horror—catastrophizing, as Ellis calls it.

The nature of being a parent means that we have much at stake in our children's futures. Our parenting is always on the line. It's easy to catastrophize. If our child gets a D on his report card, we take a D in parenting. To get ourselves a better grade, we keep harping on him to change. And in all likelihood, we feel justified in blaming him in whatever way we see fit if he doesn't bring his grade up.

If Joan assumes that Karen is trying to manipulate her, undermine her authority, and ignore whatever she says, Joan has catastrophized her initial thoughts, which, in turn, cause her to come down harder on Karen about her eating.

In the heat of the moment, we rarely question our fears. We may not say them out loud to our child, but we think them, and our **thoughts** feed our **feelings** and then our **reactions.**

Assumptions quickly become catastrophized fears:

- *He is being so mean* can instantly lead to *He's going to end up in jail one day.*
- *She'll get fat if I let her eat whatever she wants* quickly escalates to *She'll be obese, and have health issues all her life.*
- *He's lazy and doesn't care a thing about his grades* translates to *He's going to spend the rest of his life asking, "Can you spare any change?"*
- *She's can't wear that to school* projects to *Everyone will think she's a tramp.*

"I have a friend whose daughter is anorexic. I can just see it happening to Karen," Joan told the class. "I'm so afraid she's just going to keep eating less and less until she wastes away to nothing."

Events and emotions are usually out of our control. But our **reactions** are in our control. To change our reactions, we need a different emotional state. But to change our **emotions**, we need to change our **assumptions**.

The Problem

One of two things, if not both, may be going on with Karen:

1. Her mother's expectations of her problem eating lead Karen to believe that she is a problem eater. Each time her mother criticizes how or what she is eating, she is strengthening Karen's poor self-image. Karen's behavior follows her self-image.

2. Karen refuses to eat in order to gain power in their relationship. She may not feel she has enough personal power in her life—something all children require to gain self-esteem. She sees her mother getting upset and even losing control when she doesn't eat. The more she resists eating, the more upset her mother becomes, and the more power Karen gains.

The Solution

In either case, if Joan does not get upset about Karen's eating habits and stops trying to control the situation, the problem can be solved:

1. Karen will understand that her mother no longer believes her to be a poor eater. She will then fulfill the new expectation that she thinks her mother holds of her—that her eating is not a problem. She will then be able to eat in the way that is right for her, as she is able to do at school.

2. If her mother does not get upset about her eating, Karen gains nothing by refusing to eat. The power she needs will come when she is given a choice and responsibility for her eating.

Getting There

The first steps in changing your **assumptions** are to (1) identify what they are, (2) check their accuracy, and (3) make them accurate.

Think about what your assumptions are and write them down. Once you actually write them, it is likely that you will see that many of them are unrealistic or inappropriate for your child or yourself, and you can change them.

He's a monster might change to *He's very difficult to handle when he doesn't get his way.*

I'm a failure as a parent. I never should have had kids can become *I need help with handling this. I can't do it all.*

Are you reminded of someone else you have judgments about? How realistic and helpful is it to compare your child to someone you may be afraid she is turning into?

She's just like my sister could change to *She reminds me of my sister when she does that, but she is not my sister.*

These new more accurate statements will immediately reduce your emotional reaction to your child's behavior. Perhaps all you can do is adjust your assumption:

He never listens to me might only be able to change to *He almost never listens to me.* It will then be important to put more focus on the few times he does.

If you cannot change your assumption at all—if it seems completely realistic—it is important to get a second opinion from your spouse and/or a trusted friend. Ask them first to be understanding of your point of view so that they can be helpful and not push your buttons farther. Share your innermost thoughts and fears about your child or yourself and ask for their opinion on the accuracy of these thoughts. Be willing to open your mind to a new way of looking at the situation. If you find that they share your thoughts, it may be helpful to get a professional opinion.

"Can you see how you spin your emotions out of control with your assumptions?" I asked Joan after we had been working on the chain reaction model.

"Yes, I'm beginning to see where you're coming from. I definitely do that." After doing an accuracy check, Joan saw that Karen's behavior did not mean that Joan was failing in her nurturing role. She confidently related times when Karen was upset and came to her for comfort, understanding, and support. Joan also observed many instances in which Karen clearly respected her authority. They did not have any of the bedtime and school issues that many of her friends were experiencing. Joan admitted that the possibility of Karen dying of malnutrition was remote. Just the week before they had had to buy new clothes because Karen was growing so fast.

Most importantly, Joan slowly became aware that her expectation of Karen not eating played a big role. They both approached mealtime with a good deal of tension, bringing attitudes to the table along with the food. Joan was beginning to see that the problem was much different than she had originally thought.

Affirmative Self-Talk

Just as we can catastrophize with negative self-talk, we can change our emotions with affirmative self-talk. To change the talk, we need to consciously change the programming in our subconscious. We can literally talk ourselves into thinking differently.

Affirmative self-talk is mindful and intentional inner talk designed to keep our **assumptions** conscious and accurate and thus our **emotions** from getting out of control. It is a mental running commentary. Your subconscious won't buy it if you can't believe it, so make it realistic, not just what you wish for. You are simply bringing your catastrophizing fears into realistic proportion.

As a check on herself to keep her fears and emotions from spinning out of control, Joan can use the more accurate assumptions and realizations she identified to create a self-talk in times of need:

"Okay, Joan, here you go again. You've got her dead or at best rude and rejecting. Granted she eats like a bird, but she is growing. She's not sick, and she does listen around other issues. Just calm down and breathe."

This may not dramatically alter her relationship with Karen around eating, but it could very well help the tone of mealtimes.

Taking Responsibility

Before any of this is possible, we must first be willing to take responsibility for our part in the situation. It is important to recognize that our perceptions of any given situation are just that—ours—and, at the same time, to acknowledge that others hold different, yet equally valid perceptions. We don't have to agree with them. Our truth is not necessarily *the* truth—if there even is one. Understanding this is the key to healthy relationships.

When Joan saw that her thoughts and fears were not the truth but only her assumptions, she began to take responsibility for her part in the eating dilemma. She could begin to see that Karen had her own agenda that wasn't necessarily focused on dethroning her mother. When Joan realized she had permission to feel the way she did, and that it was her assumptions that were responsible for her emotions, she had something tangible to focus on. Her new self-talk—*she's a picky eater, but she's healthy and energetic; she will eat when she's hungry; she doesn't have to eat what I want her to eat*—led to new and different emotions. Another layer was being uncovered.

Sometimes It's Not Enough

It may be that all Joan needs to defuse her button—to change her automatics—is new information. If she knows more about Karen's temperament and can step into her daughter's shoes to see her point of view and to acknowledge her agenda, Joan will better understand Karen's reason for not eating and can address her needs. Members of Joan's parenting group can share what they have done in similar situations. She can learn new communication skills, change her assumptions to more appropriate ones, and thus prompt different emotions.

But the bottom line beneath Joan's anger and blame is her **assumption** *I must have failed in order to have raised a child like this. I'm an incompetent mother.* She was beginning to get a handle on her assumptions about Karen, but the ones about herself were another story. Her self-blame still sends her over the edge, and her buttons still get pushed. She will need to dig deeper to find out what is fueling these assumptions and fears.

● Identify Behaviors, Feelings, and Assumptions

Identify Your Child's Button-Pushing Behaviors

Let's look at your own buttons. List persistent behaviors (minor or major) of your children that push your buttons. Write down a phrase or two that describes the behavior, such as:

> "She never picks up her toys."
> "My son talks to me with an attitude that implies *You're a stupid jerk.*"
> "She's always demanding to be picked up. But when I give her an inch, she takes a mile."

The events/behaviors that push my button are

_____

_____

_____

_____

Next Identify Your Emotions

Name the feelings these behaviors stimulate, such as:

> "When she refuses to clean up, I feel taken for granted."
> "When he gets that attitude, I feel enraged."
> "When she demands my attention, I feel resentful but also guilty that I'm not with her enough."

When my child does this, I feel

_____

_____

_____.

_____

_____

_____

Now Go Back and Identify Your Assumptions

Name the thoughts/judgments/opinions/perceptions/fears/assumptions that you have about the behaviors or yourself that created your emotion, such as:

> "She's a spoiled brat, and I have made her that way."
> "He never thinks of anyone but himself. He's going to be a bum, nobody's ever going to like him."
> "I'll never get anything done, there'll be nothing left of me, I never get anything I want."

My automatic assumptions about my child/my child's behavior are

_____

_____

_____

_____

_____

_____

_____

_____

● EXERCISE 4: Assumptions Cause Emotions (example)

When my child *acts stubborn and persistent about everything he wants* ,
(button-pushing behavior)

I feel *angry and scared* ,

and I often react by *punishing him—sending him to his room—yelling at him*

to leave me alone .

My assumptions about my child when I see this behavior are that *he will never take*

no for an answer, he will never listen, and nobody will ever like him .
(even the horrible thoughts you would never tell anybody!)

My assumptions about myself are that *I will never have control over him and I will*

never get a moment's peace. I don't have a clue how to handle him .

I can change my assumptions to be more accurate when I say to myself that my child

doesn't like to be told "no" but he does listen when I say something he

likes , and that I *can learn how to handle him better and can acknowledge*

his agenda more often. I will get time to myself when he is older and when I take

it .

These new assumptions help me feel *calmer and a little more confident* .

If I feel this way more often, *I will stop screaming so much*

_____

_____

_____

_____

● EXERCISE 4: **Assumptions Cause Emotions**

Please complete either or both of the exercises that follow.
A.

When my child _____,
(button-pushing behavior)

    I feel _____,

    and I often react by _____.

My assumptions about my child when I see this behavior are that _____

_____.
(even the horrible thoughts you would never tell anybody!)

My assumptions about myself are that _____

_____.

I can change my assumptions to be more accurate when I say to myself that my child

_____,

    and that I _____

_____

_____.

These new assumptions help me feel _____.

If I feel this way more often, _____

_____

_____

_____

_____.

● EXERCISE 4: Assumptions Cause Emotions (continued)

B.

Describe the behaviors of your child when s/he pushes your button. What assumptions, as awful as they get, pop into your mind in the instant your button is pushed—both about your child and about yourself?

How do those assumptions translate to fears—to catastrophizing?

Check their accuracy and rewrite them.

Are these more realistic? Why?

How will thinking differently change your emotions and reactions?

How do you expect your child would respond?

CHAPTER 5

HIGH HOPES: THE STANDARDS WE LIVE BY

I hated the way I turned out, so everything my mother did with me I tried to do differently with my Jennifer. Mother was possessive, so I encouraged independence. Mother was manipulative. I have been open. Mother was evasive. I have been decisive. Now my work is done. Jennifer is grown. The exact image of my mother.
—JULES FEIFFER

S tandards are meant to be lived up to. We use our standards to determine the choices we make about every aspect of our lives, to judge and compare the behaviors of ourselves and others, and to determine what we should or should not do.

Each family and often each parent has their own set of standards and expectations. It is important for parents to hold high standards for their children's behavior and for children to understand what those standards are. Strong, conscious, consistent standards are necessary for children to know what is expected of them. Good standards motivate them to do their best. The standards by which we raise our children provide the model from which their own standards will develop.

Most of us begin our parenting journey full of high expectations. We will be the best parents and have the greatest kids—certainly not like the kids we have watched in the supermarket screaming and having tantrums. Ours will be kind and obedient, smart and generous and grateful for all we do. We assume that our standards and expectations

are correct. But what happens when those expectations are not met, and our standards are not lived up to? When our children are neither obedient nor grateful? When they do not show the politeness we expected? When we are embarrassed by them in public? When they torture a younger sibling? What happens when our standards are threatened by our child's behavior or desires?

My child's education comes before anything else.

What happens if you have a nonacademic, sports-focused child?

Proper attire must be worn at all times.

What happens when your tomboy wants to wear pants to church?

There will be no fighting or hitting in this family.

What happens when sibling rivalry rears its inevitable head?

I expect my children to be polite and considerate of everyone.

What happens when your shy child refuses to say hello?

I expect respect and attention to any of my requests.

What happens when your teenager argues with outdated rules?

Your buttons get pushed, that's what happens.

If your buttons are being pushed, it is important for you to look at the standards you hold. Your standards may be hard or even impossible to live up to. Standards may be appropriate or inappropriate for a particular child. When parents raise the bar too high, everyone loses. The child lives with the frustration and futility of never being good enough, and the parent feels like a failure, because he thinks he has not raised his child properly.

For example, my mother may have raised me with a **standard** that declared, *There is no excuse for a messy house or an unclean child*. I may have kept this standard so that when my child is dirty or unkempt, and her muddy shoes are on the carpet in the living room, my button gets pushed. I might think or even say, *You are such a slob. You're ruining my house. You are so inconsiderate. You're going to grow up to be a bum.* These **assumptions** will undoubtedly lead to yelling and blaming, and to a child who may feel uncomfortable in her own house.

Our **assumptions** are generated by our **standards.** No parent likes having muddy shoes on the carpet, but a standard that says there is no excuse for it under any circumstances puts pressure on me to enforce unrealistic rules. Whereas a **standard** that says *Having children means that my house and children will inevitably be dirty and messy at times* may lead to annoyance with messes, but will probably not push my buttons nor turn me into a fascist about cleanliness.

It is critical that parents remain conscious of the standards to which they hold their children, and that those standards be appropriate and flexible enough to accommodate the individual differences of each member of the family. If a parent's **standard** says *My children must obey me at all times,* he will have a very difficult time with a daughter who is temperamentally strong-willed and persistent. If this father is determined to uphold his standard by punishing his daughter for refusing to wear a dress to church, she will likely resist him and become rude and disobedient—his greatest fear. But if his standard allows for diverse temperaments and personal self-expression among his children, he will have far fewer battles and a much better relationship with his daughter. Who knows? She may surprise him by wearing a dress to church.

A mother may be determined when her son is very young that there will be no plastic toys, and no guns or weapons of any kind. She may fill the nursery with wooden trains and stuffed animals with strong expectations of raising a socially conscious citizen. So when he begs for a squirt gun, arguing that water can't hurt, and is fascinated with the latest craze and has tantrums for the action figures that go with it, her buttons are going to get pushed. Whether she is willing to make compromises, adjust her standards, and allow her child the play he demands ("Mom, everyone has them") or hold firm to her standards, believing that she is right and her agenda is best for him, will determine the general atmosphere and tone of family life. If she determines the standards she will uphold that only suit her own agenda with no consideration for her son's, she will be in for some battles. If she looks at her standards with consciousness and responsibility, and is considerate of her child's agenda, she can find a solution that works for both of them.

Standards

Our standards are formed from a variety of sources.

Chosen

My daughter, Molly, is an introvert. As Mary Sheedy Kurcinka points out in *Raising Your Spirited Child,* she gets her energy from being alone, so she can then be with people. I have learned that when Molly has been with a lot of people, she needs time alone before she will be ready to tell me about her experience. "So what happened in school today?" was never met with success. I adopted a standard specifically for Molly that reminded me to support her time alone.

When I forgot and asked her too soon about her day, and she rolled her eyes and said, "Whatever," I didn't take it personally and assume she was rude. My conscious standard allowed room for that behavior. I forgave the behavior and left her alone for a while. Invariably when I did that she would come to me later ready to talk in great detail.

Transferred

If I were raised with a **standard** of behavior that said, *Children should be respectful of adults at all times no matter what,* and had transferred that standard to parent Molly, my button would have gotten pushed whenever she rolled her eyes when I asked her how school was. We would be set up for power struggles each time she walked in the door. My **assumptions** might have been something like:

Why can't she ever be cheerful when she comes home?
She's always so rude. Who does she think she is anyway?
She has no respect. What will become of her?

Most likely if you have not become conscious of the standards you are holding, the ones from your childhood could be running your life. Often unconscious standards manipulate our children's behavior by putting our own needs first time after time. *You will obey me because I say so* is a **standard** that attempts to establish control for a parent who may have been overly controlled as a child. He may think his turn has finally come, and now he gets to be the parent and have all the control. Or an opposite reaction to a restrictive or abusive childhood may leave a parent overly permissive. This parent, who never got her needs met or feelings acknowledged, may not even know what her needs are, so she lives with an unconscious **standard** that says *My children's needs always come first. Mine are unimportant.* In both of these cases, the needs of parent and child are out of balance.

Standards that buoy ourselves but belittle our children or belittle ourselves while buoying our children are attempts to fill some deep emptiness in us but prevent our children from growing in healthy separation.

Dr. Alice Miller, the Swiss psychoanalyst, says in her groundbreaking book *The Drama of the Gifted Child,* children who fulfill their parents' conscious or unconscious wishes are "good," but if they ever refuse to do so or express wishes of their own that go against those of their parents, they are called egoistic and inconsiderate. It usually does not occur to the parents that they might need and use the child to fulfill their own egoistic wishes.

Reactive

I will never do to my kids what was done to me is a conscious standard that is in reaction to my upbringing. The problem is, this standard is about me, not necessarily appropriate for my child or my family. Instead of staying clear of the past, the reactive parent becomes a rebel and repeats it by default. Elizabeth Fishel writes in *Family Mirrors: What Our Children's Lives Reveal about Ourselves*, "The Rebel typically defines the parent as a negative role model and strives to do with his own children just the opposite of what his parents did with him. . . . But the differentiation turns out to be a false one, and the bold promises, bravura. The Rebel is as deeply and unconsciously linked to the past as the Traditionalist is."

Janet, a parent of three children, was treated very critically and punitively by her father. She felt his discipline to be extremely unfair and favoring of her younger sister. She quietly acquiesced throughout her childhood, doing whatever her father asked. Janet swore she would be a different parent. She would never hit or yell at her children. They would get what she never got—unconditional love. She became overly vigilant to protect them from harm and hovered closely to make sure their every need was met. However, when her nine-year-old son decided to ride his bike to his friend's house, breaking a house rule, Janet's fears led her to do exactly what she was determined to avoid. She raged and grounded him for the week with no bike privileges. She heard her son say the words she had never dared say to her father, "You are so unfair. I hate you. You won't *ever* let me do anything I want!" Janet couldn't bear the cutting remarks. She reacted with words she had not heard since her father had screamed them at her. "Don't you ever talk to me like that, you ungrateful brat. You always get your way. I can and I will tell you what to do." She could not believe what she heard herself saying.

Compensating

We sometimes unintentionally ask our children to compensate for what we didn't get or accomplish when we were young. Sometimes our deepest wishes are reflected in our present standards. *My son will be a*

star athlete and go to a division-one college might be the compensating **standard** for a father who didn't make the team, but for a son who might prefer to dance.

My children will always be able to express themselves and be heard is a **standard** that may compensate for a restrictive or neglectful up-bringing. But this standard will likely render a parent helpless when he confronts his daughter about her homework, and she expresses herself by yelling, "Can't you just get off my back and leave me alone?" This may not be the type of expression he anticipated. If he reacted to his controlling parents by rebelling and getting into trouble, he may fear that his daughter is on the same path. His standard is threatened, and he is conflicted about what to do. He may find himself reacting the way his own father did, or he may withdraw, leaving her entitled to any expression she chooses.

Many times parenting partners compensate for one another. When Carly thought that her husband, Jamal, was reacting too strictly to their daughter, she compensated by being overly permissive. Jamal reminded Carly of her fearsome, autocratic father, and she feared their daughter would experience what she had. Jamal explained that when he and his daughter were alone together he was far less strict, and they got along well. But when the three of them were together, he compensated for his wife's permissiveness.

OLD STANDARDS	ADJUSTED STANDARDS
My children must listen to me, do as I say, and respond immediately without disagreement.	I expect my children to listen to what I say, knowing that they may not like it and that they have a right to feel however they feel. I expect them to respond but give them the right to negotiate the timing.
It is my job to make the right choices and decisions all the time.	I will do my best to make good choices and decisions, knowing that I make mistakes and am not perfect.
My child's behavior is a direct reflection of my competency.	My child must learn the consequences of his own behavior, and it is his responsibility.
I am responsible for my children's feelings, attitudes, intelligence, success in school, and success in life.	I am responsible for providing the best opportunities I can for my children. I am not responsible for their feelings, thoughts, and actions.
My children should behave only in ways that make others feel good about themselves.	My children are responsible for what they say and do but are not responsible for making others happy.
A good parent has absolute control over the children at all times.	A good parent does not always know what to do and is willing to negotiate to find the right solution for all involved.
My child should have patience whenever I have something to do.	I expect that my child will have his own agenda about what he wants, as I have about what I want.
I always know what is best for my child, and he needs to listen and understand.	Often my child knows what is best for herself, and I need to listen.

Joan's Standards

Karen's mother, Joan, saw that some of her **assumptions** were either irrational or unfounded, such as *Karen will die if she doesn't eat more.* As soon as she became aware of these, she could give them up. But some—*Karen is ungrateful and disobedient; she will get sick;* and *I'm failing as a parent, because I can't make her eat*—were still creating problems that kept the old patterns of blame and resentment active at mealtime. After our discussion on expectations, Joan wrote down the **standard** she had created for herself—*It is a mother's job to know how to nourish her children properly.*

"I started out my parenting bound and determined that eating was never going to be an issue. What happened? How did I end up with such a picky eater?" Joan asked with genuine bewilderment.

"I wonder if you are setting yourself up for an impossible task," I suggested. "It seems as though you may have a standard that Karen is purposefully shooting down. When you say, *It's my job to know how to nourish her properly,* you are also saying, *It's my job to feed her the amount I think is best.* You are taking on the full responsibility and authority for her eating. That is your standard, and whether you know it or not, you are making sure you uphold that standard rather than looking at what Karen needs."

"You mean she doesn't need me to make sure she gets fed?" Joan asked incredulously.

"She needs you to make sure she gets served nutritious food. But what she eats and how much goes down is her responsibility," I said.

"Well that's just great. She might as well starve then," Joan said sarcastically.

"Why were you so determined to not have eating be an issue in your family?" I asked. Joan then told the class what family mealtimes were like when she was a child.

Her mother grew up during the Depression. Food was scarce for her family, so her mother learned to be quite creative with what little they had. Joan's mother, a stay-at-home housewife, was quite the cook. She provided three, hot, sit-down meals a day for Joan, her father, and two sisters. Using a compensating standard, she was determined that her family would never have to experience the scarcity she once had.

Mealtimes were not always pleasant for Joan. Her father was extremely critical of her and used mealtimes to "correct" her behavior. Often Joan's appetite was small in anticipation of the conversation she dreaded. If she refused anything or picked at what was on her plate, her mother muttered about Joan's ungrateful attitude. "You just don't know how lucky you are. You're spoiled; that's all there is to it," was a familiar refrain at the dinner table, along with her father's remarks about grades and laziness. "I just hope you have a child someday who puts you through the same thing. Then you'll know what I'm talking about," he would often say in exasperation.

Joan's loss of appetite was not out of ingratitude for her mother's cooking but out of fear of what her father would choose to criticize that evening. She felt vulnerable and defenseless at the dinner table and was left thinking that nothing she ever did was good enough. Never having examined what she needed and had a right to, Joan passed on her mother's high standards of nurturing her family with food. This was her transferred standard.

Joan's Set-up for Failure

"Karen perceives you controlling what she eats, and she is resisting that control," I explained. "She feels your criticism in the same way you felt your father's. Perhaps that's why she loses her appetite, as you did."

"Oh, how awful," Joan groaned.

"By controlling and criticizing, you attempt to uphold your standard. To nourish your child properly means to get her to eat what and how much *you* think is best. You are afraid you are failing as a mother if you do not uphold that standard."

"Well, right," she said. "But if I let go of my standard, doesn't that mean I am failing to do my job?"

"I don't mean to let go of your standard but to *adjust* it to fit you and your child—to make it appropriate. We need to have successful standards—ones that help our children feel good about themselves. As soon as children fall short of meeting up to them, as you did with your mother's and father's, they feel like a failure, as you did. Our children measure what they do against our standards, even if they think they are unfair, and too often come up short."

"I see what you mean," Joan said thoughtfully. "So what do I do about my standard that will help Karen? I'm afraid if I don't keep doing what I'm doing she won't eat at all."

"But haven't we established that the problem mostly arises with you? She's fighting something in you, and you are clinging to your standard. And the more you defend an inappropriate standard the more you set yourself up to fail as well. Why would you want to do that?" I asked.

"But won't I fail if I don't have that standard?"

"Not if you create a new one. Let's think about a standard that will help both you and Karen."

Together we came up with *It's my job to provide nourishing food and Karen's job to choose what and how much she eats of it.* It was still hard for Joan to see that Karen could be trusted to eat. Joan understood that she was controlling Karen's eating and that Karen was fighting that control, but her fear that Karen would never eat unless she kept after her continued to provoke her reactions at mealtime.

Joan was getting there, but something inside her seemed to be resisting. We needed to find out why it was so hard to put her new standard in place, and why her intentions were being undermined.

Your Standards

What I expect of my children is that they

1. _listen to me when I tell them to do something_

2. _____

3. _____

4. _____

And what I expect of myself is that I

1. _should have taught them to be more respectful of my wishes_

2. _____

3. _____

4. _____

Write the standards for your children and yourself that create these expectations.

1. _My children should listen and do what I say when I say it—cheerfully._

   I must always have control over my children.

2. _____

3. _____

4. _____

After you write your standards, listen to their tone.

> Do they expect you to be at your best all of the time?
> Do they expect your children to be what *you* want them to be, leaving little room for growth and individuality?
> Do they expect your family to look like The Brady Bunch?
> Are they in strong opposition or similar to the ones you grew up with?

On page 62 is a list of a few unrealistic standards adjusted to new, more appropriate ones that may help you.

● EXERCISE 5: **The Standards Exercise (example)**

One assumption I have when my child pushes my button is *my child is draining the lifeblood out of me every time he gets clingy or needy* .

What I expect of my child is *that he should be able to take care of himself, be self-reliant and not dependent on me for help* . What I expect of myself is *that I should know how to raise my children to take care of themselves* .

These expectations translate to my standard that says *My children should be self-sufficient and not need me to take care of every little thing* .

This standard stems from my past when *my mother never did anything for herself—she sacrificed her life and her career for us kids* .
(something you learned/observed in your childhood)

So, whenever my child *asks me to do things for him—get him this, do that* , I feel *afraid that I'll end up like my mother* , and I react by *yelling at him and telling him to do it himself—that I'm not his slave* .

This standard I hold either compensates for or is in reaction to *my mother's dormant life. I don't want that to happen to me* . I am afraid that *if I don't get my life back soon, I never will* . This standard is inappropriate because *it reflects my mother's life, not mine or my child's* .

I can change my standard to *Addressing my children's needs while they are young will lead to self-sufficiency later. I can take care of them and care for myself, too*

● EXERCISE 5: **The Standards Exercise**

Please complete either or both of the exercises that follow.
A.

One assumption I have when my child pushes my button is _____

_____ .

What I expect of my child is _____

_____ . What I expect of myself is _____

_____ .

These expectations translate to my standard that says _____

_____ .

This standard stems from my past when _____

_____ .
                    (something you learned/observed in your childhood)

So, whenever my child _____ , I feel

_____ , and I react by _____

_____ .

This standard I hold either compensates for or is in reaction to _____

_____ . I am afraid that _____

_____ . This standard is inappropriate because _____

_____ .

I can change my standard to _____

_____ .

● EXERCISE 5: The Standards Exercise (continued)

B.

Describe the expectations you have of yourself and your children when your button gets pushed. Are they realistic? Can you and your children live up to them? How do you react when you or they don't live up to them?

Translate these expectations into a statement that is your standard for yourself and/or your children. Where in your past does it stem from? Is it compensating for or in reaction to the standards you grew up with?

Write a new standard that is more appropriate for you and your children today.

CHAPTER SIX

HIDDEN TRIGGERS

If you can't get rid of the skeleton in your closet,
you'd best teach it to dance.
—George Bernard Shaw

When we were children, our parents said and did things that led us to believe certain things about ourselves. We interpreted our parents' tone, emotions, and body language in our child's mind to determine who we were. The value we *perceived* our parents placed on us is the value we place on ourselves.

The Messages of Childhood

Young children do not question their parent's actions or words. Instead they question themselves. When a mother says, "You are being so mean," the young child does not think, "Mommy's wrong about me. I wasn't being mean; I just took that truck because I wanted it."

Whether or not he is able to oblige his mother by giving the truck back, he perceives that he is mean. Even if his mother did not intend him to receive that message, that is the message received across the gap. He may think it's not fair that she called him mean and act out to show his distress, but he is likely to believe it nonetheless.

If a particular standard, whether conscious or unconscious, satisfies the

> "Because children see parents as authority figures and gods, they think that the way you treat them is the way they deserve to be treated: 'What you say about me is what I am' is a literal truth to your child."
>
> —Stephanie Marston,
> *The Magic of Encouragement:*
> *Nurturing Your Child's Self-Esteem*

need of the parent more than the child and is too hard for the child to live up to, the child will see it as his problem, not his parent's. He will believe himself to be wrong or bad and shove that belief into his subconscious mind. He either will behave better next time because he has an adaptable temperament and can be easily manipulated, or he will resist because his temperament is more strong-willed.

Over the years, we accumulate all that we have learned about ourselves from our parents, relatives, teachers, and friends and grow into adulthood with a self-image—a set of beliefs about ourselves. If we are lucky, we emerge from childhood knowing that we are strong, capable, important, and worthy of unconditional love. Unfortunately, too many of us emerge having perceived countless messages that were not quite so self-affirming. Hoping that they will disappear with time, we store those messages away in the attic of our subconscious mind, but they emerge to haunt us when we least expect it.

> **Parent-Blame**
> It may be tempting at this stage to blame your parents for leaving you in this predicament. But that will only keep you in the same emotional entanglement with your past as if you were to accept and repeat the old patterns. The source of blame is impossible to find. Your parents did the best they could given the knowledge and circumstances they had at the time. Their intentions were most likely different from the messages you received. Blaming your parents is an excuse for not taking responsibility for yourself and growing.

The Effects of Our Beliefs

Positive or negative, our **beliefs** about ourselves (*I'm unimportant, the pretty one, stupid, good at everything, fat, incompetent, just a girl, funny, selfish*) and **beliefs** about our parents (*parents are the bosses, mothers sacrifice for their children, fathers aren't around*) are strongly embedded in our subconscious. They influence our **standards,** shape our experiences, affect our behavior, and trigger the **assumptions** we make about ourselves and others. Our automatic **reactions** are firmly grounded in these **beliefs.**

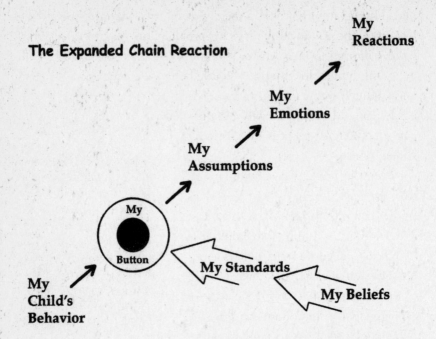

The Expanded Chain Reaction

My Reactions

My Emotions

My Assumptions

My Button

My Child's Behavior

My Standards

My Beliefs

Your button is created when an inappropriate or unrealistic standard has been established as a direct result of a deeper belief. When your child pushes that button, your standard is threatened and you react in an attempt to protect that belief from exposure.

Whatever the messages we heard, we "buy into" them, whether we accept them or spend our lives trying to prove them wrong. When we become conscious of this programming, we can choose to reprogram and change our experiences. Old beliefs lose their power, and we can rewrite our standards into ones that are useful and effective for us today.

If I have a **belief** in my subconscious that *I am a capable, worthwhile, and effective person,* I will likely be able to develop strong boundaries with my children and balance my own needs with theirs. But if I **believe** that *I am not good enough, I can't make decisions, and my needs are unimportant,* I will be less able to establish healthy boundaries, set limits, or be empathic when my children behave inappropriately. I will have set myself up to get my buttons pushed.

It is these childhood beliefs that hold power over us and get tapped when our children push our buttons. Even when we consciously choose an appropriate standard for ourselves or our children, it can get undermined by an unexamined, unconscious belief, and our best intentions are derailed. We react, and we don't know why.

Negative beliefs lingering from childhood, tucked away in our dusty, cobwebbed attic, are not easy to change. We can't just decide that they don't work for us and believe something different. But becoming aware of them—visiting the attic, dusting off the cobwebs, and bringing them out in the open where we can see them, feel them, and make conscious choices about them—diminishes the power they hold over us.

Don't Contradict What I Believe!

As we have learned, we generally give credence only to the information that confirms our beliefs. If I believe I am not smart, I will not believe anyone who says otherwise, even though I may want desperately to hear it. I might behave in a grandiose manner attempting to prove how smart I am, but if I do well on something I will likely attribute it to luck rather than accomplishment. I will, however, believe, take personally, and have my button pushed by anyone who I perceive thinks I am not smart. I will react defensively, because at least a part of me believes it. **It is easier to feed our beliefs than to change them.**

Our Beliefs Can Conflict with Our Standards

I might consciously choose an appropriate **standard** for my family that says, *It is important to address the needs of all members of my family respectfully.* That way if my daughter throws a tantrum as I am cooking dinner because I won't play with her, I can respect her anger as well as my need to cook dinner. If I am able to uphold my standard, we can work out an agreement. I might promise to play after dinner and before bath time or delay dinner by half an hour. If neither is possible, I can address her anger and empathize with how frustrating it must be when I am too busy to play. Both she and I are respected.

But if I have a **belief** about myself that says *my needs are unimportant,* I will become frustrated and angry when she insists that I play *now.* I may end up resentfully playing with her while my thoughts are stuck on the dinner that is not getting prepared, banish her to her room so that I can get dinner on the table, or yell at her to leave me alone. In all three cases, my button has been pushed, and I am passing on unhealthy beliefs of unimportance to my daughter.

What happened to my standard? It was cleverly undermined by my belief. I might be trying to heal that wound by putting my needs above my child's or by forcing her to comply, or I may fall back into my old pattern of making her needs more important than mine and resenting her. In either case, **my belief is more powerful at driving my parenting than my chosen standard.**

Sometimes we set up unrealistic standards for ourselves and others to prove we are not who we believe ourselves to be. If I felt angry that my father never gave me a chance to argue my case, tell my side of the story, or be right about anything, and if I believed that my opinions didn't count, I might react by creating a controlling standard unintentionally similar to his. I want to prove that my opinions do count and demand that my children listen to me and do what I say. With such a strict standard, my children will not measure up, and I will feel like a failure, confirming once again that my opinions don't count.

If I set high enough standards, I think it will look good to the outside world, and people will think I'm doing a good job. I'm trying to convince the world, because I can't convince myself. So I create a standard that shields my deeper belief in an attempt to keep others from finding out the truth about me. But in the proving, I put my children in the same powerless role I was in. My **beliefs** sabotage my **standards,** and I create the opposite of what I intended.

Unraveling Joan's Beliefs

"It sounds like you created a belief about yourself that you were ungrateful, unworthy, and inconsiderate since you couldn't do enough to gain your father's approval or satisfy your mother's attempt to compensate for her upbringing," I suggested. "That makes perfect logical sense for a little girl in those circumstances. You felt guilty for not doing what you thought you should be doing. You didn't know that it wasn't your fault."

"So why do I end up saying some of the horrible things my parents said to me? I try so hard to be different, but I hear myself saying those words I dreaded so much," Joan said in exasperation.

"Because your subconscious belief about yourself is more powerful than your conscious effort to parent differently. That belief is what drives your expectations and prompts the assumptions you have about Karen. When she refuses her food, it feels like a slap in the face. Your belief about your own ingratitude gets tapped. Little Joan knew it was not okay to refuse food. Little Joan couldn't be ungrateful and inconsiderate; so that's what she perceives Karen to be. It is little Joan who rises up to criticize Karen and get her to do what she is supposed to do—eat and be grateful."

Karen's refusal to eat pushed Joan's button, exposing her **belief** in her own unworthiness. She reacted defensively by strictly enforcing her **standard** to defend her worthiness by maintaining authority and control. Even though she had not wanted it, eating became an issue.

Whenever her **standard** felt threatened, she reacted with anger or sarcasm. Joan was unconsciously attempting to use Karen to heal her old wound by demanding that Karen obey her authority—authority that for Joan was associated with food. Ironically, Joan has preserved those familiar feelings of unworthiness and rejection. The cycle will continue until she decides to confront the **beliefs** she has about herself. Karen has given her that opportunity and has pinpointed exactly where she can begin.

I asked Joan to write down what her little-girl thoughts were when she sat at that dinner table. She wrote: *I have to eat what is put in front of me and tell my mother how great it is. But I don't feel like eating it, because I'm nervous and uncomfortable. I have to be good so my father won't yell at me, but I can't figure out what he wants. He changes all the time. I'm scared that he's going to yell at me.*

I then asked her to write what little Joan believed about herself based on those thoughts. She wrote, *I can't ever get it right. I'm selfish, ungrateful, and inconsiderate. What I do is never good enough, and my point of view does not even exist. If I open my mouth, I'm wrong.*

"Do you see how your beliefs are undermining your standards? If you can't ever get it right, are selfish and inconsiderate and don't even have a point of view, how do you suppose you will be able to nourish your child properly?" I asked. Joan's tears welled up. "But you have to prove that you *can* get it right, so you use your standard to do that proving by demanding Karen's obedience." Joan was amazed. She realized that she had created a button that Karen was destined to push.

"When Karen's behavior threatens your authority, you perceive that your standard is at risk and so try to enforce it harder," I explained. "But when that doesn't work, you decide that you are failing, thereby confirming your old beliefs about yourself. Your worry about Karen's health is your justification for remaining determined to get Karen to behave in a way that will validate your standard."

"Oh, dear. I'm not sure I followed all that, but I sound like one messed-up mother who is really messing up her daughter. It sounds hopeless," Joan said with a sinking tone.

"Not at all," I assured her. "We all fall into these patterns. You may only need to become aware of them. Already, I can tell that you understand enough of what we've been talking about to see the pattern and want to change it."

"Absolutely. But I don't have a clue how."

Changing Focus, Becoming Conscious

I explained that instead of being so concerned about her own job as a perfect mother, she can focus more on Karen. She can look at the facts—Karen's poor eating is not a problem at school, not a problem with Dad, and she is indeed growing—as reason to *adjust* her standard to fit her daughter appropriately. I pointed out that Karen is not little Joan. They do not require the same standards, the same parenting.

After becoming more aware of some of the self-defeating **beliefs** that were running her life, Joan asked with discouragement, "But I can't just erase them. What do I do? Just tell myself they aren't right?"

"Well, yes and no," I said. "They have been sitting in your attic affecting your agenda day in and day out for many years now. You can't expect them to disappear overnight. Actually you shouldn't expect them to disappear at all. Instead, try making friends with them."

"What are you talking about? Here you've told me how they are messing up my relationship with my daughter, and now you say make friends with them!"

"When you were a little girl, you did everything you knew how to do to survive, be good, and get love from your parents. Your beliefs served you to do this. You were in effect agreeing with your parents rather than fighting with them. It was admirable of you. Can you have compassion for little Joan, who was trying her hardest to please her parents?"

"I think I see what you're getting at," Joan said, but she still looked puzzled.

I told the class what I had once heard Angeles Arriens, a cultural anthropologist, say that hit a strong chord with me. She was talking about the personal judge that we all have inside our heads—the one who has no problem telling us what we are doing wrong at any given moment. She said, "When your judge comes knocking at your door, don't turn him away. Welcome him in. But usher him into the guest room. Don't let him take over your house.

"Your job now, Joan, is not to try to get rid of those beliefs. Your job is to put them in the guest room and not let them run your life. As you become aware of them, you are transferring them from your subconscious mind, where *they* hold power, to your conscious mind, where *you* hold power. If you can acknowledge that they were an important shield for you as a child and have compassion for why you believed them, you can then tell yourself that they belong in the past and are no longer necessary."

Joan's Defusing Process

Joan can now choose to stop taking Karen's eating behavior personally. She can see that it has no direct tie to her unworthiness. She understands that her **standards** and childhood **beliefs** play a big part in determining her agenda at mealtimes. She acknowledges that Karen's agenda is quite different and is focused primarily on getting her mother off her back.

Joan had some regressions along the way. It took a while to let go of the control, as she was strongly attached to her old beliefs. But she continued watching her reactions in these situations and writing down how she perceived them and what had occurred. At first, her emotions remained too high to stop herself in the middle of a scene, but after a while, she could walk away, breathe, and talk to herself until she was calm.

Joan's Self-Talk

As she became more and more aware of the cycle and her responsibility in it, Joan was able to stop herself in the moment, or else go over the incident in her mind later when she was calm. She would talk herself through all the steps she had learned.

Okay, here we go. She thinks the sandwich is "stinky." I'm so angry I want to scream. Why does she do this to me? No, wait a minute. She's not doing *it* to me. That's just what I'm *assuming*. I'm reacting to my fear that she is going to die, and that's not true. She is not going to die. Worst case, she gets sick. She doesn't have to be appreciative like I had to be. Maybe she's not eating because she feels stressed just like I did. I'm putting a lot of pressure on her to make *me* feel good. That's my problem. I need to pull back and let her take responsibility for herself. I am still a good mother even if she doesn't eat. I am doing my part to provide her with nourishing food. She doesn't always defy my authority. It is her decision to eat or not eat. My job is to accept her and provide for her, and I am doing just that.

Joan changed her assumptions and redefined Karen as a picky eater instead of defiant and disobedient. If Karen didn't want anything, Joan bit her tongue and said, "If you're hungry later, let me know." If Karen said, "It hurts my tummy," Joan said, "Okay, maybe later," and left it at that.

She arrived for the last class with news. "Guess what?" she said as soon as everyone was seated. "I think I'm getting there. Yesterday, I set out a few things that I know Karen likes for lunch. She characteristically criticized what was there, and I didn't take it personally! I said, 'Well just eat what you want and leave the rest,' and I went about cleaning up the dishes and didn't pay any attention to her. After about five minutes she said, 'Okay, bye' and ran off. I noticed that she had eaten only a tiny bit, but I told myself that it was okay, that it wasn't about me. Then today, I noticed she wasn't quite as critical, and she ate a tiny bit more. When she jumped down off the stool, she said, 'Mommy, I'm not going to die, you know.' And I said, 'I do know that, Karen. You are doing just fine.' And we gave each other a big hug."

Joan is beginning to respond to Karen effectively. Karen can now focus on herself, rather than on her mother's disapproval. Joan can feel good about herself as a mother *even* if Karen does not eat as much as she would like.

Joan eventually achieved her original desire. Eating became a nonissue in their family. This time it was backed with substantial awareness of what was appropriate and realistic. Karen occasionally tested her mother's new approach by not eating at all. But with assurance that this was Karen's test of her new standard and that steadfastness was necessary to pass the test, mealtimes lost their provocative tension. When Karen trusted that her mother's expectations had changed, she had the freedom to eat as she liked.

● EXERCISE 6: Your Limiting Beliefs

Write down what you think may be the negative beliefs that you perceived about your-self from your childhood experiences. You can start with what you think about yourself now. Then try to remember what you thought about yourself as a child. How did those thoughts translate into the beliefs you have carried with you? These are most likely the shameful thoughts that you keep hidden.

What I believed about myself when I was a child:

1. _____

2. _____

3. _____

What I believe about myself now:

1. _____

2. _____

3. _____

This/these beliefs probably came from the time/s when _____

_____

_____

_____

_____

_____

● EXERCISE 7: My Beliefs (example)

When my child ___*deliberately disobeys me or doesn't listen to me*___ ,
(button-pushing behavior)

    I react by ___*yelling at her, grounding her*___ ,

    because I'm afraid that ___*she'll never learn to respect or obey authority and*___
(worst-case scenario)

she'll get into trouble .

Her behavior reminds me of when I was a child and ___*I swore at my mother and she*___

slapped me across the face. I was shocked and mortified .
(state what happened or what feelings came up)

I reacted then by ___*doing whatever my parents asked me to do*___ , in order to

avoid/get ___*getting hit again*___ .

    Whenever I did that, I felt ___*alone—like I never got to do what I wanted*___ ,

    because ___*nobody ever listened to me*___ .

What I believed about myself was ___*that I was a nobody, that anything I wanted was*___

stupid or unimportant . So the belief that I still carry with me is ___*that my*___

needs are unimportant and my job is to take care of everyone else ,

which leads me to ___*yell at my daughter when she doesn't do what I did*___ .

What I wish my parent had said or done differently is ___*listened to me and let me do*___

something I wanted or at least argued with me instead of hitting or grounding
(your fantasy of how you wished your parent had been)

me .

If that had happened, I would have felt ___*more important and self-assured*___ .

    If I had felt this way, I probably would ___*listen to my daughter when she argues*___
(how you would respond differently to your child)

with me .

● EXERCISE 7: **My Beliefs**

Please complete either or both of the exercises that follow.
A.

When my child _____ ,
(button-pushing behavior)

   I react by _____ ,

   because I'm afraid that _____ .
(worst-case scenario)

Her behavior reminds me of when I was a child and _____

_____ .

I reacted then by _____ ,
(state what happened or what feelings came up)

   in order to avoid/get _____ .

   Whenever I did that, I felt _____ ,

   because _____ .

What I believed about myself was _____ .

   So the belief that I still carry with me is _____

_____ ,

   which leads me to _____ .

What I wish my parent had said or done differently is _____

_____ .
(your fantasy of how you wished your parent had been)

If that had happened, I would have felt _____ .

   If I had felt this way, I probably would _____

_____ .
(how you would respond differently to your child)

● EXERCISE 7: **My Beliefs (continued)**

B.

Describe an incident in childhood during which your parent/s were angry or disapproving of you. What were their expectations of you that you either could not or did not want to meet? Describe what they said, how you felt about it, and what you believed about yourself because of it.

Do you still hold this belief? How does it affect you today? How does it affect your parenting?

CHAPTER SEVEN

DON'T TAKE IT PERSONALLY— THEY'RE NOT OUT TO GET YOU!

But it is not what I am saying that is hurting you; it is that
you have wounds that I touch by what I have said.
—Don Miguel Ruiz, *The Four Agreements*

He's just trying to get me. He's so good at manipulating. He just wants my attention, and he's going for anything he can get." Sound familiar? Sometimes we think that our children do nothing but plot our downfall so they can get the upper hand and run the family. Rarely is this assumption true.

We take our children's behavior personally when we feel exposed and vulnerable. Anytime we take anything personally, it means it's hitting a sore spot. We don't like that spot being hit, so our focus remains on *us*, what our child is doing to *us*. *We* don't want to be disrespected; *we* don't want to be manipulated or put down; *we* want peace and quiet; *we* don't want our agenda inconvenienced. From this vantage point, we are incapable of reaching across the gap to focus on *their* problem or *their* pain—to be helpful. We are too busy defending ourselves, upholding our standards, and protecting our beliefs.

Anna, Jeff, and Sarah

Anna and Jeff are at the end of their rope. "We can't take it any longer. We feel hopeless. We can't live like this. We're even talking about sending Sarah away," they reported in class one night. It is amazing how much power a child can hold over a family, and a very nice family at that. This is not a sixteen-year-old rebellious runaway. Sarah is six. "She ruins our day. We wake up in the morning and don't do or say anything, and she starts."

Sarah's temperament has been difficult for her parents to handle from the beginning. She is extremely persistent, aggressive, and willful. Her parents' reactions intended to temper Sarah's behavior have been met with stronger and stronger persistence. They have tried punishments of all kinds and have even reverted to hitting a few times, shocking themselves in the process. "It does nothing to quiet her, to cause her to understand that she needs to back down and cooperate so that she might get approval and kindness from us."

Anna and Jeff are understandably frustrated, and they worry about Sarah's influence on her one-year-old brother, Daniel. "She is rude, demanding, and has an attitude with a capital A. She is bossy and extremely daring in her behavior. Why does she do this to us?" Anna sat in class distraught.

"I actually had her pinned to the floor this morning after she screamed 'stupid' at me and told me to 'get out of here.' She runs the family," she said. "We never know what's coming next. After I got her off to school today, I went out in my car and just screamed and cried and said life shouldn't be like this." No, it shouldn't. No one should live under the tyranny of a six-year-old.

Sarah is very successful in school. She receives accolades from her teacher, who says that she is reading at a fourth-grade level and patiently teaches other children how to sound out words. Anna thinks that the teacher has her daughter confused with another child. This told me that Sarah is strong, capable, and on track still, but has learned many unhealthy manipulative skills that she maneuvers at home. If left unchecked, Sarah could become that rebellious sixteen-year-old runaway.

The next week, Anna told the class a revealing story. "I carried Daniel into the living room to nurse. Sarah was already in there playing by herself under a blanket. When we walked in, she stuck her head out, saw us, and sneered, 'Get your stinking butt out of here.' I saw red and screamed at her, 'You get upstairs to your room this instant, young lady.' Many not-so-pleasant things were said before Sarah started upstairs, came back down for more screaming, and finally went upstairs to stay."

Later, Anna was upstairs sweeping up bits of wallpaper they had scraped off the walls in preparation for painting. "Sarah found a metal spatula on the table and began scraping more wallpaper above the floor where I had just cleaned and started singing, 'I'm making more work for Mommy!' I demanded that she stop. She walked over to the stairs and began scratching the wooden bannister with the spatula.

"Then a strange thing happened," Anna continued. "I felt myself move into this calm, detached place. It was like I didn't care, but I did. I knew that my anger would only provoke more from Sarah. It was a no-win situation. I knew I was either going to lose control entirely, or I was going to walk away. I walked away—and went downstairs. I got out a rag and a bottle of scratch remover, walked back upstairs, and handed it to Sarah, calmly saying, 'You need to fix the scratch marks in the post.' She took the rag and did just that!"

When Anna detached from her emotions, she became objective. From this new perspective, she had a choice. The choice to walk away often feels weak and powerless to a parent bound on maintaining authority. But when faced with walking away or losing the battle, walking away definitely holds the power. And Sarah knew it.

Their Two Agendas

When Sarah screamed at her mother, "Get your stinking butt out of here," Anna's agenda became loaded as her button got pushed. Her expectations of her daughter's behavior, her emotional rage, her fears of what would lie ahead for a child like this, her assumptions of how she had failed as a mother all went into her demand, "You get upstairs to your room this instant, young lady!" Anna hit Zone four on the Button Meter. Her assumptions undermined her intention of teaching her daughter not to speak rudely. All Anna could see was Sarah's behavior. Sarah's agenda was ignored, and so she turned parent-deaf. The gap was wide. The message was lost. The battle ensued.

Across the gap, Sarah undoubtedly heard, "You are so bad. You never please me. Daniel is my good child. You never do anything right." Sarah's defense was to scream back at her mother to uphold what little integrity she had left and resist the command to go upstairs until she didn't want to fight anymore. But as soon as energy returned, she took the next opportunity to retaliate by scraping wallpaper onto the clean floor, scratching the bannister, and taunting her mother.

But when Anna walked away, she changed her focus from taking it personally back to her intention of teaching. As long as Sarah heard rebuke, she defended herself and fought back. When the blame was gone, she had no need to defend herself. She knew her behavior was wrong, and perhaps she was asking to be stopped. The clear direction "You need to fix the scratch marks in the post" could be heard and acted on. There was no reason not to.

Unfortunately, this was an isolated incident and Anna was not yet able to transfer her learning to other situations. The battles continued.

"She's Out to Get Me!"

"Sarah is your teacher," I said to Anna.

The expression on Anna's face showed us that she thought I had lost my mind. I suggested that each time Sarah sent her to the brink, she ask herself, "What am I supposed to learn from this? What is Sarah trying to teach me?"

I asked Anna if she could pinpoint the instant assumption she made when she walked into the room with Daniel and Sarah erupted. Anna said without hesitation, *She's a rotten kid, and she's out to get me. Plus, she's going to end up in really big trouble someday.*

"What do you think she is out to get?"

Anna first looked confused by my question. Then she said, "She's out to get me mad."

"What good does that do her? How does it serve her to get you mad?"

"Sarah is like a knife—she cuts me." The class was quiet. "She takes my power away. She knows what happens to me. She is so manipulative." Anna was so sure that Sarah calculated her every move. She was caught in taking it personally.

"I wonder why she wants to take your power away," I said.

"Because she knows when she defeats me like that, she gets the power."

"Do you think she enjoys feeling more powerful than you?"

When Anna answered with a definitive yes, I offered that children don't feel very good when they know they have more power than their parents. When they fear their parents are not in control, they think they have to take control. It's actually a very scary place for most children to be.

I asked the class if anyone had an idea about why Sarah would be after her mother's defeat.

"Maybe she thought if her mother was vulnerable, something might happen," offered another mother.

"What do you think Sarah thought might happen?" I asked.

"I don't know. If Sarah really is her teacher, like you say, maybe she's hoping that if she goes for the jugular, Anna will break down and change in some way. Maybe Sarah thinks that Anna will listen to her if she goes at her hard enough. Maybe she hasn't gotten what she's needed, and she thinks she has to get meaner in order to get Anna to pay attention."

I looked at Anna to see her reaction. She was thinking hard. "I don't know what more she wants from me," Anna said dejectedly. "She has sucked me dry. She's gotten everything there is, and there's nothing left. What more can she want?"

"What if she isn't intending to suck you dry?" I asked. "What if you are misunderstanding her agenda? If you assume that she is out to get you—to suck you dry in order to get power—and she is intending something quite different, then there is a huge gap between you. You both have loaded agendas. What could you do to narrow the gap?"

"I don't know. Be aware that what I think about her isn't necessarily true?"

"That sounds like a great place to start," I said as others in the group smiled their support. But we knew it would not be easy. Anna had a lot of sore spots that needed protecting.

Anna's Haunting Past

When I asked Anna who Sarah reminded her of, she said, throwing her head back with emphasis, "Oh! My sister. She's ditsy and whiny, complains all the time, and is always in crisis—just like Sarah. When

Sarah was born she was very colicky, and my mother said right from the beginning, 'She's just like your sister.'"

Anna's parents immigrated from South America. They were resentful of Anna's American ways, ease with English, and desire to learn. She was reprimanded for reading and struggled to get herself to college against her parents' wishes. She has always believed, *I'm never good enough. I can't do anything right.*

Her mother was physically abusive to both Anna and her older sister; but her sister got the brunt of it, while Anna retreated into her books and got only disapproving looks. As abuse often leads to a dependent relationship, Anna's sister and mother have formed a tight bond and live down the street from one another. They have always been in collusion in their criticism of Sarah and of Anna's lack of discipline. After Anna and Jeff moved from her hometown and her parents and sister moved to Florida, Anna felt alone and depressed. She began emotionally distancing from Sarah and "buying into" her mother's and sister's cutting remarks about her. She needed the alliance of her family now.

Putting It All Together

"If I get close to Sarah, I have to separate from my family. I get approval from my mother for dealing with Sarah the same way she dealt with me and my sister," she said with perception. "If I take Sarah's side, my mother is filled with disdain and disapproval."

Anna strived for her mother's approval at great risk to her daughter's self-esteem. Whenever Sarah behaved inappropriately, Anna's agenda became loaded with ideas of what her mother and sister would think, and fears emerged about her own dependency on their approval. She was very aware that an alliance with Sarah meant a break with the familiar relationships of her past. Sarah was losing out.

In order to defend her choice, Anna had to blame Sarah. But Anna's choice was vulnerable, to say the least, and Sarah was fighting back. She was demanding that her mother see to her needs. She was trying to break down her mother's defenses. But Anna was too focused on her own insecure position to be able to understand Sarah's behavior.

Being focused on herself, she saw Sarah's defiance as *out to get her* rather than as a cry for help. So she decided that Sarah's behavior was manipulative, and her assumption demanded that Sarah be controlled and punished.

Sarah as the Teacher

If Anna is willing to let her daughter's behavior reveal the wounds connected with her past, she will be better able to see how her standards have more to do with her past than with Sarah. By caring for Sarah in the way she herself longed to be cared for—not by compensating for her past but by understanding Sarah's individual needs—they can both grow and connect. By giving what she did not get, she will give to herself as well as to Sarah. Sarah has taught her how.

How to Do It

When Anna entered the room where Sarah was hiding, Anna's reaction was understandably punitive and blaming. If she had done what Sarah demanded and left the room, she would have rewarded Sarah's rude, disrespectful comment. Either way, Sarah's need—the hurt and anger at the root of her inappropriate behavior—is unattended, Anna loses her authority, and Sarah learns that she needs to be louder and more demanding next time in order to be heard.

Sarah doesn't understand that she is acting out because of her need for acceptance and unconditional love. She doesn't know how to say to her mother, "You aren't understanding what I really need," except with her behavior. And she doesn't have the adaptable temperament necessary to acquiesce to her mother's demands and behave cooperatively. If she did, her needs, still unattended, would fester deep inside to cause problems later on.

If Anna can clear her personal agenda and reach across the gap to see her daughter's need for acceptance, her message can be sent as intended. If Anna had heard the hurt below Sarah's words, been able to refrain from taking her words personally, and detached from her catastrophizing fears of their future, she might have been able to teach Sarah an important lesson. **The key is to change her personal focus** from *Why do you have to do this to me?* to a more objective: *You're having a problem. How can I help?*

"I didn't know you were in here playing. I see that you'd like to be left alone. Would you please ask me respectfully what it is you want to say?" This response would let Sarah know that her reaction is unacceptable, but that her wish for privacy is heard and respected. She would be held accountable for her behavior immediately, rather than having her needs ignored and be let off the hook with banishment to her room.

If Sarah continues with rude remarks, Anna needs to address Sarah's emotional state. "You're sounding so angry with me. I won't allow you to talk to me that way, but you *can* tell me what's going on— why you're feeling so mad." This *might* motivate Sarah to say more. Even very young children are capable of expressing themselves, if they trust they will be heard and not judged.

If Sarah can't, Anna needs to do some guesswork based on past experience. "I wonder if you're angry because I spend so much time with Daniel. It must seem like you never get to do what you want without Daniel being in the way."

What you guess your child is thinking is probably accurate. Many parents fear putting words in their child's mouth, but your child will be delighted to tell you if you're wrong. And your conversation can start from there. Statements like these are far more likely to open the door to communication than judgments, criticisms, or questions.

Even if Daniel is screaming to be nursed, Anna could communicate in the same way while accommodating the nursing and inviting Sarah in. If that still doesn't work, waiting until after the nursing, when Anna is calmer, would be far better than reacting in the moment. Sending Sarah to her room is much easier, but affords no learning other than developing plans for future retaliation.

The only reason a child wants to "get" you is to draw attention to something she wants or needs that is not getting attended to, and the only way she knows how to do it is by pushing your button. When your reaction to her behavior is even more punitive, she thinks her behavior must get stronger next time. But her intention is to serve her need, not to make you nuts. When you address her need, pushing your button is no longer necessary.

Neither punishment nor permissiveness gets the result the parent intends. The gap engulfs communication, and more often than not, the child is left with the belief, *I am not doing this right. I am trying, but it's not working.* When we take our children's behavior personally, we focus on ourselves and our needs, ignoring our child's.

Easier Said Than Done

Anna had become addicted to her patterns of behavior, debilitating as they were. But she was beginning to see the need to change. Anna has many excuses that can keep her stuck. "That'll never work with a child like Sarah. You just don't understand how bad it gets. It's about time she learned to wise up and be nice to us. She's not going to get a free ride in life." It's hard to take our focus off what our child is doing wrong to look at what we are contributing to the problem. Like Anna, we all have many excuses not to change. The next chapter will show you why.

● EXERCISE 8: **Taking It Personally (example)**

When my child _screams at me disrespectfully_ ,

    I think that s/he is _out to get me, trying to get me to do what she wants_ .
                                  (what you think your child's motive is)

Because I take this behavior personally, I focus only on my need to _be left alone and_

to be spoken to respectfully .

    If I focused on my child's need instead of the behavior, I might see that her/his

need is _to be heard and to be accepted. He's trying to tell me what he wants,_

but he doesn't know how .

So, if I acknowledge the need behind the behavior, I might think _he's hurting inside_

and is behaving badly because he wants to be heard

    instead of _he's being a brat and treating me disrespectfully—he's controlling_

our household .

When I have this new idea, I will be able to respond instead of react. So when s/he

    screams at me and demands my attention
                      (child's behavior)

    I will be able to _go for the emotion underneath and address how he must_

feel

    instead of _trying to get him to stop talking to me that way_ .

When I do that, I will be more effective in teaching different behavior.

● EXERCISE 8: Taking It Personally

Please complete either or both of the exercises that follow.
A.

When my child _____ ,

    I think that s/he is _____

                            (what you think your child's motive is)

_____ .

Because I take this behavior personally, I focus only on my need to _____

_____ .

    If I focused on my child's need instead of the behavior, I might see that her/his

    need is _____

_____ .

So, if I acknowledge the need behind the behavior, I might think _____

_____

    instead of _____

_____ .

When I have this new idea, I will be able to respond instead of react. So when s/he

_____

                              (child's behavior)

I will be able to _____

    instead of _____ .

When I do that, I will be more effective in teaching different behavior.

_____

• EXERCISE 8: **Taking It Personally (continued)**

B.

Notice how you react when your child pushes your buttons. What is your personal agenda? What do you think your child is doing to you with her/his behavior?

Describe your need—what you want your child to do instead and why.

Describe your child's agenda—what you guess your child is after and what the need is under the behavior.

Describe how you can change your thoughts about your child when you change your focus from your need to your child's need.

CHAPTER EIGHT

WHAT KEEPS YOU STUCK IN OLD RUTS?

Our deepest fear is not that we are inadequate. Our deepest fear
is that we are powerful beyond measure. It is our light,
not our darkness that most frightens us.
—MARIANNE WILLIAMSON, *A Return to Love*

D o you ever wonder what you might have been like had you grown up differently, if your parents had given you support for your feelings, respect for your side of the story, and considered you an important member of the family? Or if they had held you truly responsible for your behavior instead of letting you off the hook by either rescuing or punishing you?

Do you need others to tell you that you're okay? Do you feel confident in your abilities and able to do what is in your heart regardless of whether someone else thinks it's worthwhile? Do you wish you were on a different path, meeting your full potential, doing what you are meant to do?

Many of us stumble through our lives clinging to the beliefs our child-selves bought into. We choose our careers, our partners, and who we want our children to be based on who our child-self thinks we are, only to find out—if we ever do—that we are trying to fill a void left from long ago. Unless we decide these beliefs don't work for us anymore, search ourselves honestly, and take responsibility for making changes, we stay stuck in our old patterns and ruts.

But you might say, "I turned out okay. What's so wrong?" Few of us are left without at least one or two voids that want filling. But we have adapted, we have established our role. Many of us also have chosen an addiction or habit in an attempt to fill that void—at least temporarily.

Parenting the old way, even if you think it was okay for you, may not be okay for your child. But we continue to do it because it's so hard to do it differently.

Old Habits Die Hard: Making Different Choices

Human nature resists change—even when we desperately wish for different results in our lives. Now, you understand that in order to change the way you react, you need to change your assumptions—reevaluate your agenda and the standards and beliefs that control your thinking. To change their effects on you, you need to understand that they are choices you are making.

If I believed as a young child that I was not good enough to get my father's approval, I have most likely hung onto some form of that belief. *I don't quite measure up to other people's standards or even to my own. I'm not smart enough for that kind of career. I'm not good enough to be what I've always dreamed of. I still don't deserve approval.* As an adult, I now have the power to acknowledge these beliefs and make a different choice. We cannot change our childhoods. But we can decide we are not who we thought we were then.

Why do we choose to keep the beliefs we had as little children? Mostly because we are used to them. It's habit. It's who we are; it's who we know ourselves to be. We can make up all kinds of excuses to keep from changing the patterns in our lives and what we believe about ourselves.

- **We think that what we believe about ourselves is true.** We'd be lying to ourselves if we thought differently.
- **There are no guarantees** that making a change in our behavior

will get us the result we want. We could change and make everything worse.

- **We're pendulum thinkers.** The only alternative we see is the
  opposite.
- **We don't know what else to do.** The problem with the "I've
  tried everything and nothing works" excuse is that we have
  drawn only on what we already know.
- **We don't have time.** We want a quick fix, and we want it now.
  We're too stressed.
- **We're suspicious** of newfangled ideas. The old way has worked
  for generations, so why change what must be right.
- **We don't want to accept responsibility.** What's wrong with me
  is someone else's fault, not mine.
- **We don't trust ourselves.** Relatives and friends are a restraining
  influence as they judge us and direct our parenting either in reality or in our imagination.

Do you ever wonder if . . .

"I can't stand it anymore," Bill complained in class. "Willa's behavior is totally unacceptable. No one in their right mind would let her get away with what she's doing. Her behavior has got to change, and I have tried everything."

Bill is a single father raising three girls. Willa, thirteen, is the oldest. "She thinks she's sixteen and knows everything. I ground her, she sneaks out. I give her permission to go to her friend's and find out she's lied and gone to a party instead. She's horrible to her sisters, and rude is an understatement to describe her behavior with me." Many parents have lived with battles for so long that specific button-pushing behavior is hard to distinguish. It all rolls into one big, cumulative problem.

When I asked Bill what she was like as a young child, he said, "She's always been a walking land mine. You never know what she's going to do. She's an angel one minute and then hits her sister for no reason at all the next. We never really knew what to do with her, and since it's been just me, she's pretty much gotten her way. Now she's out of control and thinks she can do whatever she wants. I'm afraid she's going to either end up pregnant or in jail."

I suggested to Bill that now was the time for him to do some real soul searching and have some father-daughter heart-to-hearts.

"How do I do that when she doesn't even speak civilly to me?" Bill asked.

"Do you have a story about an incident in your teens when you got in big trouble with your parents and how unfair you thought their punishment was?"

"Sure!" Bill laughed. "But I'm not sure telling her what I did is such a good idea. That's what I'm afraid she's going to do."

"Exactly," I said. "You're afraid that telling her about it will give her permission to do it herself. Your fear keeps you from connecting with her. I imagine that you also believe it's your job to keep her from getting into trouble." He nodded. "So you must insist on obedience to do your job." He nodded again. "The problem is your standard is interfering with communicating with Willa in the only way you can right now. And if you can't communicate with her, you will have no influence on her.

It's too late to lay down more rules and expect her to follow them, but it's not too late to establish a relationship with her. Are you willing to expose some of your old self to prove that you understand her?"

"I don't think so," Bill said, looking at me like I had two heads. "I'm not her buddy; I'm her father, and she has to respect me."

"I absolutely agree with you. How do you imagine gaining her respect?"

"Well, I assumed you would give me some strategies for better punishments. She's got to learn that she can't act this way. If she knows I mean business, she'll respect me."

"Respect you or obey you?" I asked.

"What's the difference?" Bill said.

"There's a big difference. Did you obey your parents?" I asked.

Bill said that his father used the belt to keep his kids in line. "We knew who the boss was, and I learned what I could and couldn't do. She's lucky I don't hit her. Sometimes I think that's what I should do."

"With obedience comes fear, and a relationship based on fear isn't a great one," I added. "We may think it's important to sacrifice the relationship for our child's own good, but ultimately without relationship, we cannot influence our children with our values."

Bill confessed that he has little respect for and no communication with his father. We also found out that Bill hates his job but stays for the security, has never felt satisfied with his life, and has been through two tough divorces.

I told Bill that if he genuinely shared some of himself with Willa, she would listen in rapt attention. He could express his fears that she will choose a life with little opportunity and could apologize for reacting to his fear with punishments that feel unfair. I suggested ways to problem solve with Willa that would honor the needs of both of them. I pointed out that his parenting had shifted dramatically from permissive to autocratic and that the inconsistent expectations for Willa's behavior did not motivate her cooperation. It would take time and patience, but I imagined the relationship was worth it.

Bill thought that what I suggested would mean lowering his standards and stepping out of the role he thought he must play. He was sure it wouldn't work and that Willa would "take the ball and run with it." He did not understand how this would get her to cooperate, and he was not able to see that his discipline efforts contributed to Willa's bad behavior. He knew he had been too soft, and now he had to "crack down." As is true with many parents, Bill was not ready to accept responsibility or dig down to see the beliefs that drove him to unintentionally push his daughter away.

How Our Beliefs Serve Us

The most critical reason for not changing our behavior is that the old way has served us for a very long time. It's like a comfortable old shoe. We actually get something out of hanging onto our old beliefs. You may say, "But what could I possibly get out of something that's not working?" It's the familiarity, the comfort that comes from sameness and routine.

When we were little, we acted in a way that we hoped would get us what we needed—acceptance and approval—whether it was by being good or bad. Being smart little children, we adapted ourselves according to what we thought our parents wanted us to be—unless we couldn't. We created a false self and either stuffed away or exaggerated the self we thought was unacceptable.

If your father convinced you that you were unimportant, it was much safer for you to go along with him than fight him. So you believed you were unimportant—you didn't assert yourself or strive for anything he thought you would fail at anyway. It probably got you a relationship, negative though it was, with your father. Or you might have seen what happened to your sister when she stood up to him and decided you wanted none of that. Believing him and adapting as best you could was the smart thing to do.

Or you rebelled. You reacted strongly to the expectations you couldn't meet by becoming the "black sheep" or the "scapegoat" of the family. That too provided you with a role that you were forced into by family expectations. Your strong-willed temperament might have made it impossible for you to meet your father's expectations, and so his demands pushed you away. But you have led an unsatisfying life trying to prove to your father that you are somebody. Your underlying belief in your unworthiness has won out, and you have never quite made a success of your attempts.

Either way, you were not heard, and your needs were not met. You had to give up some of yourself to enable this false self to develop, which continues to nag with feelings of emptiness, dissatisfaction, or hurt. You may have lived thirty or forty years with this false self and learned how to accommodate and function. Perhaps medication has helped. It is not easy to decide to just change, to decide that you *are* important. That decision entails quite a bit—possibly doing something meaningful with your life.

Continuing patterns of behavior confirms over and over who we believe ourselves to be, even if that belief is negative and causes reactions we hate. It's much easier to continue believing *I am a failure* or *I'm ugly* than to believe the opposite, because all our behaviors in life have been confirming those beliefs.

Andrea got her buttons pushed each time one of her daughters said, "I can't . . ." This phrase signaled to Andrea that her girls saw themselves as inadequate and incapable. This was in direct conflict with her standard *No girl of mine will ever think that she can't do anything she wants.*

Andrea's parents had dampened her dreams by telling her that because she was a girl or because she didn't have what it takes, she couldn't follow those dreams. Through the class work, Andrea realized that she lived with the belief *I'm not smart enough because I'm a girl.* She was determined that her girls would never feel that way. So her button went off even when she heard an innocent "I can't tie my shoe."

In class, Andrea made the connections and realized the source of her button. She believed that she was not smart enough to do anything really well and had changed jobs often, never able to settle on a career.

I asked Andrea what she got out of believing that she wasn't smart enough.

She was confused. "I don't get anything out of it," she exclaimed. "I just told you it keeps me from staying with a job and doing it well."

"Yes, I understand," I said, "but what do you gain by hanging onto that belief? How does it serve you to keep believing it? What do you get to avoid?"

"Oh, I get it," she said slowly, thinking hard about the questions. "What do I get? I guess what you're after is that I get to keep believing I'm not smart enough."

"And why is it important for you to keep believing that?"

Tears came as she worked it through and understood. "If I believed I was smart enough, then I would have to show that somehow. I would have to choose something for my life and stick with it. And what if I failed? Then I would *prove* I'm not smart enough, and my parents would win."

"Is that your payoff?" I asked. "By keeping the belief alive that you're not smart enough, you protect yourself from failing to spite your parents."

"Yes," she said softly, choking back tears. "I guess I'm the only one keeping me from doing what I want. So if I give up this belief, it leaves me in the dangerous position of having to accept that I *am* smart and capable. I might have to find a career and do something with my life. Wow, that would be scary."

In order to model self-confidence and capability for her daughters, it was up to Andrea to change what she believed about herself. Her girls pointed the way each time they said "I can't . . ." because it pushed her button. When she didn't react to their words, she was able to hear their needs. She soon saw that an "I can't . . ." was no more than a harmless way of getting her attention or help. Usually it was as simple as, "I can't zip my coat" from her three-year-old or, "I can't do this math" from her ten-year-old.

Andrea arrived the next week bursting with a success story. At 9:00 P.M., Sophie, ten, had plopped on Andrea's bed and said, "You have to help me with this math. I can't do it." Instead of impatiently criticizing Sophie by telling her she could too do it if she didn't procrastinate until the last minute, Andrea admitted, "I really don't know how to help you with that math." With a pathetic look that normally sent Andrea over the edge, Sophie whined, "I hate this. I can't do math."

Andrea was aware of her rising feeling of hopelessness and quickly used self-talk to bring her emotions back down. She breathed deeply and said, "You're really having a hard time with that math."

Sophie said, "I hate long division."

Andrea said, "I know. I hate it too. Long division is hard."

"So what's the answer to this one?"

"I don't know."

Sophie said, "Do you divide this one into this?"

Andrea said, "Yes."

"The teacher said we can use calculators. I'm going to get it." The homework was soon finished, and they both went to sleep that night feeling quite competent. Andrea beamed. "I did a great job!" she said. "I realized that Sophie's frustration did not mean the same devastating thing it meant to me. It was in fact just Sophie's frustration. It wasn't about me."

Fear Is the Bottom Line

All of the excuses we use to ward off change come from fear. Fear is an important emotion. It often protects us from harm. But when it gets in the way of self-change, it keeps us from connecting with our heart. It can also keep us from connecting with our children. We need to acknowledge our fear and put it aside—not deny it, not disown it—just put it aside. We need to have the courage to break out of old patterns of beliefs. **We need to parent today, not in reaction to yesterday.**

Resisting change, maintaining the familiar, is part of the human condition. We like stability. It feels safe. But change is also part of the human condition. The key is to take it one step at a time. Contrary to what you may think, you do not have to become a different person. What have you got to lose? Yelling, screaming, rageful accusations, and blame? Power struggles and discipline methods that don't work? When you look at it that way, isn't it absurd to keep doing the same old thing?

● EXERCISE 9: **How My Belief Serves Me (example)**

I have identified a limiting belief I have about myself as, _sacrificing my desires gets_

me approval from my mother .

I have this belief because _my mother always taught me to ignore my own_

wishes and to help others in more need than myself—and to always look to see

who might be in need .

How that drives my parenting today causes me to _never say no when I'm asked for_

anything, jump when my children want anything, volunteer for too much ,

which keeps me from _spending time with my family—relaxing—taking care of_

_me_ .

What I get out of hanging onto this belief is _knowing that I will continue to get_
(how this belief serves you)

people's approval .

This allows me to _keep believing that I'm a good person_ .
(what you can keep doing or avoid doing)

If I let go of this, I'm afraid that I will have to face _who I really am. If I don't do all_
(something about yourself)

this stuff for people, it means I'm bad ,

and then I am afraid that _I will have to prove myself some other way—like get_
(what you will have to do about it)

a job and work hard .

If I want to change this, I need to _realize that I am a good person and deserve love_

even if I don't always please others .

If I leave my belief in the past, I can _set better boundaries and rules with my_
(how you can change your parenting)

kids, do things for me, and be a better wife and mom .

● EXERCISE 9: How My Belief Serves Me

Please complete either or both of the exercises that follow.
A.

I have identified a limiting belief I have about myself as, _____

_____ .

   I have this belief because _____

_____ .

How that drives my parenting today causes me to _____

_____ ,

   which keeps me from _____

_____ .

What I get out of hanging onto this belief is _____
(how this belief serves you)

_____ .

   This allows me to _____ .
(what you can keep doing or avoid doing)

If I let go of this, I'm afraid that I will have to face _____

_____ ,
(something about yourself)

   and then I am afraid that _____

_____ .
(what you will have to do about it)

If I want to change this, I need to _____ .

   If I leave my belief in the past, I can _____

_____ ;
(how you can change your parenting)

● EXERCISE 9: **How My Belief Serves Me (continued)**

B.

Describe the limiting belief you have about yourself and how it interferes with your needs and your child's needs.

What does believing it get you? What do you get to avoid or keep doing? Why?

What are you afraid might happen if you stopped believing this?

If you no longer believed this about yourself, how would your parenting be affected? What could you believe differently about yourself?

PART TWO
THE BUTTONS

CHAPTER NINE

THE BUTTON STORIES

*[W]hen your kids 'push' your buttons, they've actually
tapped into your own struggles learning how to assert yourself.*
—MARY SHEEDY KURCINKA, *Kids, Parents, and Power Struggles*

Each of us is unique, and each of our stories is different. You may have one clear, outstanding button that you can identify. But many parents have buttons in different areas of their relationship. Whatever your buttons, they represent an unrealistic or inappropriate standard established because of a belief learned in childhood. Our defensive reactions toward our children are meant to uphold that standard and protect that belief. It is natural and logical to do this—until we understand what's at stake.

The following chapters identify eight buttons, with stories illustrating each. The first step in defusing your buttons is to identify them. These stories illustrate the buttons of many different parents in many different parenting situations—from innocuous and common to serious and potentially dangerous. You may identify with certain buttons, or you may find yourself in parts of several. You will see that some of the stories illustrate more than one button. For instance, a parent who has a responsibility button may have a fix-it button as well. I have placed each story with the button that labels the predominant theme of that story.

These buttons by no means represent all possible buttons or combinations of buttons. It is my hope that the stories inspire you to uncover and identify your own.

You will notice that some of the stories end with success and some do not. When parents persevere, progress is made. Some successes come merely with awareness and a little knowledge; others require a deeper understanding and hard work. Some of the stories are of parents who are at the beginning; some have been at it for a long time. Each success story describes only one incident. This does not mean the frustrations are over. But achieving success even once is a huge step. It is evidence that hard work is paying off. Each success builds confidence for the next time. Some of the stories dig into the parent's own childhood for the origin of a button; some show incidents where changing the assumption alone can alter the outcome.

Automatic Ideas

As you read the button stories, notice how parents "go on automatic" when they react to their child's behavior. Due to our own temperaments and experiences, our automatics are usually expressed in one of two ways: We may **explode** by expressing anger, being overly controlling and protective, manipulating our children, and blaming them for our problems and inconveniences. Or we may **implode** by giving up, giving in, blaming ourselves, withdrawing, resenting, and spiraling inward to a dark place of self-defeat.

While more autocratic parents tend to automatically say no (to convey *I'm the boss*) to their children, more permissive parents tend toward an automatic yes (or *Whatever you want*) when their children demand something. The autocratic parent, who has a harder time saying yes, feels the need to maintain power and control in his relationship with his child. He fears that saying yes means giving over his power to his child and relinquishing his role as boss. He may have cowered under the feared power of one of his parents and learned that autocracy is the parent's job. Or he may have been given so much control as a child that he holds on to that control, because it has become his identity—*I'm the boss*.

The permissive parent who has a hard time saying no has more difficulty setting limits, following through on consequences, creating boundaries, separating from the child, and letting go. She may fear being rejected by her child or seen as unloving or uncaring. She may perceive no as rejecting or shaming, as this may be how she experienced her own parent saying no. Or she may have rarely heard it growing up and never learned how to say it effectively.

We often fluctuate between the two depending on our present mood and circumstance. Think of a continuum from permissive to autocratic with your goal being a balance somewhere in the middle. When your button gets pushed it sends you quickly to your automatic—the autocratic end or the permissive end. It will be helpful to examine your reactions to find your predominant pattern.

Parent Temperaments

Our individual temperaments have a great deal to do with our reactions. For instance, a highly organized, fastidious parent has a much harder time accepting a child's messiness than a parent who is less organized. The neat and organized parent may have a tendency to be more controlling and to say no more often than not. An easygoing, more flexible parent may tend to give in to her child's demands by saying yes more often. Temperament is often referred to in these stories. It is a critical piece in understanding your child's needs. (Mary Sheedy Kurcinka's book *Raising Your Spirited Child* is an excellent source for learning more about the temperamental qualities of both you and your child.)

Which Style Is Yours?

The following questions may help you understand in which direction your buttons send you:

1. When I find myself reacting automatically, I tend to explode/implode. (circle one)
2. When I explode, I do that by _____.
3. When I implode, I do that by _____.
4. I have more of a tendency to say yes/no to my child. (circle one)

5. If I tend to say yes, it is harder for me to say no because I am afraid that _____.

6. If I tend to say no, it is harder to say yes because I am afraid that

_____.

In the following button stories see if you can identify which parents explode or implode and which ones have an easier time saying yes or saying no. What are the parent's and child's agendas for each situation? Have they been thwarted?

What are the assumptions made by each parent that cause the emotions and reactions? Think about the parent's expectations of herself, her child, or the situation. Can you see how these expectations come from the standards held by the parent? And in some of the stories, can you see how the beliefs from childhood played into the standards currently held? How do a parent's standards and agendas get in the way of connecting and being effective? See if you can determine the best intention of the parent, how it was miscommunicated, and how it was received by the child. How much of a gap has developed between parent and child? What situations close or open the gap farther?

Where there is success, what assumptions has the parent let go of or changed? How has the standard been adjusted? What has the parent done to connect?

CHAPTER TEN

THE APPROVAL BUTTON

I t is the rare parent who never sees her child as a reflection of her-self. Some go to extremes. From supermarket behavior to the col-lege choice, an approval-seeking parent watches her child while keenly sensing the eyes of others watching her. The pressure is on, and if her child does not behave according to her standards, she fears em-barrassment. The world will confirm that she has failed and will see her as the fake she fears herself to be.

Approval-seeking parents are trying to avoid their shame when they tell their children, "Say hello to Mrs. Jones," "You will wear what I tell you to wear," or "Stop embarrassing me!" These are ways to manipulate children to guarantee that stamp of approval from the outside world. "And the 'I'm the Best Parent' award goes to . . . ?"

Many parents still work hard for the approval of their own parents. The strings are still tightly attached. Often the assumed feelings of their parents take precedence over the feelings of their child. The par-ent feels caught in the middle and defers to the old pattern, risking their children's needs in the process.

When their button is pushed, approval-seeking parents feel ex-posed and embarrassed. Looking good is their ultimate protection. Children of approval-seeking parents typically feel incompetent, unlovable, ashamed, and never good enough.

When children push the approval button they are saying, "Stop lis-tening to what other people think and listen to what you and I need."

"I'm between a Rock and a Hard Place."
Eleanor and Sydney (8)

Eleanor is a tired and stressed young mother, drained of energy yet determined in her mission. She claims responsibility for everything Sydney and her younger brother do, have ever done, and will ever do. "Their happiness is my responsibility," she said emphatically. Eleanor has to make sure they never have a problem because their behavior is a direct reflection of her competence as a parent. She is exhausted by the vigilance the job requires. She says she is constantly putting out fires and fixing their problems. She relayed the following story to the class.

Eleanor's mother, Adrian, was visiting the day of Sydney's final softball game. Sydney had missed the previous two games, so this day's game was especially important to her. Before it was time to leave, Eleanor asked Sydney if she had all her gear together. Sydney said she couldn't find her glove. Eleanor suggested she better look for it, but

Sydney slid farther down in her seat and whined, "I can't. You find it." Embarrassed by her daughter's behavior in front of her mother, Eleanor insisted that Sydney look. But when the whining and stubbornness continued, Eleanor began her search in hopes that Sydney would be happy and stop whining.

Adrian had often complained that Sydney was spoiled and needed a good spanking. Uncomfortable under her mother's scrutiny, Eleanor was sure this was what her mother was thinking now. She recalled the many times in her childhood when her mother had criticized her "silly" desires and spanked her each time she heard a whine or a complaint. Eleanor had worked hard in school to win her mother's approval, but each B was criticized for not being an A, and each A was criticized for not being an A+.

The search for the elusive baseball glove went upstairs, downstairs, inside, and out. Sydney was complaining at her mother's heels everywhere she went. At one point, in the backyard, a frantic Sydney yelled at her mother, "You are so stupid! Why can't you find it? We've got to go soon." Speechless, Eleanor darted a warning look toward Sydney. Adrian began muttering about a spanking just loud enough to entangle Eleanor with familiar feelings of inadequacy. Even as an adult, she could never get it right.

As Eleanor's anger continued to build, she took a last trip upstairs with Sydney tagging behind. While Eleanor scoured the bookshelves, Sydney, who up until this point had not helped in the search at all, picked up her pajamas from the floor of her closet and uncovered the "holy grail." Shrieking with delight, pride written all over her face, Sydney exclaimed, "Mom, look, I found my glove!" It was all Eleanor could do to contain her rage. Seeing the look on Sydney's face, she realized that Sydney had instantly forgotten all that had just happened and was now ready to go to the game.

Eleanor was frozen. She glared into Sydney's sparkling eyes with a "how dare you embarrass me in front of my mother" stare and sternly told her to sit on her bed and be quiet. She staggered into the hall and sat on the stairs heading down to the kitchen, her head in her hands. She was trapped. Above her were the wails of her daughter, now fearing the worst, and below her was her mother pacing back and forth, tossing critical glances up the stairs.

Adrian won. Eleanor knew she could not let Sydney off the hook without being accused of raising a spoiled brat. She told Sydney that she would not be going to the game after behaving the way she had. She went back downstairs to face her mother's criticism of Sydney's "astonishingly rude behavior" while screams of "It's not fair!" rained from upstairs.

Clearly Sydney's agenda was different from her mother's. She intended to go to the game and win. She wanted her mother to be proud of her. She knew playing well was important to her mother. Plus, she had missed the past two games. She had to be there. Perhaps her friends on the team would give her grief for missing again. Sydney fully expected her mother to find the glove, as she always had—mothers just do that. When her mother couldn't find it, Sydney got anxious. Her surprise at unearthing the glove herself filled her with pride and elation. She assumed her mother would be proud of her! But, no. What were those glaring, accusing eyes telling her? This wasn't her mother. What was happening?

No warning—"Unless you help with this search . . . " or "Until you stop these rude remarks, you will not be going to this game"—had been given to Sydney. And it was a familiar scenario. Sydney had never before been expected to take responsibility for lost objects. Why would this time be any different? But she didn't take into account the powerful influence her grandmother held over her mother.

Putting her children's happiness first, Eleanor had actually set Sydney up to treat her disrespectfully. Eleanor had taught Sydney over the years to expect her to take responsibility for Sydney's things, so when her mother was not behaving as she had come to expect, Sydney got angry. Not an appropriate response, but a logical one. Eleanor could not see what part of the situation was her responsibility and what part was Sydney's. She felt trapped. She went for her mother's approval.

Had Adrian not been there, Eleanor probably would have given in and taken Sydney to the game, fuming inside with resentment but putting her daughter's happiness first. As it was, Eleanor was caught between a rock and a hard place—between her mother's approval and her daughter's happiness.

If Eleanor believes that she is incompetent and worthless, then her children's behavior is critical to her self-worth. When they are happy and behaving properly, she can relax. But when Sydney is rude and disrespectful, her belief is triggered, and she feels threatened. She reacts with anger but has no idea how to find balance in the situation. Her ability to hold Sydney accountable for her behavior is too hard given her need to make her happy. But her need for her mother's approval beats all else. It's too easy to fall back into her pattern of incompetence when her mother is glaring over her shoulder. It keeps her relationship with her mother safe, but it puts her at high risk in her relationship with her daughter. But she's been in a relationship with her mother a good deal longer than with her daughter.

Had Eleanor felt more competent in her abilities, she would have been able to set up clear guidelines with Sydney. If her button were defused, she could have said with no emotional stake at all, "Sydney, I'd like you to spend ten minutes looking for your glove. If you haven't found it by then, I will help. But better get started now, because we will need to leave in half an hour." If Sydney had refused, a detached Eleanor might have been able to say, "When you've looked for ten minutes, let me know whether you've found it or not. If you don't want to look, that tells me you don't want to go to the game." It would then be Sydney's choice whether to look for her glove or miss another game.

"Don't Embarrass Me in Public."
Leslie and Brian (6), Beth (8), and Peter (12)

Leslie came to the "When Your Kids Push Your Buttons" class quite distraught because her son's teacher suggested that she get him evaluated for Attention Deficit Hyperactivity Disorder (ADHD). She did not want Brian to be coded with a label that would live with him throughout his school years. She felt sure she could handle him; she just wasn't sure how.

Brian is the youngest of Leslie's three children and is the one who pushes her buttons the hardest. "He's in my face all the time," she protested. "He just never stops. I'm exhausted. God knows how I'll make it to, let alone through, his teens!" Leslie's fear of the ADHD label has made her determined to figure him out. After a few classes, she shared with us the following story.

One day, while shopping, Leslie experienced every mother's worst nightmare. She had promised her kids a trip to the lake, but wanted to do two errands on the way. Her first stop was a quick pickup at the grocery store while the kids stayed in the car. When she returned, Brian was miserable. He complained about how hot he was and whined, "Didn't you bring me anything to drink?" The tone of his voice, although familiar, set Leslie off, and she retorted with annoyance, "How was I supposed to know you were hot and thirsty? You'll have to wait till we get to the lake."

The second stop was at Marshall's to get the boys some socks. Brian insisted on coming in, much to Leslie's dismay. She hated going into stores with him. She tried to find the socks quickly and escape, but Brian hung on her, persisted loudly about getting to the lake, and complained that he was dying of thirst. She prayed that no one was watching.

As she turned to tell him to let go of her arm, an older woman appeared, pointed her finger at Brian, and snapped, "Your behavior is not only distressing your mother, but every other shopper in this store!" Leslie looked at her in horror, too shocked to speak. The woman gave them both a disdainful shake of her head and disappeared behind ladies' dresses.

Leslie was mortified. This woman embodied all her fears of what other people must be thinking. She blew. "You see how your behavior bothers other people, too?! Now maybe you'll listen when I tell you to stop," she yelled loudly for the benefit of those who were watching, waiting to see what she would do. Brian kept on about the lake.

In this moment of confrontation, Leslie's small voice that knows Brian is unique and requires unique parenting, shut down. Instead, a louder, harsher voice spoke, telling her that she had failed to raise a child worthy of approval. It confirmed her fears that Brian really is an ADHD child, that she really isn't cut out for parenting, and that indeed this woman was absolutely right.

Hindsight helped Leslie see that her sudden reaction to Brian resulted from her embarrassment at being seen as a bad mother raising an uncontrollable child. Not until much later did she consider that the woman's intrusive remark was highly inappropriate. Leslie was willing to forgo being her child's ally to believe wholeheartedly the judgment of a total stranger—to, in effect, betray her child.

Leslie's standard tells her that *Children should do what their parents tell them whether they like it or not*. Her first two children were proof to her that that standard is appropriate. "If I told them to leave the room because I needed to make a phone call, they would do it. If I tell Brian to leave the room, he will find every possible excuse not to and insist on talking to the person himself," she said with disdain. Leslie's standard does not allow for a child who is temperamentally different. If she is shopping in a crowded store and he begs to leave, her attitude is, *I have to do this, and you're coming with me because I say so*—even though she knows that noises and too much stimulation set him off. Leslie is confused by Brian's temperament rather than understanding of it. She assumes that she should be able to teach him to behave like her other two children.

After her work in the class, Leslie understood that at the time of the incident, her agenda was all that mattered. When he didn't go along with it, she clenched her teeth and tried to remain calm, but her tension was picked up on his radar screen. He knew she wanted him to behave properly in public. The problem was that her definition of proper was not something he knew how to do. He became rigid whenever he sensed he was not meeting her approval, and his behavior accelerated.

After a number of classes, Leslie had a success story. She and all three children were in the dentist's office waiting for Brian's appointment. Leslie was making a plan with Brian's older sister to go Christmas shopping. Brian looked up from the toy box on the other side of the room and cried, "I have to go, too!"

"No, I'm taking Beth. I spend a lot of time doing things like that with you; now it's her turn." Leslie said she was amazed at her calmness and clarity, even though she feared his reaction. She knew that the empty waiting room helped.

Brian continued crying, forgetting how much he hates shopping. His agenda was to be included. Too often Leslie said okay when Brian complained, and her daughter felt resentful whenever he tagged along. This time she said, again calmly, "If you want to scream, why don't you go in the coat room." To Leslie's amazement, he did. He feigned a few fake screams, stomped back into the waiting room, plopped down in a chair, and pulled his coat over his head. Leslie continued the book she had started to read to the other two.

In a few minutes, Brian pulled the coat off his head, sat straight up, and declared, "You're right. I realized under my coat that I do get to do a lot of special things with you. It's okay. You can go with Beth."

I pointed out to Leslie that she hadn't blamed him for his initial re-action. She gave him something to do with his frustration and allowed him to work it through. The empty waiting room was a good place to practice her new skills.

Leslie's standard, *Children should do what their parents tell them whether they like it or not,* is what gets threatened when Brian's behavior embarrasses her in public. She is working on letting go of what others will think. At first, she worried that this meant letting him get away with being rude, but she soon saw that the tension she felt while trying to uphold this standard in public actually aggravated Brian's tension and inevitable rude behavior. The tension was not there in the dentist's waiting room. She could try out her new understanding of what lies beneath his behavior instead of reacting to it as usual.

"What Must People Think?"
Barbara and Lily (3)

She's making my life so difficult. I'm a total loser. She's being a brat. These were the assumptions that were hard to draw out of Barbara. She was so afraid the others in the group would think she was a terri-ble mother that it wasn't until several weeks into the group that we heard anything from her. "I was so afraid of what people would think of me," she said after she understood how common her struggle was. She became more open about sharing what a bad mother she thought she was. Barbara is a twenty-year-old single mom struggling to balance a full-time job and a very strong-willed three-year-old.

"Why do you think you're a bad mother?" I asked.

"Because I can't get Lily to do what I say. She won't eat, and she won't use the toilet when I tell her to. I know she's doing it just to get me. She's perfectly capable of going to the toilet, but now she's withholding her poop. When I put her on her potty seat, she refuses to go. She's fine at day care, which really gets me. She'll do it for them but not for me. I exploded at her when she woke me up in the middle of the night to tell me she'd pooped."

"Why do you think it's your fault?" another group member asked.

"Because I can't get her potty trained. What's wrong with me anyhow?" Barbara began to tear up. "My friends come over and say, 'She's not potty trained? What's with that?' I get so upset. And I blame myself for divorcing her father and having to work such long hours. I have to do everything alone." She hung her head silently for a minute and then continued. "But the worst is my father. He has this 'I told you so' attitude about my ex-husband and won't help me out, because he says I made my bed and now I have to lie in it. But whenever Lily has an accident—and of course that happens every time we're at my parents' house—my father gives that look. I know he's saying, 'What's the matter with you? You can't even mother properly.' I can't ever get it right."

When she was a child, Barbara's father never actually told her she was bad. She just knew it from the way "he exuded his disapproval." Barbara admitted to being "slightly" rebellious as a teenager, but mostly she remained a "good girl" to avoid her father's "evil eye," as she called it. "It was that look. That's all he had to do," she said, "and I knew I was in trouble."

"What kind of trouble?" I asked.

"That's the funny thing," she said. "We never really got spanked or grounded or anything; it was just that look that told us we had been bad. It gives me the shivers now just to picture my father's face. And about anything—if I came in late for dinner, or said something he didn't like, or wanted something he didn't want me to have. I just felt so incredibly guilty."

It was the withdrawal of approval from their father that kept Barbara and her sisters in line. Their father's silence and stony look signaled his disapproval and disappointment. "I saw that look, and I felt about as small as an insect. Then I would have to win it back. I would do all sorts of nice things for him until I got a smile once again. Sometimes it was days before he'd change. Then it was touch and go until the next incident. It sure did the trick."

The "trick" resulted in Barbara seeking approval anywhere she could get it—even from three-year-old Lily.

"When Lily behaves properly—uses the potty, eats a good meal, is cute and charming when we're with anyone else—I give myself this huge pat on the back. It's like she is my seal of approval," Barbara confessed with a little embarrassment.

Barbara's father had managed well to teach his daughters how to behave the way he wanted. But the fallout was great. What he probably didn't intend by withdrawing his approval was the resulting insecurity his daughter felt about anything she attempted, even with her own child.

"But most of the time, Lily makes me feel like a total loser as a mother," Barbara said. "It's like she's throwing in my face everything I doubt about myself."

"Isn't it amazing how that happens?" I said. "Our children are constantly pointing out to us our greatest faults and then rubbing salt in the wounds! What do you think she's trying to tell you?"

"I don't get what you mean." Barbara was confused.

"When Lily refuses to eat or use the potty, she is pushing your button, and that button is causing you to think she's a brat and is out to get you. If you think that, you will of course react with anger." Barbara nodded. "But when she pushes that button, she is attempting to tell you something about yourself. If you think you are a loser at mothering because she won't use the potty, that means you're using her behavior for your validation. So if she fails, you fail. You're asking from her what you wanted from your father."

"Wow. So if he had approved of me, I would be better able to handle Lily?" she asked quizzically.

"Well, I don't think you would take her behavior so personally if you felt more confident of yourself. She is most likely asking for more power when she resists eating and toileting. She's telling you that—not what a bad mother you are. You perceive your father criticizing your mothering and project that onto Lily."

When Lily pushes her buttons, all of Barbara's needs for approval rear up to smack her in the face. She does not want to be reminded of what a bad girl/bad mother she is, so she turns her blame on Lily. The pressure is on Lily to perform, to show what a good mother Barbara is, but Lily is her mother's teacher. She will persist in her resistance until her mother learns that her button is about herself, not about Lily.

I told Barbara that when little children feel powerless, they take it out on their parents in the areas of toileting, eating, and sleeping, where they know they have ultimate control. We talked about the many ways she could give Lily more control in her daily life by giving her choices, taking her agenda into consideration, and validating her feelings even if Barbara doesn't like them.

Another working mother in the group asked Barbara if she thought Lily might be angry about the hours her mother is away. This was hard for Barbara to talk about because of the guilt she felt at leaving her daughter in day care for long hours. But when she heard other mothers discussing not only their own guilt but their strategies, she perked up. She decided to talk to Lily about how unhappy she must feel about being separated from her mom all day. She would tell her that each day after playground time, Barbara would arrive and then Lily could choose what they would do together for the first half hour at home.

"But what about the potty training?" Barbara asked.

"The key is not to expect potty training to validate your worth. When you don't have that pressure on yourself anymore, you will let up on Lily, and she can relax. You may never get your father's approval, but if you can give unconditional approval to Lily, whether she is potty trained or not, you will be able to give yourself approval for a job well done. Listen to Lily. She will keep pushing you until you give yourself what you are demanding from her. She cannot give it to you, but she can provide you with the opportunity to give it to yourself."

Barbara was still struggling at the end of the class, but her final exercise showed that progress was happening slowly. Her new standard, *My daughter is in charge of her own body, and I can give her my approval even when she has an accident,* says that Barbara's perception has changed. She understands the importance of Lily taking responsibility for herself in the areas of previous resistance. When she can give Lily what she longed for from her father, Barbara will help herself as well as Lily.

CHAPTER ELEVEN

THE CONTROL BUTTON

Parents with control buttons are in constant fear of losing that control to their children. In order to maintain control, they require obedience and perfection from their children. Controlling parents fear that if they are not in control, they will expose imperfection in themselves—that they will be out of control. They must be the boss in order to keep those "bad" parts of themselves hidden.

When controlling parents "win" a power struggle, they are deceived into thinking they have maintained authority and control. In fact, the opposite is usually the case. What eludes these parents is the fact that in the winning, they set the child up for rebellion and retaliation, and the seed of the next power struggle is planted. On the other hand, a more complacent, adaptable child willing to submit to the control as a means of avoiding the parent's wrath may give the parent a sense of a win and a job well done. The child, however, is at risk of feeling invisible, unheard, and dependent on the approval of others in later years.

When their button is pushed, controlling parents get enraged. Children of controlling parents typically feel unimportant, wrong, unaccepted, and not good enough.

Pushing the control button is a child's way of saying, "Lighten up and let go of always having to be right. You may find more power in sharing it with me."

"Do What I Tell You to Do."
Matthew, Ruth, and Cindy (15)

Matthew and Ruth called me in a panic. Their daughter Cindy had run away. It was not the first time. They were frantic, angry, and lost.

Cindy was forbidden to have friends at the house after school when her parents weren't home. She had broken that rule before. Drugs were missing from the medicine cabinet and alcohol from the liquor cabinet. The rule had been broken again, and Cindy was grounded again, but this time, she had escaped through her window. Ruth was worried and scared. Matthew was just plain enraged.

"She's turning into a no-good druggy, her and all her druggy friends!" he stormed. "Well, they can't do their drugs and have their sex in my house. They've already stolen my money, my pills, and my liquor. She lies all the time, and she knows I will not tolerate a liar. I told her next time, I would call the police."

I asked more about her history, knowing that primarily I needed to help them with an immediate plan. Matthew began by saying that

Cindy had low self-esteem, so I used that opportunity to approach the cause of her behavior.

"What makes you think her self-esteem is low?" I asked.

"Our older two kids have turned out fine," Ruth added. "But Cindy's always lived in the shadow of her popular older sister."

Matthew continued. "I don't know what's wrong with her. She's never listened or done what she was told. I said she could have her friends over when we're home, but they always go somewhere else. Just as well."

I asked, "Why do you think she doesn't want to bring them home?"

Matthew snickered. "When I told her she could, she just rolled her eyes and said, 'Yeah right, Dad.' I should have smacked her right then."

"Slip into her shoes," I suggested. "Be her right now and tell me what her parents think of her friends."

"That they're no-good losers," he said with no hesitation.

"So why would she want to bring her friends home when you're there?"

He cleared his throat.

Ruth joined in. "She's never had friends that we would have chosen for her. She's never been able to make friends easily, like her older sister. And then last year, she started hanging out with these kids and getting into drugs. I think she's had sex with one or two of them."

"Think?!" barked Matthew. "Know is more like it!"

"How do you know?" I asked.

"Because I found a condom under the couch cushion. She's been lying to us for a long time." Then he muttered almost inaudibly, "She's just like my niece."

I asked him to tell me why he thought that.

"My niece is a good-for-nothing. She ended up a drug addict, lost her job, lost her husband and kids. My brother won't have anything to do with her anymore. I don't blame him."

"Are you willing to lose your daughter, Matthew?"

"If she keeps on with her druggy friends and her criminal behavior I am."

"Do you love her?" I asked.

"Of course I love her, but I will not tolerate this behavior."

I had an inroad. "Of course. You can't tolerate the *behavior*, but you love *her*. It's her behavior you abhor. Let's see if we can figure out where the behavior is coming from."

I explained how our intended messages often get misguided en route to our children. I suggested that from Cindy's point of view, she's probably feeling controlled and unaccepted. "It sounds like she's trying desperately to get you to see her. Her behavior is her only way of saying, 'You're making me feel like I don't belong here. You need to accept me for who I am.'"

Ruth said softly, "She does tell us that, actually. She'll scream at us that we don't get her, we never have, and so what's the point. But we've tried giving her what she wants, we've tried doing what her counselor suggested, but she refuses to go anymore. It didn't help anyway. And grounding certainly doesn't work."

"What you *think* she wants might not be what she really wants. Often when we think we are doing the best for our children, it inadvertently pushes them away and breaks our connection," I explained. "Right now, what Cindy needs more than anything is to be accepted. She has found friends who are doing that, and to keep them, she thinks she has to do drugs with them. She may not care about the drugs. But she does care about being accepted. Do you want them to be the only people in her life who accept her? When you can do that for her, she may not need those friends. But it will take a while. She probably doesn't trust you any more than you trust her."

"But what do we do right now?" Matthew said in a more neutral tone than I had heard before. "We've got calls out to all her friends and to the police."

"Hopefully she will come home on her own. Let her know you love her, no matter what. Acknowledge to her that you have made some mistakes. That you are sorry for some of the things you have said. That the mistakes are reactions to your fears about her safety. Tell her you want to trust her, and you want her to trust you. Refrain from any blame. The only thing that will work now is making a connection with her. Any more restrictions, groundings, or criticism will push her farther away. The only choice you have to bring her back is to accept her with everything that comes with her. You might start by accepting her friends."

"I can't do that!" Matthew stormed. "What do you want me to do? Tell them it's fine with me to ransack my house; it's fine with me to come over and do their drugs and screw my daughter?"

"Accepting them does not mean you are condoning what they do. Think of it as a serious illness. It wouldn't be helpful to tell someone who might be dying that they shouldn't have done what they did to get sick."

"Okay," Matthew conceded, "I'll try. I'll say you can have your friends over next Wednesday when we're not here if you behave properly. But if I find out they got into anything, that's the end of it." The rage began to rise again.

"Can you say the same thing but with a positive tone?"

Matthew planned his words carefully. "I know you'd rather have your friends over when we're not here. We can try next Wednesday after school. But please let them know that they are not allowed to do drugs here."

"Can you do that?" I asked. Matthew agreed that he could. He also agreed to change his assumption *She's lying to me* to *She's protecting herself from getting into trouble*. I warned him not to expect much from her, that it would take a while for her to build trust and for them to give it.

I agreed that they had a lot to be angry and scared about. Cindy had made some bad decisions. Their worst fears were becoming reality. Everyone was reacting automatically, and those reactions were widening the gap between them. I explained to them that when in crisis mode, parenting standards must be put on hold. The only option now was to work for connection. In that connection, Cindy could come back without losing face. Only then would their influence have effect.

Matthew was loaded with automatic assumptions: *She's a druggy. She's a liar. She has never listened.* In a situation like this, it is easy to catastrophize to *She's a slut, and she'll end up in jail if she's not dead*. He has also associated Cindy with his niece, increasing his fears. These assumptions seem realistic given the circumstances. But when I suggested to Matthew that he change *her druggy friends* to *her friends* and *she's a liar* to *she's protecting herself,* his tone changed, and his mind opened.

Matthew and Ruth's standards, which probably include *No child of mine will get into trouble with drugs and sex,* fuel the adamant conclusions they have drawn about Cindy and her behavior. In times of crisis, assumptions and perceptions are what need to change immediately. Often when that brings results, new ideas can prompt new standards.

Cindy did come home that day and did not react negatively when she heard her parents' attempt at connection. She listened and agreed to try their suggestion. A lot more work is needed to repair some deep-set patterns, but if Matthew and Ruth are willing to accept her, resist their past expectations, and adjust their standards to suit Cindy's needs at the present time, they will be able to save her from drowning and save themselves from losing the daughter they love.

"Because I Say So, That's Why."
Robert and Kelsey (3½)

Robert and his daughter Kelsey butt heads much of the time. Kelsey is spirited, strong-willed and tests her father's patience every day. Robert does not experience the same problems with his six-year-old son. Robert thinks he is a delight. Kelsey on the other hand, even though he admires her determination and spunk, pushes his control buttons.

Robert is a charming young father with a delightful sense of humor. But he likes to have things go his way. He feels off balance when plans get changed. Adaptability has never been his strong suit. When he has a problem, he likes to maintain control. His problem takes center stage. Nothing else matters. And family members usually let him have his way. All but Kelsey, that is.

Mostly their power struggles are over relatively insignificant issues like Kelsey not putting on her shoes when Robert wants her to. He will argue and yell at her until she has a "meltdown" and Robert has won. He relayed a typical scene.

"Kelsey, get your shoes on. We're going now."

"No, I'm playing house, and Amanda has to go to sleep now."

"Kelsey, get them on now, I said."

"No, wait a minute."

Further stalling provoked Robert to grab her arm and plunk her down beside her shoes. Kelsey cried and kicked him, yelling, "You're no fair. You never let me do what I want."

"Oh, yeah, you always get your way. Now do something I am asking you to do for once. Get those shoes on now, or I'm taking Amanda away for a week," Robert yelled in that voice that sometimes scares her into submission. But Kelsey continued to scream as he pinned her down, put her shoes on her—"quite forcefully," he added—and dragged her to the car.

"That's a common morning in our house," Robert said smugly. "What am I supposed to do? Let her run the house, do whatever she wants? No way! She's got to learn that what I say goes!"

Robert added that he doesn't get particular satisfaction out of winning, but he cannot stand to lose. If Kelsey "gets her way," Robert thinks that she has robbed him of something essential. "My being in control, I guess. Having the final say" is how he put it.

Robert's standard, written at the beginning of class stated, *My children will learn about reality if the unreasonable way they act elicits irrational, negative responses from me.* He could then justify his angry reactions by convincing himself that those reactions would teach his children about the real world and influence them to behave appropriately.

After Robert read it aloud he said, "I guess they're pretty negative and unrealistic."

"And I might add, rather complicated and elaborate," I said with a smile.

I suggested he try an experiment. Having a plan that he would be in charge of sparked Robert's interest, and he immediately rose to the challenge. I suggested that for one week he try allowing Kelsey to win, to refrain from arguing and observe what happened. Since it was a finite period of time and letting her win would be by his design, Robert willingly agreed.

He arrived the next week with several success stories. One involved

Kelsey wearing her shoes on the wrong feet all day long—a typical scenario that would have normally driven Robert up the wall. "She didn't seem to mind, and to my surprise, neither did I," he said with a smile.

The choice story involved bedtime, a usual nightmare for Robert. He and his wife alternated putting the two children to bed, and Robert always dreaded his turn with Kelsey. But this night, he tried another premeditated experiment. He decided his only goal for this particular bedtime was to get Kelsey in bed with a diaper on. He would let her call the shots on everything else.

When they walked into the bathroom, Robert said, "Okay, Kels, do you want to brush your teeth and get washed up?" Kelsey defiantly grunted, "No!" Robert obliged even though she was quite sticky and dirty, reminding himself of his goal.

Normally, getting her into her night diaper required firmly holding her down on the bed, as she always resisted him. But this time, Robert was able to detach and watch the process. He was very aware that under normal circumstances, he would be yelling at her to lie still, that she would complain that he was hurting her and would then scream for her mother to come. He would yell back that she had to deal with him until he finally got the diaper on. She usually refused his good night kiss.

Now, he was focused on his goal instead of her cooperation. As he put her diaper on, she lay quietly, telling him about the dog who had licked her face that afternoon. They both giggled. Robert astounded himself. The diaper went on smoothly and he found that he was actually enjoying their time together. He asked her if she would like to pick out a book, and she snuggled next to him as he read the one she chose. When he finished, he gave her a hug and commented on what a nice time they had had together. As he leaned in to kiss her good night, Kelsey said, "Daddy, can I brush my teeth now?"

Robert had to convince the class that this was a true story. "It was amazing. The less I controlled her, the more in control I remained."

"What should he have done if Kelsey hadn't said that?" a group member asked. "Let her go to bed sticky and dirty?"

"Yes, that was my plan," Robert said. "That was the experiment. To let her win."

"I think what you found out," I added, "was that relinquishing your control allowed Kelsey to take control of herself." I said to the class, "This doesn't mean that Robert should continue allowing Kelsey to choose whether or not she wants to brush her teeth or wash up. It means that he needs to be more detached from controlling the outcome. It is that control that Kelsey is fighting. From a detached place, he will be much better equipped to give warnings, set consequences, and empathize with Kelsey's point of view."

After several sessions of the class, Robert began to see that his re-actions were coming from inside himself, not directly from Kelsey's behavior. He began to understand that he was the one who needed to do the work, and then his daughter's behavior would follow. When it came time to write his new standard, Robert wrote, *When I am stressed and my children stimulate feelings that are simmering below my surface, I will remember to step away emotionally and find a rational way to defuse the situation.* Robert was beginning to take responsibility.

"Don't You Ever Do That to Me Again!"
Bonnie and Casey (2)

When my first child was born, I was sure that I would be the per-fect mother and that my child would be the perfect child. I was well prepared and had waited several years. I knew what I was doing. And because I was so sure, flexibility was not one of my strong points.

One day, my son, Casey, and I were traveling home to the Upper West Side on a New York City bus. The bus was nearly empty when we got on at Columbus Circle, and Casey was thrilled to have a seat to himself. I clearly spelled out to him, knowing that giving him a warning was "good parenting," that it was fine for him to sit on the seat, but as soon as the bus filled up, he would need to sit on my lap. He nodded his head but was busy feeling very grown-up, stretching his neck to look out the window.

Sure enough, after a few stops, the bus began to fill with people. I said to Casey, "It's time for you to sit on my lap now."

He said, "No!" He was on his knees, watching the sights out the window.

My perfect child was not obeying my perfectly delivered instructions. I had allowed him to do what he wanted. I had given him forewarning. What I hadn't considered was the egocentric development of a two-year-old focused only on what he wanted to do—his agenda.

I said, "Yes," and reached over to pick him up.

He screeched and kicked and squirmed his way off my lap, slipping under the seat in front of me. I was mortified but desperately tried to maintain control. As his screams filled the bus, narrowed eyes glanced and even rudely stared my way. My stubbornness dug in and met Casey's head-on.

Not only had no one taken the seat next to me, but the rows in front and in back of me had emptied even though people were crowded in the aisles. I tried grabbing Casey's arms and pulling him up, but he held on to a bar under the seat with the strength of a linebacker and screamed even harder. Eventually I gave up and tried ignoring him. I stared straight ahead, also trying to ignore the angry stares.

I knew people expected me to pick up my child and get off the bus. We had many stops to go, and I was damned if I was going to spend another token to get back on another bus just because my child wouldn't do what I told him. I wasn't going to let him control me. He was going to learn who was boss.

When we finally reached our stop, I pried Casey out from under the seat and carried him to the back door of the bus. He was still crying. As the bus came to a stop and the doors opened, the entire bus applauded our departure. I was mortified. I reached the sidewalk, put Casey down, dragged him through the foot traffic, backed him up against the side of the bank building, and screamed at him, "Don't you ever do that to me again!" I grabbed his wrist and pulled him the rest of the way home, feeling completely justified in my anger and my behavior. Now he was crying for a different reason.

It seemed clear to me that Casey's behavior was the reason for my anger, the anger of all those on the bus, and my humiliation at their applause. *He was being unreasonable. I did it right; why shouldn't he? What a spoiled brat.* These were the assumptions that sparked my outburst when my control let go. My standard that *I know how to do it right* locked me into an inflexible trap. I feared that if I let him sit on the seat, I would be teaching him that I didn't mean what I said and would be giving him all the control. As I saw it, it was me or him. I left myself no options.

Flexibility might have saved a number of people from a very unpleasant bus ride. If I had taken his agenda into account and realized that my two-year-old was not able to let go of his anger to satisfy me, I would not have been so locked into my own agenda and rigid standards.

In hindsight, I realized that if I had taken him off the bus, removed him from the scene, and acknowledged his anger at not getting to sit on the seat, he most likely would have soon calmed down. If I had not taken his behavior so personally ("Don't you ever do that to me again!"), I would have remained calm and told him again about letting a grown-up sit down. I did not have to sacrifice my values for his agenda. But if I had taken both our needs into account, he would have felt heard (yes, even at two), and I could have solved the problem. I would have validated that it is much more fun to sit by himself, offered a motivation like letting him stand on my lap to see outside, and asked him if he was ready to try again. But my need for control and my unwillingness to spend another token did not allow me that alternative. I had a deeper belief that defined my standard and prevented me from letting go when I needed.

When I was about seven, I hid my father's cigarettes. He was a heavy smoker, and I didn't like it. He always kept his carton on the top of the bookcase in the living room, and every day at lunchtime before returning to work, he took a fresh pack. I knew how important his cigarettes were to him. I also knew the power of his wrath. I had witnessed it over and over again, watching him discipline my older brother with a fierce, rageful control that led to my compliance with his authority.

I can only imagine how nervous I must have been as I hid the carton in the kitchen pantry drawer underneath the place mats. I undoubtedly thought that would stop him from smoking. When he discovered the cigarettes missing, he got very angry. I must have looked guilty, because he demanded that I show him where they were. I decided that confessing was a better option than feigning ignorance. Although he did not yell or hit me, I will never forget the disapproving look he gave me when I uncovered them in the drawer. He grabbed the carton, scowled sternly, and roared, "Don't you ever do that to me again!"

My action had no influence on my father. My disdain for his smoking probably seemed to him no more than a little girl's mischief. His determination to have what was important to him and his dismissal of my motive may have been the fuel that led me to cling to control when I had the chance with my child.

I learned that when a child's agenda is not considered in the resolution of a situation, power remains unbalanced, and the child will fight to regain it. This does not mean that Casey had to have as much power as I in the bus dilemma, nor did I have to give up and let him have the seat. But if I had acted like a grown-up, gotten off the bus instead of stubbornly fighting to win (thereby reducing myself to his two-year-old level), I could have respected his agenda and given him a choice that worked for both of us. Yes, even a two-year-old is capable of cooperating in a situation like this if he feels respected.

CHAPTER TWELVE

THE APPRECIATION BUTTON

The appreciation button gets pushed when a parent who most likely felt unappreciated as a child goes out of his way for his children but gets no show of gratitude in return. He is asking his children to give him the appreciation he longed for. But in fact, he often ends up passing on the legacy when he expects the same gratitude demanded by his parents.

The old story, "I had to walk ten miles to school barefoot!" is a good illustration of this button. "You should appreciate how good you have it." This parent's need for appreciation blinds him to the fact that his children should not be obliged to show their appreciation for something that he missed out on many years back.

The parent who demands appreciation is usually overcompensating for his past by giving all that he wished for to his children. Often his child doesn't want it, certainly didn't ask for it, and now is being expected to be grateful for it. The agenda is clearly the parent's. He expects his child to know how lucky she is. But his child has nothing to compare her own experience to and is left feeling unfairly blamed.

When the appreciation button goes off, the parent feels resentful and taken for granted. Children of appreciation-seeking parents feel confused and misunderstood. They know they are expected to be something they're not and think it's unfair to have to be grateful for something they have come to expect.

By pushing the appreciation button, the child is saying, "Your life was then. This is now! Let me live my life, not yours."

"I'll Give You Everything I Never Had— and You'd Better Be Grateful."

Greta and Cloe (11)

When she had Cloe, all Greta ever wanted was to give her daughter everything: a beautiful room, beautiful clothes, a chance to be one of those girls who has what it takes to be somebody in school—to be accepted, approved of, even admired and emulated. Everything Greta always wanted.

As Cloe grew, Greta was well aware of the dangers of projecting her own desires and dreams onto her child. Or so she thought. It became apparent that Cloe had a mind of her own and different ideas about things. Greta adapted. Cloe was chunkier, more tomboyish, more willful, and more stubborn than the delicate, amiable little girl she had planned on having. Greta adapted.

Cloe was given everything. The play kitchen Greta always wanted, a tricycle with Minnie Mouse pedaling on minipedals on the handle bars, an electrified dollhouse with every accessory stores had to offer. The bins of perfect toys were scrupulously maintained by Greta so there was never a missing piece. Cloe would have it all when she played. Christmas always had a theme, like the "costume Christmas" when Greta hung beautiful new dress-up costumes across the living room on red cord with green clothespins. When Cloe's face lit up Christmas morning as she walked into Greta's dream, Greta felt triumphant. She thought she had become the mother she always wanted.

Christmas for Greta and her younger brother had been socks, pajamas, and a couple of dime-store toys. It wasn't that her parents couldn't afford more. Greta's mother, Lillian, was an accomplished pianist who wrote popular children's piano instruction books. She was quite the "grande dame," as Greta described, but her money and accomplishments did not make her generous. When her mother took her piano students out for ice cream, Greta was instructed to say she didn't want any. From the age of five, she was left alone much of the time. When she was seven, she was in charge of caring for her younger brother as well. Greta's father committed suicide when she was thirteen.

Her fall and winter clothes were purchased every August, when they went to the dime store. Lillian picked out five fabrics that Greta had no part in choosing and then visited the seamstress, who outfitted her in two-piece pleated skirt and tuck-in blouse sets. "There," her mother would say, "there's plenty of clothes for Monday through Friday for the year. Two-piece outfits are handy, so you won't grow out of them."

Every time her mother dropped her off at school, Greta was expected to say, "Thank you very much." If she forgot, Lillian would honk the horn and glare at Greta. "I was expected to be appreciative of every morsel that came my way and to dote on my mother," exclaimed Greta resentfully. "I did a remarkably good job."

So Greta put all her hopes and dreams into tiny, unsuspecting Cloe.

The only problem was that the mother Greta always wanted wasn't the mother Cloe needed. Cloe was growing up in a middle-class community where her riches were ostentatious. She was embarrassed by them. And as much as Greta longed to get away from her mother's influence, Lillian continued to control Greta by criticizing Cloe and the lavish gifts and opportunities Greta provided for her. "She's a spoiled brat. She's rude and selfish. You ought to be beating the hell out of her," was Lillian's familiar remark when her granddaughter did not show her the love and politeness Lillian expected.

For a while, Greta focused on trying to be a good mother. But soon, she confessed in class, "A rage has begun to build inside me like some volcanic boil. I realized it's because Cloe doesn't appreciate anything I do for her. She has everything I never had. She doesn't get how hard it could be for her in a different life."

When Cloe needed art supplies for a school project, Greta took her to the store, where she all but called the store manager in an outrage because the boxes of twenty-four colored pencils were gone.

"But Mom, the teacher said a box of six," Cloe complained, embarrassed by her mother's anger.

"But wouldn't you rather have twenty-four and be able to choose from all those colors?" Greta sounded just like the little girl who had wanted all those colors so badly—who had wanted her mother to insist on the biggest box. But Cloe didn't want the biggest box.

Greta described a recent scene to the class. "The other night before a project was due, Cloe, of course, had something else she *had* to do. So I cut and pasted and colored a map of the European countries long after Cloe went to bed. Then I left the finished gem outside Cloe's door to be found in the morning. I assumed Cloe would be surprised and thrilled with it—and with me. Not even a thank-you! In the hustle and chaos of the morning, it was loaded carelessly into the car along with her backpack and books. I could feel the rage building inside me, but I kept a lid on it—until the car door slammed behind Cloe as she ran off toward the school building. Nothing had been said about it. That was it. My button exploded. I got out of the car and screamed across the playground at Cloe, 'You are the most selfish and unappreciative child in this school! You have a heart the size of a green pea and the sensitivity of an ice cube.' Cloe ignored me and slinked into the building, I'm sure hoping that no one connected her with this maniac of a mother. I got back in my car and cried."

"Imagine if your mother had done something like that for you," I said.

Greta, a bit choked up, said sadly, "I can't imagine it."

"You expected the appreciation you know you would have felt. You were doing for Cloe what you could only have dreamed of. But if you had had a caring mother, you probably wouldn't have wanted her doing your projects for you either."

Greta looked up. "Huh, I hadn't thought that far."

"Cloe has come to expect your indulgence. No reason for her to be grateful for it. You were satisfying you, not her. Maybe she gets that and is trying to make you get it by not responding. Her appreciation would keep you doing it."

"Of course, that's right. I never saw it that way before," Greta said pensively.

Greta learned from her mother, *I am worth nothing*. This belief led her to establish a reactive standard: *I will give my child everything I never got, and I will finally be appreciated and be something*. But the frustration that neither her mother nor her daughter appreciate her, no matter what she does, leads her to rage. Her emotions cause her to automatically react in the same way her mother did.

Greta compensated for what she never received with grandiose parenting, never suspecting that she was asking Cloe to heal her wounds by giving her the appreciation she always needed. She was caught up in her own agenda of filling the role of best possible mother and couldn't see that her daughter had come to resent the lavishness because of the strings attached.

When Greta can focus on what Cloe needs from her, rather than on what Greta fantasizes, she will be giving Cloe the kind of attention she needed from her mother. In doing that, Greta will begin to fill the void left from the lack of attention that Lillian was unable to give.

"Who Do You Think I Am, Anyway?"
Charlotte and Lauren (13)

During the first session of a "Buttons" class, Charlotte piped up after hearing my introduction of what it means to get our buttons pushed. "Boy do I have a good example of that!" she exclaimed.

For almost two years, Charlotte had battled with her daughter, Lauren, over laundry. Charlotte would bring a basket of clean, folded laundry to her daughter's room. Lauren would leave the clean clothes in the basket, and throughout the week, she would throw her dirty clothes on top of them.

"It totally pushed my button," Charlotte said. "I tried telling myself that the stupid laundry should not be such a big deal." All her friends, even her own mother, wondered why she got so upset over such a little thing. But Charlotte couldn't stop herself from yelling at her daughter time and time again: "What do I have to do to get you to put your clean clothes away? Why can't you do this one stupid little thing? Who do you think I am anyway? Your maid! I go to all this trouble for you, do your laundry, fold it even, and what do you do for me?" Lauren would either ignore her or say, "I don't care about it. Leave me alone."

"I actually decided I was going nuts to make such a huge issue out of the laundry. But it was on my mind constantly. Every time I walked by her room, I would make some kind of sarcastic or mean crack." Charlotte smiled and shook her head at the memory.

When I asked Charlotte what it was like for her growing up, she told us that she is the youngest but only girl of six children. Her job throughout her childhood was to take care of many of the chores around the house, one of them being the laundry for all her siblings. It was the "girl's job." Her brothers had more "manly" chores. She vowed that her children would not be the servant she had been. So in her present family, she has never been strict about assigning chores. "I just ask at the time for someone to help me with the dishes or cleaning the house or whatever, and the kids usually chip in with little or no problem," she said. But putting away the laundry was a different story.

Laundry had been Charlotte's most hated chore growing up. Her brothers were slobs and left their dirty socks and underwear every-where. She would complain to no avail. She grew to hate her brothers, as they would mock her when she yelled at them to pick up their dirty clothes. Her mother was a distant autocrat, depressed most of the time and often belligerent when the house was not kept in order. Charlotte knew there was no support from her mother in getting her brothers' co-operation. So she resentfully picked up their messes and put their clean clothes away.

Charlotte didn't want her daughter to suffer the same degradation. She didn't even require her to do her own laundry. But when Lauren refused to even take her clean clothes out of the basket and put them away, Charlotte exploded. Exaggerated fears of what a slob her daughter was and that her life would always be a mess because she would never be able to organize anything flew through her mind.

Charlotte wanted the appreciation she never got from her mother or brothers. And deep down, she was resentful that her daughter was getting away with not doing what she had to do. Lauren had been let off the hook that had dragged Charlotte down for so many years, and "she can't even put away her damn clothes! What kind of respect is that?" Charlotte remembered thinking.

One evening when Charlotte went into Lauren's room to get her dirty laundry, she noticed the neatly stacked clean clothes underneath the dirty ones. This time she really lost it. "Who do you think I am any-way, your servant? Do you expect me to put them away for you, too?" she screamed. Lauren looked up at her mother, rolled her eyes, said, "Looks that way," and went back to her book.

Charlotte's rage was rooted in the conflict between her present standard—*Children should not be servants in their own home*—and her belief: *Children are servants in their own home*. This conflict fueled her assumptions: *She doesn't appreciate what I do for her. She's a slob and will never be able to organize her things*. Most likely if Charlotte had had the tools presented here to discover this conflict between her past beliefs and present standards, her torture over this issue might have ended sooner.

Finally exhaustion and surrender led Charlotte to a happy ending.

One day after almost two years of this battle, Charlotte sat down in Lauren's room, spent and somehow detached. She said calmly, drained of anger or blame, "Okay, what do I do about this clothes thing? I give up." Her daughter, released from having to be defensive against her mother's rage, said, "Mom, I don't have any room in my bureau for any more clothes."

Charlotte admitted that she even knew that. But her irrational assumptions of her daughter's incompetence, disorganization, and lack of gratitude had far overshadowed the facts. She finally detached enough to hear the simple truth that overcrowded bureau drawers was the root of the problem all along.

On the spot, Charlotte and Lauren made a plan. Charlotte took a couple days off from work, and she and her daughter spent Thursday through Sunday of school vacation week going through everything in Lauren's room. At the bottom of her drawers were little-girl's clothes that she hadn't worn for over five years. Outdated clothes and recyclables were put in a bag for Goodwill. They made piles and more piles; and by the end of the four days, not only were the drawers half empty, but the room was rearranged. Together they went through catalogues and ordered new school clothes. They listened to music, reminisced over each piece of clothing, and laughed till their stomachs hurt. Charlotte claimed it was the best time they had ever had with each other. Her only regret was that it took her almost two years to get there.

If Charlotte had been able to clarify the fact that she was resentful of her daughter because Lauren didn't have to do something she was never asked to do in the first place, she would have seen the deeper roots of her anger. But all she could dig up was the fact that laundry had always been an issue for her. It took complete surrender and detachment from her emotions for Charlotte to give up her fight and look for the reason beneath her daughter's behavior. When Lauren did not feel blamed she could express that reason.

"You Don't Appreciate Me!"
Paula and Tess (9), Maggie (7), and Beth (3)

The morning of the two-hour snow delay, Paula's three girls were ecstatic. They had been rushed, as usual, to get ready for school, and now they had an extra two precious hours to play. Beth was thrilled to have her two sisters home for a while longer. Paula was not so happy. The snow was deep, the driveway had to be shoveled, and her husband was already at work.

Maggie pleaded with her mother for a special favor to watch a video, something they only got to do on weekends. Tess had put Maggie up to the task and was eavesdropping from the other room. She knew her mother would be against the idea and didn't want to be the one yelled at. Paula had wanted them to read or color quietly, but she was impressed with Maggie's argument. "We've had our breakfast, brushed our teeth, put our breakfast dishes in the dishwasher, and have our backpacks ready to go. And we did it all very cooperatively, didn't we?" Maggie had bartered well for her age, Paula thought. It was all true. She couldn't argue with it. She agreed, knowing that she had to shovel the driveway and that watching a video would keep them quiet.

Paula believed that a good argument presented with strong convictions should be encouraged in her family of all girls. She had never been given this opportunity in her childhood. In fact, her mother and father had squelched any convictions she ever had. She was determined that no daughter of hers was ever going to believe she was incapable of doing what she wanted. Feeling proud that she had just honored her daughter by acknowledging her debating skill—something she herself had always wished for—Paula put on her boots and went out to tackle the driveway.

It took her an hour and a half to finish. She came in to gather the girls for the drive to school. Expecting to tell them they would have to finish the movie Friday night, she was startled to see they were nowhere in sight. What was in sight was a huge mess. The couch cushions were scattered around the living room floor, toys were everywhere, juice boxes had left sticky puddles on her favorite table, and her best teacups were lined up on the floor.

Her button went off. She was in shock as she heard herself screaming at her daughters, "You ungrateful brats. Here I am out there working, letting you do what you wanted, and this is the thanks I get! We're not going anywhere until every bit of this is picked up and put back together again. And there will be no more movies for a month."

The girls slinked down the stairs with heads hung low. Paula barked, "Hurry up. I don't have all day, you know." They set to work to put the living room in order. When Paula saw the looks on their faces, the avoidance of eye contact from all of them, she realized she had shamed them into good behavior. She was appalled by her outburst, but felt justified in her anger. She was confused about what to do. Guilt and anger merged, and once again she tallied another mark on her long list of parenting failures.

Paula shared in class that the first two assumptions that popped into her head were *My children are ingrates* and *They are unappreciative of my liberated parenting*. "I expected them to be grateful and to show their appreciation for my gracious gift with impeccable behavior. I wanted a pat on the back for not bringing them up under the same restrictions I had and to be assured that my progressive parenting worked." She laughed after she said this. "I guess I'm asking them for that pat on the back. But I still think their behavior was out of line."

Paula recognized that she had two strong beliefs from her childhood: *I must be grateful* and *I am never good enough*. When I asked her where she had learned them, she said, without hesitation, from her father.

"He always wanted things his way," she told us. "He was always right, never wrong. He never apologized for anything in his life. No one crossed him. We all learned to appease him for fear his wrath might suddenly erupt. Arguments with him were never won and so were rarely entered into. I was the good and dutiful child, but still I wasn't good enough."

She recalled a time as a teenager when she had borrowed the family car shortly before her parents were leaving on a trip. She was rushing to get her errand done to get back in plenty of time. As she was on her way home, she noticed the gas tank was close to empty. She wondered whether her father would be more pleased if she got home ahead of time or if she filled the tank, risking being a couple minutes late. She decided on the latter. After all, they would have to stop for gas if she didn't. She raced home realizing she was golden! Not only had she filled the tank, but she would be back in plenty of time for their departure. However, when she proudly told her father that she had filled the tank for him, he criticized her for not recording the mileage.

As she shared this story, her eyes widened as she recognized the fact that she had not been appreciated for her thoughtfulness. She got it! She exclaimed, "So my anger at my girls comes from thinking that I'm *still* not being appreciated for what I do! My belief is that *I'm not good enough or worthy of appreciation!*" She had hit the nail on the head. But then her expression dropped as she said, "Well that's stupid! I can understand feeling that way as a child, but as an adult I know I shouldn't expect my children to tell me or show me how much they appreciate me all the time. It's amazing how that stuff stays in there from childhood."

She went home that day, gathered the girls together, reminded them of the snow day, and told them how much she appreciated their speedy cooperation in getting the living room back in order. She apologized for her reaction. She then asked them to take responsibility for their part. They apologized and said they had decided not to use up their precious time cleaning up their toys. Paula acknowledged their desire to play, but asked them to go back over the situation and come up with a better solution. They agreed together that they should have just gone upstairs to play when they were bored with the movie rather than getting out all the toys. And they agreed never to use her teacups for play again. Paula taught her girls that *her* rage was *her* problem. They did not have to take responsibility for their mother's feelings as she had done with her father. But they did have to take responsibility for their behavior.

CHAPTER THIRTEEN

THE FIX-IT BUTTON

Fixers are parents who want to make life easy for their children and themselves. They have to solve their children's problems, because either they don't think their children are capable on their own or it's just "easier to do it myself." If they can fix their children's problems, then they can rest easy knowing they have done the right thing. But when problems don't or can't get fixed, or if fixing efforts are fruitless, resentment, guilt, and anger build, and the fix-it button gets pushed.

Fixers generally have poor boundaries and are unclear about where their responsibility ends and their child's begins. They think they are doing the right thing, being a good parent and making their children happy by helping them out. But their children never have the opportunity to figure things out for themselves; so they end up believing they are incapable. Fixers need their children to feel good, and this gives them the impossible job of rescuing them from any unhappiness. They want to be loved and think that making everything okay for their children will get them that love. They will give and give, but if it's to no avail, they will suddenly explode at their irresponsible child, not realizing their part in setting up that irresponsibility.

When their button is pushed, fixers feel both resentful that their efforts do not win the love and appreciation they expect, and guilty that they could not fix the problem. Children of fixers are left feeling frustrated and incapable, because they have little or no chance to work out their own problems.

Children of fixers are telling their parents to let go of trying to do it all and to let them solve their own problems and learn by their own mistakes.

"I Have to Be There."
Susan and Luke (3)

Susan is a "fixer" and the daughter of the ultimate "fixers." Having been brought up by parents who took care of everything for her, protecting her from experiencing any pain or responsibility, she is left with a legacy that is hard to follow. Susan is extremely close to her parents and thinks she should parent with similar standards. Her conflict is between what she thinks she should be doing and what she wants to be doing.

Susan found herself reacting to Luke's periodic nighttime waking with irrational anger and frustration. Not many parents enjoy nocturnal one-on-one's with their children, but most realize the child is having a problem going to sleep. Like many fixers, Susan thinks that it is her fault that he is not sleeping, because she thinks he is not capable of falling asleep without her. It is therefore her job to get him back to sleep. If she fails, she blames herself, because, as she has confessed, her assumption is *I'm afraid I'm abandoning him.*

Luke had been waking a lot lately, and one night, he seemed to be making a concerted effort to keep himself awake between 11:30 P.M. and 4:00 A.M. After Susan rocked him for two hours, dad went in to take over, but "No! Mommy!" brought her back to him. Unable to calm him and exhaustion at its peak, they resentfully brought him into bed with them, where he continued squirming for two more hours. Susan dragged him back to his room kicking and screaming.

Her rage got the better of her. She heard herself scream at the top of her lungs, "You get back in that bed and you go to sleep, do you hear me? I cannot do this anymore. You can't do this to me!" She was spent. Her adrenaline had risen suddenly and rapidly. In her ravaged, post-rage state, she made her way back to her bed to lie awake full of guilt for the rest of the night listening to Luke crying, trying to bring her back until he finally fell asleep.

Susan had spent the night trying to fix Luke's problem. Rocking, holding, cuddling, apologizing, taking him into bed—nothing satisfied him. She felt guilty that she couldn't fix it and guilty that she had finally abandoned him for her own selfish desire. Her sense of failure sent her into a rage that she dumped on Luke. The guilt from that was almost unbearable.

Susan is an only child, as is Luke, and remains the object of her parents' doting. She says she feels "ten years old" whenever she is with them.

"I got everything I ever wanted," she said with a note of resentment. "So now I want time to work at my sewing machine, time alone with my friends, time to read a book, when I *should* be wanting to play with Luke. Every time I see him by himself, I think I've abandoned him. I'm afraid I'm a spoiled brat," she said.

"Why is that?" I asked.

"Well, aren't I supposed to be putting my child's needs first? I'm really afraid that because I got everything I wanted as a child, I don't know how to put his needs ahead of mine. Maybe I just want Luke to be happy so it'll be easier for me," she confessed with embarrassment.

"Why do you think his needs should be ahead of yours?" I asked. "Don't you think your needs should be considered as well as Luke's to bring balance to the relationship?"

"Balanced needs, huh. Sounds nice! I haven't the foggiest how to balance them."

The morning after their sleepless night, Susan was still consumed with guilt. She tried everything to fix it again for Luke. She played with him, took him for ice cream, and came home with his favorite video. "I gave him everything he wanted all day long," Susan said. "He was especially clingy, whiny, and demanding. And I resented having to hold him constantly. I couldn't do my sewing or even get dinner ready. I felt so selfish—again, like a spoiled brat. I was caught in my own trap."

Susan's parents continue to lavish gifts on both her and her husband, much to her husband's dismay. Her parents refer to them fondly as "those kids." Susan hears, "Aren't they cute? They're pretending to be grown-ups."

"I fluctuate between love and gratitude for my parents and anger and resentment for fixing all my problems and treating me like an incompetent baby."

Luke's nighttime crying, clinging, and demanding has triggered Susan's assumptions of *Luke needs my undivided attention all the time* and *I'm abandoning him,* because her standard of parenting tells her, *A mother's job is to fix her children's problems*—a standard she was brought up with. This results in guilt whenever he is alone or wants her attention. When she acts on this by going to him all night long or playing with him all day, she reacts with rage and resentment, because she believes *I should get all my needs and desires taken care of by someone else.* She never had to experience anything unpleasant. Now it is her turn to handle the unpleasantness of her child's feelings, but she has not learned that Luke has a right to them.

I must fix everything for him all the time is an impossible standard to live up to and one that inhibits the individual growth of both Susan and Luke. But Susan chooses to blame herself (*I'm a spoiled brat* or *I'm a failure as a mother*) rather than her inappropriate standards. As soon as Susan began verbalizing her standards, she saw how impossible they were to live up to. She began working on a new one that said, *I can both play with Luke and do things that I want and still be a good mother*.

Susan needs to be needed. It is a role she has always played with her parents, a role that is hard to step out of. If she believes that Luke feels abandoned whenever she is not with him, she gets to feel needed by him all the time. Ironically, it becomes important for her to nurture Luke's neediness, as her mother nurtured it in her. Susan's old pattern is thus served by holding on to the belief that Luke needs her and feels abandoned if she is not with him.

With her new standard in place, Susan can take care of her own needs in balance with Luke's and still consider herself a good enough mother. When her own needs are as important to her as Luke's, she will know that her sleep is as valuable as his and can find a balance in the middle of the night. She will no longer believe that she is abandoning him whenever she is not playing with him, and he will be able to learn how to solve some of his own problems and be better able to entertain himself. They will both be in a better position to respect each other's needs.

"I'll Give You Everything I Always Wanted."
Connie and Max (17)

Babying, pampering, physical closeness, and cuddling was what Connie assumed her only child, Max, would want from her. After all, that was what she had longed for throughout her childhood.

Connie's mother was verbally abusive to her, and her father, an alcoholic, was verbally and sexually abusive. Connie never knew loving touches and closeness from either parent. But Connie could count on her mother's food. Three meals a day, including a hot dinner at 5:30 P.M., seven days a week were her only reliable connection to her mother, even though she was told to stay out of the kitchen and out of the way. Her father continually criticized Connie's physical appearance and weight. He forced her onto the scales regularly and controlled her with strict, regimented diets. So the only lifeline she had to her mother, which was food, was controlled and withheld by her father. No surprise that Connie has had a problem with weight all her life.

When Connie became pregnant with Max, she began reading parenting books. She latched onto one that encouraged responding empathically to a child. This philosophy gave Connie permission to satisfy an emotional closeness that she needed desperately. But unable to establish a healthy boundary and see Max's needs separately from her own, Connie compensated for what she had missed and indulged her longings on her son. In reaction to her father's insensitive, cruel controls, an appropriate disciplinary structure was missing. She was determined that her son feel safe and cared for at all times. Never would he endure the tortures of her childhood. She would fix things right for him.

Indeed, Max did feel safe and cared for. His inborn, sensitive temperament fed right into Connie's need to pamper him. The combination of the two resulted in Max's inability to handle any pain or problems himself.

When Max was seven, a friend he had been playing with knocked on Connie's door. "You'd better come. Max needs you." With fear in her heart, Connie ran to the edge of the woods, where she could see Max lying on the ground. When she got to him, Max sat up and said with a whine that he had fallen down. In helping him up, she saw that he was perfectly fine. After she brushed him off and gave him a kiss, he ran off to play. Connie realized then what she had so unintentionally created.

Now, at seventeen, Max is a popular high school senior. However, he takes little or no responsibility for himself, blames his problems on others, and is highly intolerant of anyone differing with his opinions.

"It's all my fault; I know it," Connie said. "I take responsibility for everything, including how he feels. I can't set down rules about anything for fear that he might feel even the least bit like I did with my father." She has never expected Max to do chores around the house, even though she is a full-time, working, single parent. Although he has a car and time on his hands after school, Max expects her to do all the shopping, have his favorite foods in the house, and meals prepared when he wants them. She feels immobilizing guilt whenever he complains, "There's nothing in the house to eat or drink. I'm starving and dehydrated!"

Connie came into class one day concerned over a history paper

Max had not done. She feared he might fail U.S. history and could not bear the thought of his disappointment at not graduating with his class. The look on her face convinced us that she took full responsibility for making sure this paper got done on time.

The paper was due midsemester, but Max had been given an extension by his teacher until the end of the semester. When he still had not written it by Christmas vacation, his teacher extended it farther, but insisted it be handed in as soon as school started in January. Although Connie knew these extensions did not promote responsibility, she was relieved with each one. "I felt like I got the extension," she exclaimed.

But Christmas vacation came and went, and there had been no sign of even page one. Connie was beside herself with guilt over the fact that she had raised her son to be so nonchalant about something this important.

"I didn't want to nag Max about it, but that's all I've been doing," she said. "I say things like, 'So Max, how's the paper coming?' and he glares at me. I didn't want to open my mouth, but I just couldn't help it. I have no clue what to do about this. I feel at a total loss. And I'm realizing as I'm saying this that I'm here hoping you'll fix it for me!"

When I said, "Do you understand that this is not your problem, it's Max's problem?" she looked confused. "He doesn't have to take responsibility for himself if you take it for him—especially if he thinks you will find a way to solve it."

"Oh, I never thought of that," she said. "That makes sense."

Connie's belief in her unworthiness drove her fears that she was not taking care of him properly if he wasn't doing his history paper—or anything else she thought he should have done. It was her fault. She was not meeting up to her standard *I must make sure my child feels safe and cared for all the time,* which permitted her to indulge in babying him but prevented him from learning to be responsible for any of his own care and safety. She never expected him to do chores or get groceries because it put him out, but she also unintentionally taught him in the process that he didn't have to do a paper if he didn't want to. It never occurred to Connie that the babying she had wished for as a child might be smothering for Max.

She exclaimed in class one day, "Why would anyone not want to be babied?"

Another parent in the group quickly responded, "Boy, not me. I hated being babied, and my mother still does it. I hate it when my daughter comes crying to me and wants me to kiss her all over." Connie was amazed. This was the first time she realized that her desire to be babied was not universal. She could see that she had projected her desires onto her son and that that had led to his dependency. But this was the first time she realized that he might not even like how she protected him.

Connie made the connections quickly, and soon she had a different story to tell. Max had come home distraught after finding out that he had to repeat U.S. history to graduate. He could either take it in his last semester and not take the courses he had planned on, or take it in the summer, or fail and not graduate with his class. We held our breath.

"Normally I would have been drawn in and tried to come up with answers that would make him feel better. We would have gone out for comfort food. But I held myself back, empathized with the difficulty of his decision, but left the decision up to him!" The class applauded. Connie smiled with pride.

"He tried to put the responsibility back on me by saying, 'I know how much you want to see me graduate with my class, and I don't want to disappoint you.' I assured him that I would not be disappointed, and that I would support him in whichever decision he made." Connie cleanly handed full responsibility over to Max, who was left with no choice but to make the choice himself.

Max deliberated for several days and finally announced that he would add the course to his present schedule and graduate with his class. "Besides," he added, "I guess it was my fault." Connie could hardly believe her ears. Max has since successfully satisfied his history requirement and is now a high school graduate.

While Connie was busy taking all the responsibility for Max, he got quite handy at manipulating her feelings. When he said he didn't want to disappoint her by not graduating with his class, he was provoking her once again to take responsibility and make the decision. When she didn't, she set a boundary, on the other side of which he was left with responsibility for himself.

"It felt so liberating. Like this huge weight had been lifted off my shoulders," Connie said, beaming from ear to ear. "I was so proud of myself." Connie is now in a position to let go of Max and allow him to find his own way without her.

"I Have to Make Everything Right."
Charlie, Fran, Melissa (3), and Betsy (1)

Melissa is a strong-willed, persistent child and pushes buttons in both her loving, eager, and concerned parents. Although both parents admire and cherish Melissa's dynamic, outspoken personality, it wears thin by the end of each day, since her parents think it is their job to give her only their support. Charlie said, "Betsy is already a breath of fresh air. She knows how to take care of herself."

Trying to meet the needs of both girls has created tension between Charlie and Fran. Charlie is building a new business and working long hours, and Fran designs computer software in her home but is on the road a lot. Both feel guilty about the little time they have with their girls and compensate by sacrificing their own needs to focus on making their girls happy all the time.

Charlie comes from a large, Irish Catholic family where there was a loving environment but not much one-on-one attention. He spends far more time with his children than his father did with him and gets resentful when he is not appreciated for it. Fran's father was a workaholic, and rarely around. Her needs went repeatedly unmet, as her mother felt overburdened and overwhelmed, blowing up at the slightest inconvenience to her.

Charlie stifles his anger when Melissa insists on the yellow plate *not* the blue plate, or when she yells, "Daddy, that's wrong! You can't do it that way," as he is adding ingredients for her oatmeal. He knows how angry Fran gets with him when he does explode or say anything that she defines as "inappropriate."

"I have to do everything just right, say everything just right, to satisfy Fran," Charlie complained. Not wanting to ruffle any feathers, he politely pleads with Melissa to *please* do whatever it is he wants her to do. That seems to be her cue to take control.

"We both feel like we are walking on eggshells around her. It's the same way we felt around my mother," Fran added. "I don't want them to experience anything like I did. So I work really hard to do everything just right, to make things work out for them. But I never know how Melissa's going to react. We always have to keep ten steps ahead of her."

These self-inflicted demands on their time have left no time for Fran and Charlie. Fran feels pulled in two directions at once. Feeling dismissed and unappreciated much of the time, Charlie complains that neither of those directions lead toward him. Whenever Fran is alone with both girls she gets extremely stressed trying to anticipate every situation. So when Charlie is home, she assigns him one of the girls, and they spend most of their home time in separate parent/child pairs.

Charlie complained, "I always come in third. If Fran and I are talking, I'm the one given the invisible shove when one of the girls interrupts. I just withdraw."

"Well, they're just children. They don't know how to wait for us," Fran snapped.

Fran described a typical situation in which she felt drained trying to manage both girls. "Betsy was practicing climbing the stairs, and Melissa called to me from the other room to see her drawing. I felt so torn. I wanted to let Betsy continue climbing, but I didn't want to ignore Melissa. I called, 'I'll be right there, just a minute,' and then felt all this pressure to get Betsy to finish, saying, 'We need to go see what Melissa wants.' And then I was overwhelmed with guilt. I didn't know how to take care of both of them at once."

"Did you expect that you could or should?" I asked.

Fran looked at me quizzically. "Isn't that my job?"

"It is if that's what you think it is. Sounds like your standard is making it impossible for you to meet the expectations you have of yourself. You need to be two people."

"Exactly," she said. "That's why I need Charlie to take one of them."

I asked Fran what assumptions flew through her mind while she was watching Betsy on the stairs. She thought for a minute and said, "I was letting Melissa down. If I had been better prepared, I could have done it differently so that I could have handled them both."

"You're running yourself ragged to fix every problem, anticipate every want at once, ignoring your husband's needs in the process." I suggested that she call to Melissa and say that she is with Betsy right now and either she must wait until they are done or bring her drawing to the stairs. Fran said it felt as if I was giving her permission to be with just one of them at a time and making that okay. The relief drifted over her, and her shoulders noticeably dropped.

Fran came back the next week complaining about Melissa pushing her feet into Fran's face and then laughing when she asked her to stop. "Of course, she didn't stop. I got really mad and gritted my teeth asking her *please* to put her feet down. It was so annoying. I finally had to get up and walk away. Then I felt really guilty."

"What kept you from holding her feet and insisting she stop, putting her feet down yourself if need be?" I asked.

"It would have felt so forced. I couldn't bring myself to do something like that," she said, surprised that I would suggest such a thing.

"Before you can expect her to stop annoying you in that way," I said, "you need to give her a clear signal that you are not to be treated like a punching bag. But before you can do that, you need to know that you deserve not to be treated like a punching bag. As it stands now, she has permission to walk all over you, because you fix everything for her and ignore yourself. You never learned that your needs count." Tears came as Fran started to get the picture.

Neither Fran nor Charlie got the attention and care in their own childhoods they were both giving their girls. Fran's belief—*My needs are insignificant*—has driven her to develop a reactive standard to ensure that she never minimizes her children's. Charlie's belief—*There's never enough time for me*—carries into his relationship with Fran and triggers his resentment of Fran's attention on the girls.

We do our children no good when we sacrifice ourselves, no matter what the driving force prompting the sacrifice. Of course we must sacrifice much of our agenda when our children are young, but sacrificing our need for self-respect and ignoring our own wishes gives our children a very poor model of adulthood. An adjusted standard—*Good parents meet their children's needs better when their own needs are met first*—will help them develop important boundaries with their girls.

I reminded them of the instructions we always receive on an airplane. If the oxygen masks drop, be sure to put one on yourself before helping your child.

I suggested they begin a once-a-week date night by hiring a baby sitter as well as teach the girls not to interrupt when Fran and Charlie are talking. By balancing their own needs with the needs of their children, Fran and Charlie will model self-respect and teach their girls the importance of respecting the needs of others. As a bonus, it will prevent Fran and Charlie from sabotaging their marriage as well.

CHAPTER FOURTEEN

THE RESPONSIBILITY BUTTON

The responsibility button is similar to the fix-it button in many ways, but where the fixer is concerned about his child's needs, the overly responsible parent is more concerned about her own. Responsibility becomes a button when parents take on more than their share, do too much for their children, overprotect, and then react when their children don't make them look good. They are in fact asking their children to give them good grades.

These parents see responsibility as their job description. Instead of taking over their children's problems, they hover and nag them to get it right, patrol them to make sure they do what is expected, and overprotect them to prevent them from failing. They nag their children to brush their teeth, do their homework, and look their best. And if their children fail, the parents fail, even though that failure is projected as blame onto the child.

The overly responsible parent usually believes her children cannot cope, get things done, or exist, for that matter, without her constantly telling them what to do and when to do it. Dependency is at the core of their problems; so inadvertently these parents raise children who either rebel and fall on their face or transfer their dependence onto others to hold them up.

For overly responsible parents, their children's lives rest in their hands. It's a huge job. So when this parent's button gets pushed, she feels resentful and often reacts by controlling in an attempt to show the world what a good job he has done.

The child who pushes the responsibility button is saying, "You take responsibility for yourself and teach me to take responsibility for myself."

"I Have to Keep Them Safe."
Hannah, Paul, Eric (9), Cyrus (7), and Whitney (1)

"Could we talk about fears?" Hannah asked in class one morning. "I'm afraid about everything my kids do. I'm always worried they're going to hurt themselves or get killed. I feel so responsible. I remember when I held my first baby in the hospital. I cried and said to my mother, 'I'm responsible for him!' It was overwhelming. And what makes it worse is that Paul doesn't seem to care whether they live or die, the way he deals with them."

"Hey, I teach them how to take care of themselves," her husband argued. "I teach them what's safe and what's not. They need to learn how to have fun, too." Hannah said that Paul thinks she is smothering them like his mother did to him and that he's getting back at her by not focusing on their safety at all.

Hannah worries that letting her boys go into the woods around their house, ride in the back of the pickup in the driveway, ride on the tractor with their dad, or leave the upstairs windows open is asking for trouble. If they leave Legos around, she is afraid Whitney "will choke and die." She catastrophizes, racing to worst-case scenarios even though as a child, she spent most of her time wandering in the woods far from home. "It was my favorite thing to do, and I never got lost; I was lucky. But I could have, and my mother didn't have any idea where I was," Hannah said with a judgmental tone.

I asked her what she was afraid might happen. "If I don't protect them, something terrible will happen. The other day both boys rode their bikes down to the end of our long driveway. When they came back, they said they had talked to a man who lives down there. I was horrified. I didn't even know they had gone. They could have been abducted!"

"Is that what scares you the most?" another parent asked. "That they'll be abducted?"

"It's that I wasn't there to protect them," she confessed.

When Hannah was two and her brother was six, their father left the family. She later found out that he had served time in jail. Her stepfather moved in about three years later and ruled with violence. Hannah's brother, Tom, got the worst of it. Fearing the same, Hannah became a "good girl," but she got her share of name-calling and belittling. Tom took out his aggressions on Hannah.

When Hannah was twelve, she and her brother were fighting at the dinner table when their stepfather pushed his chair back, threw his napkin down, and said, "That's it, I can't take it anymore. I can't live with this," and walked out. Hannah took full responsibility—for making him leave and for the loss to her mother. She felt so much guilt that she had to make up a way to live with it.

"I had this great fantasy that he had gone off to buy a big, beautiful, white farmhouse with animals and lots of space. I waited for him to come back and take us there, knowing we would live happily ever after," she said, still with dreamy hopefulness. After three weeks, he did come back. There was no house, but Hannah turned on her best behavior, convinced that she could make him stay. But he left shortly after, never to return again.

"I truly believed it was all my fault," she told us. "I saved up all my baby-sitting money to buy my mother extravagant gifts. I did all the household jobs I wasn't even asked to do. I tried to second-guess everything my mother might need. I found out years later that my stepfather was having an affair with his secretary." Hannah laughed to downplay the irony and shame.

To make up for the abandonment of both her fathers, Hannah has to be there to protect her children. Her mission is to prove to them— unlike her father and stepfather—how much she cares, how much she *is* there, and how responsible *she* is. Hannah is taking on the responsibility for the whole family.

"I hate both my father and my stepfather so much. They didn't care whether I lived or died."

"Men can't meet up to your standards, can they?" I asked.

Hannah was silent as she realized what she had said. She saw what she was projecting onto her husband, another important man in her life.

"No, I guess they can't."

"So that puts an awful lot on your plate. What if you gave a little bit of the parenting responsibility to Paul?" I asked.

"They'd be dead!" she exclaimed. Paul rolled his eyes.

She came into class the next week and said, "I read an article in a magazine about people who don't believe they deserve anything good because they're just waiting for it all to be taken away. That's me! I have a wonderful husband, wonderful children, and a wonderful house; but I can't relax because I'm so afraid it's all going to disappear."

"And so it's your responsibility to hold it all together. And you can't risk letting up for a second."

"Right," she said. "No wonder I'm so exhausted all the time."

"And no wonder you can't let the boys just have some fun," Paul added.

We uncovered Hannah's childhood belief: *I am responsible for everyone abandoning me, and I have to be perfect to make up for it.* Her belief in her need to be perfect sets her standard: *I have to be there to protect them at all times. If I'm not, I am abandoning my children and showing them I don't love them.* Hannah maintains her watch over her children, fearing that at any moment catastrophe will strike if she's not prepared and on her best protective behavior. *He'll be killed; he'll get lost; she'll choke and die* are all catastrophizing assumptions that lead Hannah to her exhausting vigilance and defense to prove her love and to compensate for Paul's easygoing approach.

Awareness first helped Hannah "bite her tongue" and allow her sons a bit more freedom. She now sees the pattern she is bringing from her past and is working hard not to pass it on to her children. With self-talk, she is learning that she had nothing to do with her father and stepfather's departures and that she was dealt a raw deal. She is working with her new standard, which says, *My children are capable of handling themselves responsibly.*

Hannah has relaxed considerably since her work began. Although her worries are far from over, she is taking responsibility for them and not asking her boys to take care of her needs with conservative behavior. It will be important for Hannah to be realistic with her rules and not let her fears determine them. As she is growing more aware of their origin, she is able to put them aside, know they are her responsibility, and not let them interfere with her expectations of the boys.

One of her sons asked if he could go on an overnight with a friend. She realized after she had said yes that she had not even felt the familiar tension. "I didn't catastrophize a bit," she said proudly. "I asked him to give me a call sometime while he was there, but that was it!"

"Your Report Card Is My Report Card."
Carl and Tommy (16)

Carl is the distraught parent of Tommy, an angry, frustrated, and almost lost teenager. Carl described Tommy as "basically a good kid" who doesn't accept responsibility, is lazy, and doesn't apply himself. Carl has many of the typical catastrophic fears of parents of teens: *He'll never get a job. He'll become a drug addict. He'll get into trouble and end up in jail.* Carl's fears serve to camouflage his deeper feelings of his own unworthiness, which Tommy triggers with his behavior.

When Carl began classes, he listened for a few weeks before sharing with the class that Tommy was doing very poorly in school. Carl had always expected Tommy to get As and Bs, because he knew he was capable of them. He had done fine in middle school. In high school, Carl had accepted his son's Bs and Cs, but they had since dropped to Cs and Ds, with a couple of Fs looming. Carl felt ashamed and angry about his son's performance and let him know it. He was always on his back with nagging questions and remarks:

> "How much homework do you have tonight? Don't you need to get to it?"
> "How did you manage to do so poorly on that test?"
> "You can't go out until you do your homework."
> "How do you think you're ever going to get a job with grades like these?"
> "No son of mine is going to drop out of high school."
> "How can you be so lazy?"
> "You're wasting whatever talent you have left."

"I feel hopeless," Carl confessed. "I can't understand what has happened to Tommy. His behavior feels like a disrespectful slap in the face." Tommy had begun lying about his test grades and assignments. Carl initially began by bribing him with favors if he did well, but that brought no results. He started grounding him from baseball practice and soon from every social event in his life. Carl and his wife, Sharon, began arguing more and more in disagreement over Carl's punishments. Sharon wanted Carl to leave him alone. But the more she tried to prevent him from interfering, the more he interfered. Carl was convinced that his son's future was up to him and that he must act aggressively and immediately. "If I lay off, Tommy will go down the tubes. He'll never do anything worthwhile on his own. It's my responsibility to push him—isn't it?"

Carl sheepishly told the class about the previous Saturday morning when Tommy had slept late. Carl was fuming, waiting for Tommy to get to his chores. All that kept him from dragging Tommy out of bed was Sharon's plea to "let him sleep just this once." To appease Sharon, Carl gathered the trash to take to the dump, a job he expected Tommy to do with him. About 11:30, Tommy stumbled downstairs and was confronted by his father. Carl immediately began to lecture.

"I have to confess I called him every name in the book," Carl told us. "But then Tommy turned to me, said, 'Fuck you, Dad!' went upstairs to his room, and went on a rampage. He began yelling obscenities and punched his fist through the wall in the hallway, making a big hole. Then he grabbed his backpack, pushed past me, and ran down the stairs and out the kitchen door, yelling, 'Fine, you hate me, you don't have to put up with me anymore. I'm outa here!'"

The next two days were a blurred nightmare for Carl and Sharon. The police were searching; Carl and Sharon had his friends searching. Two days later, he silently appeared and locked himself in his room. "He was at his girlfriend's, and all his friends had covered for him. He went to school the next day, but it was several days before he spoke to either of us." Carl hung his head and spoke softly as he relayed the details. He was now ready to hear what the group had to say. He had reached rock bottom. "What do I do?" he pleaded.

Several people suggested to Carl that he had to let go of the control he was trying to maintain. Carl panicked. "He'll fall apart; he can't make it unless I push him. He'll be a failure. I'll be a failure."

"Who tried to control you?" I asked him.

"Ha!" he laughed sarcastically.

Carl was an only child. His parents had high expectations of him, but not of their marriage. He knew his mother had stayed in the marriage for him. She was "desperately unhappy and hanging on by her toenails." So Carl always did his best to make her proud of him. He struggled in school, hating it almost as much as Tommy, but diligently made it through college and worked his way up to a stressful but financially secure job. Carl's father was strict and controlling.

"I toed the line in order to hold my mother together and to make sure everything looked good to the outside world," Carl said. "I've followed in the footsteps of what I hated," he realized.

"And now you're asking Tommy to do the same," I added. Carl's eyes grew wide.

The next week he came to class and announced, "My armor will have to come off if I let go of my control. I realized that I have built this armor to protect my anger toward both my parents. And now it's protecting my anger toward Tommy, who's getting away with what I never could. If I let down my armor, I'm afraid I'll kill him!"

The group rallied their support and encouraged Carl to talk about his anger. He realized that Tommy was very strong-willed and wouldn't buckle under Carl's control as Carl had under his father's. Carl's rage grew when Tommy refused to obey and accommodate the way he had.

Carl came in the following week and told us that his son had announced that he wanted to quit school. Letting go seemed impossible. "How can I accept this? How can I accept his terrible grades even if he doesn't quit? What will it look like if I have a dropout for a son?"

"Carl, it sounds like Tommy's report card is your report card," one of the group members illustrated. "If he gets a D in math, you think you're getting a D in parenting."

"You're absolutely right!" Everything clicked. "I have been asking him to make it right for me so I can justify all these years of making it right for my parents. So I can finally win their approval. If I let him go, all that goes! Now what do I do?"

"Nothing right now other than to stay aware of all you've discovered," I said. "See what happens over the next week." Carl left that day feeling helpless.

Carl had made the link. His assumptions—*Tommy is lazy and incompetent and will end up in jail*—provoked his rage, resulting in more attempts at control. His standard, transferred directly from his past—*It is my responsibility to make sure my children do their best*—was unrealistic, because *their best* was by Carl's definition, not his children's. Carl had had to do his best for his mother and father to avoid shame and harm. Now he expected the same *best* from Tommy. But Tommy was a different person and didn't need what Carl needed.

For Carl, a floodlight had flashed on in his head. He knew he either had to change his parenting or lose his son completely. He immediately pulled back from his nagging and shaming and shared with Tommy what he had learned about himself. The risk of letting go and allowing Tommy to take control of his own life was monumental for Carl. It resulted in Tommy dropping out of school. He is still floundering, but he has a job that he is handling responsibly. Carl had to risk Tommy making mistakes in order to hand him over responsibility for his own life.

Carl is a different man. "I can't believe it," he said, beaming, the last week of class. "We talk to each other. Tommy listens and responds, and I'm actually supporting him in his decision the best I can. When I slip back into the familiar nag, I apologize and remind Tommy that I need a lot of practice to parent so differently, but he seems willing to give me some slack. There are plenty of times when Tommy doesn't want to be around, but we don't have outbursts of anger anymore."

Carl knows that all he can do now is present opportunities, but Tommy must be in charge of what he does with those opportunities. Carl knows that Tommy's difficulties have resulted from the responsibility he took on single-handedly. "If Tommy wasn't doing it right, I thought I had to make him do it right. The problem was he never cooperated with my idea of what was right!"

Tommy may have to fall a few times before he accepts the responsibility and knows his father won't prop him up. Carl must stand by to make sure he doesn't fall so far that he can't get up, but he must know that as with an infant learning to walk, falling is part of learning. Tommy is now free to turn his focus to himself instead of toward his resistance to his father.

Carl wrote on his class evaluation, "Tommy pushed me to the edge. Instead of losing control, I learned what he was trying to teach me all along—that he needed to be trusted with his own life. It means a whole new approach, but it gives me permission and freedom to be more loving. Our relationship is now something I never thought possible."

"I Just Want to Make It All Better."
Jennifer and Alex (6)

"I think I do a pretty good job of listening to Alex and reflecting his feelings. But it just seems to make it worse. He keeps going on and on until I'm sick of listening to it. The other day, I told him his friend couldn't stay for dinner. He started screaming and calling me a meanie. I said very patiently that I understood he was mad and that he had a right to be. I didn't even add a 'but' to it. He stomped off, still telling me how mean I was, and was crabby all through dinner. I finally lost it and yelled at him to stop being such a brat and that he couldn't get his way all the time." Jennifer was frustrated that her new effective listening skill did not appear to be working with Alex.

"What do you expect to happen?" I asked her.

"I want him to get over it. I want to make it better."

"You're on the right track, but you're still taking responsibility for fixing Alex's problem. You want and expect your listening skill to re-solve the situation the way you want it resolved—for him to be done and happy. Can you see how strong your agenda is to have the outcome that you want?" I asked. "When you think it's your job to make it all better, then Alex believes that, too. He will keep at it until you do make it better. When you can trust him to handle his own feelings, he will. And he will learn to trust himself as well."

"Hmmm." I could see the wheels turning in her head.

"What was it like in your house when you were little? How were your feelings handled?" I asked.

Jennifer began, "I was the youngest of four and kind of left on my own."

"What did you want most from your mother?"

"It wasn't that I wanted more attention, I don't think. It was just that I wished she cared more about me," Jennifer offered. There were nods from the rest of the group.

"So, I wonder if you are compensating for the lack of care you got from your mother by taking on the responsibility of all of Alex's bad feelings. Maybe you're trying too hard to give Alex what your mother didn't give you. And you're afraid it's not working."

Tears started to fill her eyes. "Exactly," she said.

Jennifer recalled an evening at the dinner table when she was about eight. There was always commotion with six family members in their small kitchen. She had presented a project at school that day and had received praise from her teacher. She kept trying to tell her parents about it, but something always got in the way.

"Jenny, can't this wait? I have to get everyone fed," she remembered her mother saying impatiently. When she tried her father with no success, her mother piped in, "Jennifer, your father has had a long hard day. He doesn't have time for your foolishness. Leave him alone." The word "foolishness" rang in her ears.

Jennifer tried to hold in her hurt all through dinner. When she was asked something, she whined, "I don't know." Her mother said, "Well, if you're not going to be pleasant at the table you can just go to your room."

The event, and others like it, left a deep wound. Jennifer did not feel heard by her parents. She came away with the belief *I don't count. What happens to me is not important.* She shared very little about her life with either of her parents after that. "I kept everything in because I always thought that if I ever cried or got sad or angry, I would make people mad, and they wouldn't like me."

Jennifer approached her parenting with the standard *I will make sure my child is heard, so he will be happy.* But hearing him and making him happy are two very different things. Now Jennifer was caught. Consciously she wanted to be there for Alex, to listen to how he felt, but she had never experienced that kind of compassion and didn't know how to do it. So when she learned the skill of listening and reflecting his feelings, she had a hard time putting it into practice. She thought she had to make his bad feelings go away. When that didn't happen, she tensed up, and her acceptance and compassion disappeared.

She came in the next week feeling better. "I think I'm getting it," she said. "The other day Alex was having a fit about not getting a third cookie. This time I said, 'Alex, you're really mad that I won't let you have another cookie. I can really understand how you feel, and you can cry about it as long as you need to. I'll be right here if you need me.' And then I sat down on the other side of the room and just waited. Normally I probably would have either given him the cookie to make him happy or not given it to him but been riddled with guilt. He kept on crying, but I felt detached. I didn't have to stop it. Even though I was detached, at the same time I somehow felt more involved than ever. Soon he finished his crying and then came over and asked me to read him a book!"

Jennifer had learned that she couldn't express herself to her parents without deep hurt and feelings of unworthiness. She was determined that her son would not feel the same. But wanting him to feel the happiness she had wished for got mixed up with her duties and responsibilities as a mother. She needs to see that her parents were not responsible for her unhappiness. They were responsible for the things they said and did to her. She is not responsible for her son's happiness, only for what she says and does.

CHAPTER FIFTEEN

THE INCOMPETENCE BUTTON

can't do anything right. I'm a mess" is the lament of the parent who feels incompetent. When a parent considers himself incompetent, inadequate, or a failure, he feels powerless to influence, to teach, to be authoritative—to parent. He looks to everyone else for the answers, cannot trust himself, and certainly does not trust his child. The incompetent parent is at risk for giving over power, being overly permissive, and becoming a "doormat" for the rest of the family, perhaps burdening others with the responsibility of doing the job that he doesn't believe he's up to.

It is natural for this parent to lay blame on his child for his own shortcomings, asking his child to compensate—to make it better for him so he won't have to feel badly about himself. This parent can present himself as the victim when he says he's incapable of doing anything about the problem. Victims feel powerless but often exhibit power in their victim role by being helpless and requiring someone else to compensate for their inabilities. They also tend to take on too much responsibility, being convinced it is their job, even though they don't know what to do about it. It becomes another reason to blame themselves.

When their button is pushed, incompetent parents feel helpless, hopeless, or invisible and give themselves little or no credit. Children of these parents may either play on the parent's subservient role, take the power and run with it, or they may be left with guilt for what they are not able to do to make their parent happy.

When children push the incompetence button, they are asking their parents to step into their power, feel confident in their decisions, and take control.

"It's My Responsibility. Isn't It?"
Shelley and Tyler (7)

"Okay, what did I do wrong?" a frustrated Shelley asked the class. "I bought Tyler this Lego Robotron he's been wanting for a long time. We got in the car to go home, and he begged me to open it. I told him that he would lose the pieces and would be upset. He said he would be careful and kept begging, so I gave in. Sure enough, he was putting it together in the living room, and eleven pieces were missing! I was furious. I yelled at him, 'I told you so,' and then he cried and told me it was all my fault. The whole thing was a horrible mess. I've been upset about it ever since. I set out to do something nice for him, and it turned out rotten."

"So did you look in the car for the pieces?" another mother asked.

"Oh, yes, but four are still missing."

"So can't he build other things with it?" they asked.

Shelley said, "I don't think so. I think that's it. Anyway, I took it away and put it in the closet."

"Of course he can build other things with it. Is he upset about the four pieces?" a father asked.

"No," Shelley said, a little embarrassed. "I'm the one who's upset about it."

"Why have you made it your problem?" I asked Shelley. She looked confused. "He lost the pieces. It's his toy; he is responsible for the lost pieces."

"But I'm the one who is so mad!" she said.

"Exactly. That is what tells me that you have made it your problem. Can you identify the assumptions you had at the time?"

She listed them: "*He's disorganized and careless. He's going to grow up without any care for his things. I haven't taught him how to be organized.*"

"So what standard are you using that generates those thoughts?" I asked. Shelley was stumped. We all came up with them together. *My child must be organized and careful with his things at all times. It is my responsibility to teach him organizational skills.*

"Are you organized?" someone asked.

"No, I'm terrible, and it makes me so mad. I don't want Tyler to grow up like me. I can't keep anything straight, and then I get mad at my husband for not knowing where something is."

"But, Shelley, aren't you forgetting that Tyler is seven? He's a kid, and kids lose things. If it doesn't upset him, what's the big deal?" one of the class members asked.

"It's also the money. That's a big issue with me. I just spent money on this toy and already it's wrecked," Shelley added.

A different mother piped in, "But you bought it. It was your choice to buy it for him. That's done. Now it's his. Can you let go of it?"

Someone else said, "It sounds like you're expecting him to be perfect. Like a doll." Shelley looked pensive.

Shelley was listening hard, but she still felt stuck. "The problem is I don't think there's anything wrong with my assumptions. I think they're true."

"Okay, let's look at the whole piece," I said. "First, do you like the way you reacted? Was it helpful?"

"No, I hated it. I was very upset, and it definitely was not helpful."

"So your reaction was caused by your emotions. You were furious with him and furious with yourself. We've said that your emotions cannot be controlled, only suppressed or acted on. But your assumptions are what cause your emotions. So if you don't like your reaction, the problem must be in your assumptions. If your assumptions seem accurate, there must be another way of looking at it that you haven't thought of. Are your expectations appropriate? Several others seem to think they are not."

Shelley thought for a minute. "I think I'm beginning to see something. I'm putting more importance on Tyler's things than I am on him. It's the material objects that are getting in my way of letting go of taking responsibility for everything."

"If everything is your responsibility, then you are always at fault when something goes wrong," I said.

"Absolutely," she responded. "And when we went over the situation later, and I asked him what we could have done differently, I said, 'Do you think I should have let you open the box?' and he said, 'No, you shouldn't have let me.' I was left feeling blamed—again."

"It sounds like you set yourself up to feel incompetent. Which happens when you think everything is your responsibility. Tyler had his out. He could make it all your fault, and you took it. So he never had to take responsibility for himself."

We discussed how the situation could have gone differently. Shelley could have said in the car, "The risk of opening the box is that pieces will get lost. Do you understand that?" If he still wanted to open it, she could have noted that it was his choice and then *let go*. When pieces were missing, it would then be his problem, not hers. He would then be given the opportunity to understand cause and effect, trial and error. He could internalize the risks of making that choice and learn something for next time. If he gets to blame his mother, he doesn't learn anything.

"But what should she do then?" someone asked. "Should she help him find the pieces?"

I suggested that it didn't matter whether she helped him or not. If she knew it was his problem and not hers, she could empathize with his being upset about the missing pieces, she could offer to help him, or she could let him do it on his own—whatever felt right. If she is upset about the pieces but he isn't, the problem is hers. If he continues not to care about his things, it might be a good idea to let him start saving money and buy them himself. The important piece is to allow him to have his problem so that he can learn from it.

"I get it!" Shelley said. "He can't learn if I take the blame. And I give myself the blame so he won't be unhappy. The problem is, I end up feeling like a failure. But he has a right to be unhappy, and his unhappiness might motivate him to take better care of his things."

"Yes, you did get it." I beamed back at her. It seemed like everyone in the room got it. "I think it will be wise for you to write a new standard for yourself that releases you from all the responsibility you carry. Parenting Tyler will be much easier when you do."

"I'm Nothing, So You'd Better Be Something."
Kate, Tucker (5), and Misha (3)

When I asked a new "Buttons" group what had brought them to the class, Kate said, "I hit rock bottom with Tucker the other night. But it was the best thing that happened to me. We were both out of control, and then, all of a sudden, it hit. I'm thirty-six, and he's five. I'm the one who has to change.

"Misha is just like me," Kate said. "She's built just like me; she looks like me; she acts like me. Tucker is much more out there, putting it in your face. And he puts it in Misha's face all the time." Kate was worried about the sibling rivalry between her two children. She saw Tucker as the instigator and Misha as the victim. I asked Kate where she fit in her family of origin.

"I'm the youngest of four," she said. "I have two older sisters and an older brother. Plus I'm the youngest of all my extended family. All my siblings and all my cousins teased me and put me down constantly. They treated me like nothing."

"Where were your parents in all of this?" I asked. "Did they do anything to protect you?"

"They made sure it didn't happen around my parents. My father actually didn't care. He treated me like nothing, too. But my mother didn't really know about it."

"You didn't tell her?" I asked.

"No, I didn't want her to have any more to deal with than she already had dealing with my father."

"It sounds like you have identified with Misha, the youngest and the girl, and don't want her to suffer what you did. I wonder if Tucker reminds you of your older siblings, and it pushes your buttons when you see him taunting Misha like you were taunted. You fall right back into your sibling role and resent what he is doing. What is your standard for Tucker's behavior?"

Without hesitating, Kate said, "That he always act in a way that makes others feel good about themselves or do nothing at all." I suggested that that was a tall order.

"What about Tucker's feelings?" I asked. She looked pensive. "Did you do that in your family?" I prodded.

The story came out without reservation. "My father was a violently angry man. He blamed everything on someone else. If any one of us opened a door that knocked against a chair that bumped his foot, he would yell, 'You did that on purpose.' He never hit, but he sure blamed us a lot. I was envious of my older sister because she didn't take it. She would say back to him, 'Don't be ridiculous. Why would I *want* to make you mad?' and he would back off. I was just scared. I lived on fear and guilt. So I did everything I could to avoid his rage and to make him happy."

She added that everyone made fun of her and called her "big Katie" and "fattie." She confessed that she has struggled with weight all her life. She hates her "solid" build and once again said how Misha is built just like her. She has tried all kinds of diets, but nothing has worked to get her weight where she wants it.

"I was always trying to avoid teasing and criticism, so basically I tried to be invisible. My mother was my savior," Kate added. "We're like each other's best friend, but strangely, I don't go to very deep places with her. I keep her at bay. Actually I keep most people at bay." Kate gestured with her palm facing out. "I don't really know why. My mother did blame us for doing whatever we did to set my father off."

"It sounds like your mother needed to side with her husband, possibly to keep the marriage intact," I suggested. "Maybe you learned that she wasn't completely trustworthy."

"Now that you mention it, I always blamed my father for everything, but lately I've been feeling really angry with her. I guess that's why. And you're right—I don't trust her. She's always making these subtle, backhanded comments about my weight like, 'You don't want another cookie,' when she's handing them out to everyone else. Or telling my niece right in front of me how trim she keeps herself and how beautiful her clothes are, saying, 'Don't you wish you could wear something like that, Kate?' It makes me want to kill her!"

I suspected that the abuse she grew up with was the reason for her protective layer. The shame that Kate felt as a child—shame that told her she was the problem, she was at fault for making her father mad, for being too big, for being a "nothing" for all to make fun of—had seeped into her subconscious. As a result, she keeps herself in hiding from others in order to keep them "at bay," so that they don't see the real person inside.

When Tucker makes fun of Misha, hits her, and gets in her face, it triggers Kate's shame and reminds her of those unpleasant memories. She projects her experience onto Misha and doesn't want Tucker to treat Misha like a nothing. She wants to protect Misha from feeling the deep agony she felt, so she reacts with blame toward Tucker, who is quickly learning to see himself as the problem.

"It seems as if you are trying to make Tucker treat Misha the way you wanted to be treated," I suggested. "A natural and logical goal. However, with your standard telling you *Children must act in a way that makes others feel good about themselves or do nothing at all,* you are taking responsibility for Misha and giving Tucker no room to have his own feelings. If he is expected to make Misha feel good and she doesn't, you are unintentionally setting him up for feeling bad. It's not his job to make Misha feel good about herself. You are asking him to be responsible for other people's feelings and ignore his own, a job you had to

take on to survive. But Tucker doesn't have to do that to survive. And
Misha is not learning to stand up for herself if you protect her."

We looked at how all the pieces fit. Kate's belief—*I am worthless
and a nothing*—leads her to develop the standard—*Children must act
in ways that make others feel good*—that makes her children compensate
for what she never got. Paradoxically, this standard is beginning to create
the same bad feelings in Tucker that Kate experienced, because her
father expected her to behave in ways that made *him* feel good! But Kate
took it all inside to try to be invisible. Tucker is acting his feelings out.

As soon as Kate realized that she was unintentionally passing this
pattern on, she immediately stopped herself. She could see that she
had been defending Misha against Tucker, setting him up as the bad
guy, and he was buying it. Tucker needed what she had needed—to
have his feelings accepted, to be treated with respect.

Kate came in the next week feeling stronger. "I had a great week
with the kids." She beamed. "My standard has changed, and I think
Tucker feels it. He was poking Misha, and she was whining at him to
make him stop, all the while looking at me pleadingly. I told her that
she had every right to tell him how mad she was, which she did. Tucker
complained that she had taken the book he was reading and hid it. I
said, 'Wow, really! I can see why you would be angry at her. Can you
tell her what you want instead of poking her?' He looked at me as if I
had handed him a huge present. He said with a rather fierce tone,
'Misha, please get my book and give it to me.' Lo and behold, Misha
went and got the book! Tucker looked at me, and we shared a knowing
smile. It felt great! It's amazing what just being a little more aware of
the layers underneath can do to change things. I could let go of taking
care of Misha, and I saw that she is perfectly capable of taking care of
herself."

"If Only I Were a Better Mother . . ."
Lee, Jerry, and Robbie (4)

Lee had put up with Robbie's stinky, dirty feet for a long time before she realized she was actually capable of doing something about it.

Robbie loved his red rubber boots. Whenever he was at home, his shoes would come off, and on would go his rubber boots. Often his clothes came off, as well. He loved the feeling of no restrictions on his body. But his rubber boots had become a second skin. Lee and Jerry had no problem with their son running around at home with no clothes, nor did they have a problem with his rubber boots. But Lee did have a problem with his feet when the boots came off.

No matter how often she washed out the insides of the boots, after a few hours of hard playing, Robbie's feet were still a problem. The smell and the grime between the toes were leaving spots on her new couch and interfering with an otherwise pleasant dinner hour. Anytime Lee suggested washing Robbie's feet, he would shriek, "Noooooo!" and Lee would leave him alone. Jerry, on the other hand, would drag him off and clean them himself, telling Lee she was too easy on him.

"Jerry's reactions make it even harder for me to be firm," she confessed. "I don't want to ruffle Robbie's feathers," she said with a laugh. "So, I would say, 'Please take your feet off the couch, Rob,' being as polite and respectful as I could be. Robbie would say, 'No, I don't have to!' I could feel my blood start to boil. But I would bite my tongue and say, 'I would really like you to, sweetie.' I would be ignored, and then I couldn't say any more about it. It was like he was pointing out to me what a pathetic, worthless parent I was."

"So actually Robbie doesn't have to take his feet off the couch, does he?" I asked.

"You mean because I let it go? You're right. When he says he doesn't have to, he knows he doesn't have to! I'm such a pushover. I can't make him do anything."

Lee desperately wanted to be a good mother. She and Jerry had tried for a long time to get pregnant. After thinking it would never happen, they tried fertility drugs, but even that didn't work. Just as they had given up hope, she became pregnant. Lee was so grateful to have a baby that he could do no wrong—until her button started to get pushed.

"It feels like I am taking something away from him if I tell him no," she admitted genuinely. "I look at him and think, 'Oh, the poor thing.' I can never willingly or knowingly cause his unhappiness. I know I am spoiling him, but I feel so guilty and blame myself unmercifully if I say no to anything; it just isn't worth it."

The fear of being a bad mother had Lee trapped. Meeting Robbie's needs was her first priority. She ended up pleading with him to do whatever she wanted. Her pleading automatically put her in a submissive role, and she let him win every time. But when her button began getting pushed, she imploded into anxiety and self-doubt for fear of getting mad at Robbie.

Lee had been pampered as a child herself. She worried that she was too spoiled to be a good enough parent. Desperate to prove herself wrong, she compensated by never doing what she wanted, never putting her own needs first. So Robbie had come to "rule the roost."

Robbie had taken all the power in the relationship, and his behavior had become quite aggressive. His resistance to her requests for him to be calm and polite got louder and louder. "Occasionally, I blow," Lee confessed. "It's like I have torn him apart. He screams at me, 'You hate me!' I can't stand that, and so I apologize and get him a present or something," she said.

The turning point came on Easter morning in church. "He was demanding, loud, and rude. The whole congregation heard him when he told the man next to us to move over and give him more room. I wanted to crawl under the pew! I realized then that I had no control over him, and I had to do something fast. We took him out, and I sent him home with Jerry and told him he could not go to his grandparents' for Easter dinner. He had a major tantrum. He adores his grandparents, who of course dote on him like they did on me. But surprisingly he quickly settled down. He almost seemed happier and went home without a fuss. Later on when I got home, he was sweeter and more cooperative than he had ever been. We went for a bike ride and had the best time together."

"I wonder if all this time his aggressive behavior has been a signal to you to stop him and set restrictions on his behavior," I said.

"I thought the same thing," she answered.

Lee had to learn that her own needs were not only important to her growth and development but also to Robbie's. Her fears of being an incompetent mother only led him to take advantage. Respecting herself was in his best interest, too.

After her success on Easter, Lee felt ready to tackle the boots and grungy feet. She worked it out with self-talk first, telling herself that her desire for clean feet on the couch was justified and that the balance of their needs was her ultimate goal.

The next day, she said to him, "Robbie, from now on you will have a choice. Either you will wash your feet after you take your boots off, or you will not be allowed to wear your boots again. It is important to me that our furniture stays clean and that we do not have to smell dirty feet. The choice is yours."

"Okay, Mom, I'll wash my feet." Lee was dumbfounded. She regularly has to remind him, but he does wash his feet with only a mild grumble.

Lee's new perception includes her own needs. *I count. I can ask him to do what I want, too, and still be a good mother, meet Robbie's needs, and claim my authority.* She repeated this over and over to herself until it sank in. She came to the last class with a new story.

"Robbie was going out to ride his bike, and I was on the phone. His motorcycle goggles were not fitting under his helmet the right way, and he got very angry. He pulled off the helmet and hurled it across the room, breaking my antique vase. I hung up the phone, picked up the helmet, and without a word put it on top of the refrigerator. Before, I would have thought, 'Oh, the poor thing,' and put his helmet on the right way and sent him off to ride seething over my vase. But I didn't," she said proudly.

"Robbie lost control. He raged and flung himself at me, screaming, 'No, I want my helmet. I have to ride my bike!' I held him tightly with his back to me, but he began crashing his head into my chest. I picked him up kicking and flailing, took him to his room, and sat with him while he had his tantrum. When he finished, I held him for a few minutes. He said, 'Can I go out now?' I said, 'If you're ready to change your behavior and be calm, you can.' He was cooperative for the rest of the day. We discussed how he would take responsibility for the vase and agreed that he would pay five dollars toward a new one to be taken out of his allowance over the next two months."

Lee learned that in order to be a "better mother," she must find a way to say no. Her automatic reaction is to give in and give up. If she had reacted in the old way, Robbie would not have been held account-able for his behavior. Typically this style of reactive parenting results in children feeling entitled to what they want with no respect for the rights of others. Responsibility always belongs to someone else, com-munication with potentially influential adults is near impossible, and a deep gap develops. She has shared many setbacks into her self-critical judgments, but she is learning that when she falls into the victim role, she gives Robbie way too much power. It is that imbalanced power that causes his anger and unhappiness, not hearing her say no.

CHAPTER SIXTEEN

THE GUILT BUTTON

Guilty parents tend to place far more importance on their children's needs than on their own. When asked, they usually can't tell you what their own needs are. They feel guilty if they do and guilty if they don't. Often they were taught in childhood that the needs of the adults in their lives were more important than their own and were left feeling responsible for meeting those needs. Guilt was a useful motivator for teaching that responsibility. Guilty parents are not very good at taking care of themselves, honoring their own needs, and creating appropriate boundaries because their focus is on what they haven't done right.

Many positive moments with a child are completely ignored, because the guilt over just one thing will be exaggerated. And when guilty parents decide they have come up short, their fuse is short, too. Guilt is often used as an excuse for the parent's behavior. If a parent fears that she has done something wrong, feeling guilty often gives her permission—"If I feel guilty, I can't be blamed"—when she either can't or won't rectify the situation. Finding other compensations, like presents, trips, or sweets offers the parent the illusion of making the child happy, so the parent can be relieved of guilt—temporarily.

The guilty parent is always wishing, "If only I were a better parent . . ." Children of the guilty parent often feel guilty and anxious themselves, sometimes acting out when they feel responsible for the guilt that drives their parent.

Children who push their parents' guilt button are telling them to "get a life" and get on with what's important now instead of stewing over what could or should have been.

"Separation Is a Horrible, Destructive Thing."
Rachel and Greg (8)

"How could a decent mother drop her child off with someone she barely knew?" Rachel was amazed that tears still came when she talked about putting Gregory in day care almost eight years ago, when he was three months old. "I don't think I'll ever get over it. I still feel so guilty about it. I know I messed him up. I was a terrible mother."

On the contrary, Rachel is a terrific mother. She has worked hard learning about temperament in order to understand Greg's intense nature and to gain neutrality in handling the years of his daily tantrums. She continues to take parenting classes but is still convinced that the intensity of his tantrums were due to those first few years in day care. "I'm sure I harmed him by leaving him. His struggles wouldn't have been so bad if I had stayed with him. I did a terrible disservice to him. I'm sure we could have made ends meet, but I trusted my husband's judgment that we needed more money. I'm still angry at him about it."

"How did the guilt affect your life during that time?" I asked.

"I never stopped. I tried to keep everyone happy all the time. I just kept pleasing everybody. I spent every minute with the kids and did the laundry and all the housework after ten at night. I was just exhausted. I took care of all my husband's emotional needs. But I wasn't taking care of myself at all. So I got really sick. I got a terrible case of the flu that kept me home for weeks. I was worn out for a couple of months. That was what stopped me. It gave me the excuse to quit working. Besides, the cost of two kids in day care was practically what I was making anyway."

Rachel left work after Greg had been in day care for three and a half years. Although the stress lessened, Rachel missed her work. "They were like my family," she said, "and I loved my work, but I just couldn't take the guilt anymore."

"But it sounds as though the guilt is still with you," I noted.

Another class member piped up. "That was almost five years ago, Rachel. You're doing a great job now. You've got two great kids. Why are you still so upset about it?"

"I just feel that I did permanent damage to him. He's always been such a homebody, and separating is so hard for him. That's it, I think. Separation is my biggest issue." Rachel began tearing up again.

"What is it about separation, Rachel?" I asked.

"I was brought up to believe that separation is like death," she answered. Everyone was startled by her response. "My mother is a total narcissist with a 'borderline personality.' She has never seen life from anyone's perspective other than her own. She's constantly off to the hospital with some new made-up disease or condition. She's always been jealous of anything good that has ever happened to me and has basically made life miserable for everyone around her.

"My father has committed his life to taking care of my mother purely because of his marriage vows," Rachel continued. "He can't take her either but would never leave her. I was always his way out. He created this triangle between the three of us. I had to be there. I felt guilty if I went out for a night in high school. My brothers got to do whatever they wanted, but when I told my father I wanted to go to college, he offered to buy me a car and give me money if I would stay home. He dreaded being alone with my mother. I actually made it to college, but

I think I hurt him very much. I feel so guilty about the life I left him with. He was shocked when I didn't move back home after college."

"So what did you learn about yourself growing up in this triangle?" I asked.

"You do not separate from someone you love. I got that message loud and clear—from both my parents. My father couldn't separate from my mother even though he desperately wanted to, and I couldn't separate from either of them because it was seen as this huge betrayal. Doing something for myself is the hardest thing in the world."

"So you got left with all the guilt."

"Bingo!" Rachel said emphatically.

"So when you separated yourself from Greg by going back to work, what did that tell you?" I asked.

"That I was about the worst person in the world. Like I said, separation meant death—the end. It was the worst thing you could do. Separating from someone you love is a betrayal. It's the ultimate in selfishness. I was never allowed to be selfish. My job was to always keep Mom happy at all costs. And to keep Dad from having to deal with her by himself."

"Do you think you have to keep Greg happy at all costs?" I asked. Rachel looked pensive. "I wonder if you couldn't deal with the death/betrayal aspect of what you had done to your father and to Greg, and so you turned it into severe guilt to punish yourself. That self-punishment somehow allowed you to live with it. What would it feel like for you to say that you did what felt right, what you needed to do?"

"It would feel selfish. It would be admitting that I was a bad girl," Rachel said.

"So is the guilt your punishment for being that bad girl?" I asked.

"Yes, I guess so. I was a bad girl for leaving my father to deal with my mother and for leaving Greg in day care to deal with all those people. It still makes me feel so bad," Rachel said, shaking her head.

"What's the risk in stopping the punishment? What do you get out of still feeling guilty?" I asked.

Rachel thought for a moment and then said, "I looked at Greg in the car the other day, and I was enjoying his company so much. I thought, *How dare I not take advantage of him when he was little?* He is this gentle soul. How could I have left him alone to fend for himself? I operate most of my life out of anxiety. It feels like a safety net so I don't have to deal with what's really going on. If I didn't feel guilty, I would be a bad mother. How could a good mother leave her three-month-old and feel good about it?"

Rachel had created a standard for herself that said, *Good mothers do not separate from their children*. But to get her family's needs met, she had to separate. So as not to feel like a supremely selfish person who deserves to die, she felt self-deprecating guilt instead. That way, she could live with herself.

"Even though you needed the money and the support from work, you couldn't feel good about it because it would have meant breaking from the family—both families. *People who love each other don't separate* is the belief you grew up with. It translated directly to your standard. Since you couldn't live up to your standard, you compensated by putting yourself down with guilt. Your assumptions—*I harmed him, I did a disservice to him,* and *I made him have intense tantrums*—feed your punishing guilt. If you didn't feel guilty, you would be a selfish person in your eyes—too bad to live with yourself.

I asked Rachel to think about how accurate it was that she had indeed damaged her son and that his tantrums were due to his three years in day care.

"I know it's not entirely accurate, and I know how much I needed those days with other adults. They gave me the support I didn't have. And I loved my work," she said again.

"I think the guilt has nothing to do with working, only with separation. The guilt goes back to your childhood wound, which is tapped every time you separate."

"Well I'm already freaking out about him going off to college. I don't see how I'm going to be able to stand it," Rachel added.

"What do you get from the guilt?" I asked again.

"A lot of anxiety," she said with a laugh.

"Don't you also get to be a virtuous person?" I asked. "When you express your guilt, don't you get to have people say, 'Oh, Rachel, you shouldn't feel guilty about that?' You get to have people focus on you and feel sorry for you." Rachel looked embarrassed. "And isn't that what you would have loved from your parents?"

"Oh, my goodness. So I'm setting this all up to get what I wanted from my parents all along? Wow, that's amazing. So if I let that go, I wonder if I could lose the guilt?" Rachel pondered.

"It's worth a try," I said. "Each time you feel that guilt, do some self-talk connecting the guilt to your parents, not to work or Greg, and see what happens."

The last week Rachel came in with her new standard: *Separation allows for independence and growth.* "It's a hard one, and I don't entirely believe it yet. But I know now that my guilt protected me when I thought I had betrayed my parents and didn't deserve to live. That's ridiculous. So I keep remembering that my guilt was from then, and it's not about Greg. It helps me see that it is true, that he really is fine. And occasionally I get that I am fine, too."

Rachel continues battling her guilt. It often pops up after she has dropped Greg off at school or puts him on the school bus. When she is able to talk herself through it, the anxiety is less and she is through it sooner.

"How Can I Make It Up to Her?"
David and Cally (10)

"Cally's a shop-aholic!" David complained as the group was discussing what their children do to push their buttons. "Everywhere we go, she says, 'I have to have that, Daddy, pleeease!' It drives me nuts."

"Does she get it?" another group member asked.

David looked a bit sheepish and said, "Yeah, mostly. But we're really trying to cut back. But every time we say no, she throws a fit right there in the store. What are you supposed to do? I mean the girl has everything she could possibly want. She's even got one of those American Girl dolls that cost a hundred dollars. You'd think she'd be satisfied. I'm working my butt off to keep her in goods!"

"What motivates you to buy her the things she wants?" I asked.

"So she'll get off my back!" he said with a laugh. "I don't know, actually. She spends a lot of time playing by herself, so she needs things to play with. There aren't a lot of kids in the neighborhood, and she's an only child."

"Does that bother you?" I asked.

"What, that she's an only child? I don't know. I guess so. It makes me sad when I see her playing alone. She can't be having any fun. I mean, we didn't give her a sibling."

"Did you have siblings?" I asked.

"Yes, I had two brothers. I didn't have much to do with my younger brother, but my older brother and I were very close. We did a lot together. You know, sports, drinking beer, listening to Jimi Hendrix, stuff like that. And we spent hours commiserating about our parents. Cally won't have anyone to off-load her frustrations on. We try to have a good relationship with her so she can off-load on us, but it's not the same."

"Why did you decide to have only one child, then?" another person in the group asked.

"Purely selfish reasons. We weren't even going to have one, but we somehow got talked into it by our friends. We really like to travel and thought more than one would make it prohibitive. Cally has more frequent flyer miles than most adults. I'm really afraid it's going to backfire on us one day. She'll be in therapy complaining that her parents didn't give her a sibling."

"Why are you so sure she wants a sibling?" a mother in the group asked. "I'm an only child and wouldn't want it any other way. Maybe you're assuming she's going to be miserable because you would have been without your brother. I just went off in my own little world and loved it."

"That's really good to hear," David said. "She did say to my wife about a year ago that she wished she had a sister. It's funny. When I ask her, she evades the question. She gives me this patronizing look and says, 'It's okay, Daddy.' That makes me feel worse. I've told her that I was sorry about the whole thing, but she doesn't respond."

"It sounds to me like you want her permission to let you off the hook for something she may not even care about," I suggested. "Why do you need to be let off the hook?"

David continued talking about how much he thought she was missing out on, and then it finally came out. "We actually did have another child before Cally who died at birth. We named her and had a memorial service for her and everything. It was pretty heavy. Do you think it's okay to tell Cally that we did have another child? Would that be enough to appease her do you think—to let her know that we did try?"

"What strikes me is that you think you need an excuse for her being an only child," I said.

"Oh, I'm making assumptions again, aren't I?"

"Since you had already decided to have only one child, would you have had Cally if the baby had lived?" I asked.

"No," was David's immediate response.

"I wonder if your guilt is more about the fact that Cally wouldn't even be here if the baby had lived. Do you want to talk a little more about the baby?" I asked.

David looked uncomfortable but said, "Maybe I should. We did decide at first that that was our one shot at it, that we wouldn't have another. We were pretty depressed for a long time. It was really hard. But time helped, and we decided that we really wanted a child. We had gotten psyched for one, and now we didn't have any. It was a scary pregnancy not knowing what would happen, but then Cally arrived and has been a handful ever since! She definitely makes up for two!"

"Do you think you're compensating for the loss of the first child by giving Cally everything she wants?"

"Oh, maybe that's it. It certainly feels like compensating." David continued to tell us that he had made a decision to be self-employed so that Cally wouldn't be alone or have to be put in day care. His wife works with him. But because of that, his options were limited and he works at something he doesn't enjoy. He has to work long, exhausting hours to make travel affordable and now feels guilty about the fact that Cally has to play alone while they are in their home office. "I feel chained to this damn business. But I'm starting to cut back."

I asked how Cally does playing alone. He described her wild imagination and her closeness with their dog and cat.

"So it sounds to me like Cally is doing fine," I offered. "Perhaps you have hung onto the guilt over the fact that Cally wouldn't be here had your first not died. And that guilt continues to be fed by your assumptions that Cally is not getting what you had when you were a boy. If she does wish for a sibling, which could have been a momentary desire, it could be the result of your projection. You have expressed to her real concerns and apologies. She must think that there is something important she's missing out on. You have been breaking your back to make it okay for her. But what you're really doing is trying to make it okay for you to have made the decisions you did."

Through the class work, David realized that the standard that fueled his remorseful guilt was *Children are better off with siblings,* which has led to his assumption *I have to make it up to Cally for not giving her a sibling.* David realized that he had transferred his own experience onto Cally and had decided what she would want. His agenda then left him with the remorse over not giving it to her as well as his guilt over the baby who died. He has attempted to assuage his guilt by working at home and buying Cally whatever she wanted. The result, however, is a demanding "shop-aholic"—more reasons to feed David's guilt.

We worked on David taking responsibility for the decisions he and his wife made to have one child in order to travel and live an affordable life. His perception that their decisions were based on selfish motivation kept him steeped in the guilt that was creating the problem he needed to address—an entitled child who was learning to take advantage of his guilt.

I asked David if he could find a way to look more wholistically at their decisions. He came into class one evening and said, "I guess I have been asking Cally to validate my decisions by apologizing to her for not providing a sibling, hoping she would say that she didn't even want one. So now I have to bite the bullet and accept the fact that this is what we wanted, and she has to live with it."

"As you've heard right here in the group, some people thrive on being an only child," I pointed out. David rewrote his standard to say *We made decisions that felt right for us. Children adapt to the world they experience, which makes them who they are.*

By the last class, he reported that their commitment to saying no to

Cally over things she wanted was beginning to get little or no negative reaction from her. "And when she did balk, I could say, 'Not this time,' without feeling drenched in guilt. It didn't bother me so much that she was unhappy about it," David said, pleased with himself. "I think the guilt is beginning to break up."

"If Only I Could Do Something."
Kristen, Nelly (5), and Will (18 months)

"I have a bright, beautiful five-year-old girl who has completely stopped talking to me." Kristen announced this fact as blithely as if her daughter had stopped eating Cheerios. "Nelly doesn't answer when I speak to her; she doesn't respond when I make requests; she ignores me when I try to discipline her. I find myself yelling at her just to get her to acknowledge me. I've screamed things like, 'You little pain in the ass!' I grab her; I push her; sometimes I just want to smack her. Nothing has ever made me so mad in my entire life!"

Kristen stopped, took a deep breath, then continued. "After it's over, I feel such guilt that I can hardly get through the day. I am literally heartsick. Sometimes I just sit and stare out the window. I can't even do my job. I wait, and I watch the clock, counting the hours and minutes until I can pick her up from school to see if everything is okay—to see if I've really done it this time, if I've ruined her for good. I rush to school, filled with anxiety, call to her, and search her face for some clue that I've been forgiven or that perhaps this time it wasn't so bad. Often she'll look toward me but just past me, not making eye contact. Some days she acts like everything is fine. Either way, I feel so guilty."

Then Kristen began to describe Nelly's aggression and mistreatment of her little brother, Will. "She hates him. She won't ever let him play with her. She pushes him away or swats him and hurts him. I just can't stand it. I suffered through a second pregnancy to give her someone to make her life journey with. Someone who will be there for her after we're gone. It kills me to hear her say she hates him."

"Can you see how their relationship is your agenda, not hers?" I asked. "You're asking her to be happy about what you want her to want! It's not her responsibility to take care of your hopes and dreams."

"But why wouldn't she want to have a brother—someone to play with?"

"She may eventually, but right now he's usurping her position in the family, and she's mad about it. She has to share you now, and she used to have you all to herself," I said. "So when you get angry at her for her behavior toward him, she hears that she's not acceptable to you but he is. Her behavior reflects how she feels when she hears that."

"So is that why she wouldn't wipe his nose in the car the other day? I handed her a Kleenex and asked her to, and she flat-out refused. I got so mad at her. I guess I'm expecting her to want to help him."

"Exactly," I said. "Why is it so important to you that they have each other? Who did you have?"

"My younger sister," Kristen said quietly. She began a tale of a very hard childhood.

"My sister and I were very different, but we had this alliance that helped us survive our miserable family. My father was a good-for-nothing alcoholic, and my mother was useless in shielding us from his rages. We were incredibly poor. We never seemed to have enough heat. We wore our coats in the house and our clothes to bed. We often didn't have enough food in the house. My sister and I have a solidarity having suffered through the same childhood—a kind of 'we're in this together' bond. There isn't anything we wouldn't do for each other. I was the strong one, and she was weaker. I spoke for her and protected her against my father. He never hit us, but he swore at us. That's why I use such horrible language when I get mad—it's in my database."

"So, you want Nelly and Will to have what you and your sister had. But you and your sister were the victims of a circumstance that Nelly and Will don't share. They have no need to bond against you and your husband."

Kristen was quiet for a moment. Then she described how the shame she felt as a child still haunts her even though she has created a professional life to mask it as much as possible. "It's like this shadow that is always following right behind me," she said. "No matter how hard I try, I can't seem to get away from it. And when I'm in front of people making a presentation at work, I feel like such a fake—like any second they're going to find out who I really am."

"And who is that?" I asked.

"This unlovable, no-good failure. When I'm yelling at Nell for being mean to Will, I'm just passing on what was done to me. I'm horrified at how I've screwed her up with my garbage."

"Did you feel guilty as a child?" I asked.

"Did I ever," Kristen exclaimed. "My father was a professional musician and demanded that I play the same instrument that he did. I never liked it, because it wasn't my choice; so I always felt riddled with guilt that I let him down—let down his belief and hope in me. Plus I was always guilty about how miserable my parents were. They always told me their financial woes. My childhood mantra was 'If only I could do something.'"

I suggested to Kristen, "Your shame gets tapped each time Nelly pushes your button, and so you feel ineffectual. When that wound is poked, you react by screaming at Nelly to get her to stop poking. But you need to let the poking in and feel the pain to become aware of how your past is creating the gap between you two. When she pokes, ask yourself what the poking it trying to tell you."

"We're so much alike," Kristen said. "It's like we're twins. And I'm so afraid I'm treating her like my father treated me. I hear him coming out of my mouth."

"No wonder you want Nelly to take care of Will. That's the role you played, and you expect it of your older and stronger child. You are projecting your role onto her and resenting her for not filling it. And it's only based on fear."

When I asked Kristen what her expectations for her children were, she spoke more about the responsibility she and her sister felt for one another. "We were the parents for each other that we never had. We were each other's safety zone." When we got it written into a standard, it said, *My children should have unconditional, absolute, sincere, and lifelong commitment to each other.*

"That's a pretty tall order for two little kids," I said. "Quite a setup for failure." Thinking she could make her standard work, Kristen demanded that Nelly do things for Will. Nelly most likely heard her mother's requests across the gap to mean that Will was more important than she was and resented him for it.

"What do you think the guilt protects you from?" I asked. "If you didn't feel guilty about your reactions to Nelly, what would that mean?"

"It would mean that I meant it all, that I behaved consciously—that it was thought out and acceptable. To me, the guilt means that I have the desire to be a better parent."

I pointed out that Kristen's resentment of Nelly directly led to Nelly's resentment of Will. But the good news was that her resentful guilt was motivating her instead of immobilizing her. We discussed ways in which Kristen might regain connection with Nelly. After a few weeks, experiencing both immediate progress and disappointing regression, Kristen came in declaring a breakthrough.

"I told Nelly the story of her birth and how my secret wish had been for her to be a little girl. She looked at me like she couldn't believe what she was hearing. I told her how much I understand how annoying Will can be, and how I wish at times that it were just us again. She agreed, fully expressing her loathing for him, how much she hates him and wishes he were dead. I had to bite my tongue to keep from telling her not to say things like that. I was sure this was just making it worse. But finally she said to me unprompted, 'Mommy, it's just that I wasn't expecting a boy.' Everything started to change after that. Almost all their fighting stopped! She and I are like best friends again. I feel such joy at rediscovering who she is.

"But here's the best part," she continued. "One day they were at a friend's house, and the friend's little brother hit Will in the face. Will cried, and Nell ran to him, screaming, circling his body with her arms. When the friend's mother got to them, Nell said, 'He was hurting my brother! No one can hurt my brother!' When we talked about it later, she said, 'I was protecting him. He was trying to hurt my brother.' A week later she announced to me that she is *in love* with Will!"

In allowing Nelly to express her anger toward her brother, Kristen showed her acceptance of Nelly—feelings and all. Nelly knew she was okay and no longer felt threatened by Will. She was free to accept him.

Once Kristen made the connection between her past shame and her reactions toward Nelly, she could give Nelly what was never given to her. Her new standard declares simply, *All family members are to respect one another*. The demands for commitment are gone. The chances of it happening are now greater than ever.

CHAPTER SEVENTEEN

THE RESENTMENT BUTTON

The resentful parent expresses her disapproval or anger when she thinks she has been taken for granted. She will blame her children when they don't do what she expects, but they will never be able to fulfill her expectations, because resentment is important for her to hang onto. Her anger feels justified because she thinks the parenting required for her button-pushing child holds her back from her life. She will blame her child instead of seeing that her resentment is really about something else. Her resentment keeps her protected from her shame. When she blames her child, her secret is safe. She is off the hook of having to face her pain.

The resentful parent often reacts from the fear and shame of not being good enough and the responsibility to please others in her past. So when her child does not do what she expects, that old wound created when she had to do what others expected gets tapped. She may think her child needs her too much, is taking something away from her, is draining her of all her energy, or is holding her back—and certainly isn't grateful for the sacrifice. The problem escalates because the more the parent resents, the more the child demands.

When the resentment button is pushed, the parent feels used, taken for granted, trapped, and depleted of her resources. Her reaction is often an attempt to get her child to leave her alone. The child of the resentful parent feels put-upon, confused, and unfairly accused.

When children push the resentment button they are asking their

parents to stop blaming them, own up to their own problems, so that the parents can set clear rules, expectations, limits, and boundaries.

"You Take Me for Granted."
Phil and Jessica (13)

"Come *on*, Pop, we're going to be late!" were the words Phil heard his daughter yell, but her tone added, "you stupid jerk!" Phil heard that tone in a lot of Jessica's sentences, and it pushed his button every time. She was running late, as usual, and he was impatient, as usual. He had decided that instead of yelling at her to hurry, as usual, he would go out to his shop in the garage until she was ready for school. But Jessica didn't know where he had gone, went to his truck, saw that he wasn't there, and called for him—with "that tone."

"I never know what to do when I hear that," Phil explained. "I feel like I'm in a trap."

"So what did you do?" asked Eli, another group member.

"I just took it in, muttered that I had been out there all the time waiting for *her,* got in the truck, and silently fumed all the way to school. This sort of thing happens all the time. I do all these things for her. It's like she's the queen and I'm her servant. It burns me up."

"So why do you keep doing them?" Eli asked. "I do the same thing."

"I don't know how to do it differently. I suppose I should sit down with her and tell her that these are the rules if I'm going to take her to school, but I never do. It's too much trouble," admitted Phil.

I suggested, "What if you just said to her at that moment, 'I don't like to be spoken to with that tone. Can you tell me what it is you want in another way?'"

"I can't do anything like that in the moment. I just hold in my anger and resentment until it passes," Phil said.

"Except that I bet it doesn't pass—for good anyway," Eli added.

"Right," Phil continued, "and then once in a while, I'll really blow, and she cries and then doesn't talk to me, and my wife gets upset, and it's a mess!"

We identified Phil's assumption *Jessica thinks I'm a stupid jerk and treats me like a lowlife.* I asked him if any part of that seemed unrealistic. "I suppose she doesn't really think I'm a stupid jerk," he said, "but her tone sure sounds like she has such disdain for me. She takes me totally for granted."

"So, it's the tone that really gets you. Do you remember being taken for granted as a child?" I asked.

"Not exactly, but I remember a time when my mother probably thought I was taking her for granted. I was watching television, and she asked me to take out the trash. I said okay, but the next thing I knew, she stormed across the living room in front of me, trash in hand, and huffed as she slammed the door, clearly to make a point."

"What did you think?" I asked.

"That she thought I was a lazy, good-for-nothing slob, and she didn't love me anymore because I didn't do it. Her love always seemed conditional on what I *did.*"

"And from your perspective now, what do you think your mother thought?"

"I don't know. It's possible that she asked me a f[...]
there was a lot more time between her request and [...]
Like I said, she probably thought I was taking her [...]
ways wanted me to do what she asked, when she [...]

"It sounds like her button got pushed, and you ended up w[...]
sad message. What a perfect example of the gap," I pointed out. "And
it sounds like you might be doing the same thing with Jessica."

"What do you mean?" he asked.

"When you think Jessica is taking you for granted, you storm inside
with resentment. And she probably thinks something that you never
intended. Her intention is probably not to take you for granted. That's
your perception."

Phil identified the belief he took from the trash scene, and many
similar incidents with his mother, as *I won't be loved unless I do things
for people*. This translates to his parenting as *I have to do whatever my
children want*. And when he doesn't see clear evidence of appreciation
for that, his button is pushed.

"So you do things for Jessica because you're afraid she won't love
you if you don't?" I asked.

"No, I wouldn't say that. It's just that that's what people who love
each other do."

"Do you think that if you said no to her, it would mean that you
were telling her you didn't love her?"

"Well, I would know I love her, but I guess that's what I would be
afraid she would think. That makes sense now, but it seems absurd. I
know she loves me. That's the thing. In the moment of reaction, if you
said to me, 'Are you not saying no to her because she'll think you don't
love her?' I would say, 'Of course not. I'm not saying no because I don't
know how.' I don't know how until the resentment builds and builds,
and then I blow. Then I say no in a way that scares everybody."

Phil thought of another piece. "I also want everything to be pleasant. I don't want anyone to be unhappy. Whenever my mother was upset, I had to do something to make her happy. I thought her happiness
depended on me. So the resentment builds in me when I think I'm doing all these things to make people happy, and it doesn't make them

py, or they don't think anything about it at all. They just take what
. m doing for granted."

"But you don't want Jessica to have to take care of you the way you
took care of your mother, right?" asked Eli. "But it's that old stuff that
takes over when you least expect it. Now I get it!"

If Phil can adjust his standard to *I can still be a good parent by taking care of some of my children's wants and saying no to others, because
I'm important, too,* he can begin to develop a healthy boundary that he
never learned from his mother. With a boundary between him and Jessica, he will be able to say no and not take responsibility for how Jessica feels about his no. Then he will not blame her for his resentment.
He will be honoring himself and his needs, not just hers, and a balance
will result.

"You Should Know Better."
Katherine, Bailey (4), and Alice (14 months)

"Usually Bailey and Alice get along fine," said Katherine early in a
class session. "Bailey loves playing with her little sister. There's just one
incident that keeps recurring. It's not a very big deal, but it pushes my
button, and I don't really understand why."

Katherine told the group that whenever the girls are playing together on the couch, and she is there with them, the same thing occurs
and has ever since Alice was born.

"Bailey will get on top of Alice, Alice starts making fretful noises,
and I move in to tell Bailey she is too big to be playing that way and to
please get off. When I'm rested and calm, I will take Bailey away and
get her into another activity. When I'm impatient, I react and reprimand Bailey, 'You're too big, Bailey. Now get off. You should know better. Alice is too little.' Bailey invariably gives one last strong nudge into
Alice's stomach or back, which sets Alice off crying. It actually seems
to be getting worse instead of better."

"What's the assumption that pops into your head when you see Bailey?" I asked.

"That she's being a brute and she should know better. And I don't
know what to do to stop it," Katherine answered.

"What if it's not up to you to stop it?" I suggested. "What if it's up to Bailey?"

"But Bailey's only four," Katherine said. "How is she going to stop it?"

I asked Katherine to tell us about her own sibling situation. She is the fourth of seven and got it from both ends. Her older siblings pushed her around, but the only intervention from her parents came when she pushed and shoved her little brother.

"I got labeled the brute," Katherine said, and the light dawned. "Oh, my goodness, I'm passing on that horrible label even though I don't actually call her a brute. I never realized it before. What do I do now?"

"If Bailey is getting the message that she is bad in this situation, which is the likely result of being told she should know better, perhaps she needs to get the opposite message," I offered.

"You mean, tell her she is being good?" Katherine asked.

"Not good, but competent and helpful. Sometime away from the couch and Alice, ask Bailey if she thinks Alice talks," I suggested.

"Oh, she tells me all the time what she thinks Alice is trying to say."

"Excellent," I said. "Ask her what all her different sounds mean. What she sounds like when she's happy, unhappy, et cetera. Ask Bailey as if she is the expert interpreter, as if you need her help when you don't know what Alice is trying to say. Then the next time the couch incident happens, and Alice starts fretting, ask Bailey what she thinks Alice is saying. But you must ask with a tone of genuine curiosity rather than with the expectation that Bailey should know that Alice is telling her to get off. If you empower Bailey to do the interpreting of Alice's fussing, rather than tell her that she's too big, Bailey's focus will shift to listening to Alice rather than defensively reacting to your blame. She may test you a few times and say that Alice is saying she likes it. Go with it if you can until Alice's sounds are obvious and then ask Bailey again what she thinks. It will be hard to not jump in to protect Alice. If it gets too rough, pick Bailey up and take her in the other room, but refrain from the all-too-familiar lecture."

The next week, Katherine couldn't wait to share. She had talked to Bailey about Alice's language, and Bailey was only too happy to inform her mother of all the words and phrases only she could hear in Alice's "talk."

"Well the couch scene happened again, and I lay down with them all prepared to do what you said. As the scene familiarly played, I lay there watching the same pattern unfold that happened with me and my mother. I began recalling scenes. Not only did my mother call me 'the brute,' but she also called me 'dumb.'"

Katherine described her mother as "living under the intellectual shadow of her father," who had scored in the genius range on his IQ test and often reminded them of this fact. She said that her mother tried to keep up, always doing the *New York Times* crossword puzzles, but continually fell short. Her husband always knew the answers that she didn't. Katherine finally understood as an adult that it was to make herself feel superior that her mother ridiculed her for being "dumb," "not very bright," and "having a few loose marbles." It took Katherine many painful years before she learned that this wasn't true.

"As I lay there on the couch remembering all this, it became extremely clear to me how important it was to turn this around and instill competence and ownership in Bailey, so I became more focused than before. I told Bailey that it was up to her to interpret Alice and to decide for herself what was the right thing to do. Bailey started saying things like, 'I think Alice is telling me something, Mommy. I know what she is saying. She's telling me to kiss her cheek and shake her hand and blow a kiss to Mommy.' And she started doing those things."

"But," Katherine continued, "the most amazing thing was the piece that I had completely missed by being so focused on Bailey's bad behavior. I couldn't believe my eyes, but it was true. As I watched two or three of these couch scenes from a new perspective, I saw how fourteen-month-old Alice—little innocent Alice—was actually setting her sister up! I saw that Alice's fretting began soon after they got on the couch, before Bailey did a thing to her. She had learned how the scene was going to unfold in her favor! But when I handed the situation over to Bailey and stayed out of it altogether, Alice stopped making the fretting sounds, and the incident disappeared completely."

Katherine deeply resented her siblings for the labels that got fixed upon her. She projected her resentment directly onto Bailey by accusing her of bullying her little sister. Even though Bailey was only four and *shouldn't* have known better, Katherine's projection gave her justification for the blame. She became more and more conscious of her assumption that Bailey was being a brute each time the scene happened.

Katherine was appalled that the words she hated so much were the very words she was thinking about her own child. She saw clearly how her belief—*I am too big and too dumb*—played right into creating the pattern with her own daughter. Because she had done so much work on relearning who she was—that she was not a brute, not dumb, that these were her mother's issues, not hers—Katherine was able to break this last link quickly.

"Why Do I Always Have to Be the One?"
Sally and Andrew (7)

"Why is it always me? Why do I have to be the one to change, be understanding, do everything? Why can't anyone ever do something for me for a change?" Sally was angry as she sat in class listening to advice on how to empathize with a child's feelings and point of view.

"I'll tell you exactly what my agenda is all about and what message I'm sending with it! My agenda is loaded with anger, stress, and resentment every single morning. My intention is to get Andrew off to school, clothes on, teeth brushed, and on the bus. His younger sister gets herself ready just fine, but he can't do a thing without a prod up his butt. He'd let me breathe for him if I could. There's going to be nothing left of me. What he hears is, 'Hurry up and get down here. Why haven't you brushed your teeth yet? Stop drawing. Turn off the TV. Get your clothes on. How many times do I have to tell you?' I know that, but he still should do it."

Another parent in the class chuckled and said, "That sounds like my house every morning!"

"He knows how to do all this. He's just being obstinate to get my goat. He's so damn lazy. Now, why can't I expect him to do this? This is not rocket science for a seven-year-old."

When I suggested trying to connect by reflecting back to him that he is having a hard time getting it together, that he would much rather draw or watch TV, and that it's hard to get up and off to school when he doesn't want to go, Sally looked disgusted. "You know what?" she said, "That's just 'pop psychology.' That's just being manipulative to get him to do what I want him to do in the first place. It's giving over my control and authority to a kid."

"I know trusting him and listening to his side feels very strange. It's like a foreign language to those of us who never experienced it growing up," I said. "And it seems, at first, like we're letting our kids get away with anything they want."

As we got into backgrounds, Sally revealed a story that explained her resistance to Andrew. Her childhood was lonely and dismal. Her parents' attention was paid to her brother eighteen years older, who was sick and expected to die. He did die when Sally was eighteen. Her entire childhood was about taking care of the household both emotionally and physically. Sally can't tolerate doing it for her children as well. It should be her turn now. She feels drained of every shred of herself. She's afraid that to give any more, there will be nothing left. At this point, she sees her needs as much greater than Andrew's, and she resents any suggestion to give him any more.

"No one ever did this stuff for me. Why should I do it for him? How come it's always me who has to give?" she said resentfully.

Perhaps to keep Sally where she needed her, her mother gave Sally the message that her hopes were futile and her ambitions unrealistic. Sally lost herself in television and dreamed of one day having the perfect family. "*The Donna Reed Show* and *The Partridge Family* combined," she said. To everyone's amazement, Sally added, "And now I pretty much have that, and I feel guilty about it, because I don't think I deserve it."

"I wonder if you nag and yell at Andrew to unconsciously prevent yourself from being like Donna Reed. That way you can maintain your comfort zone and not have more than you deserve," I pondered out loud.

"That's an interesting thought," Sally said. "Better than having a child who is seriously ill, I suppose."

The following week Sally came into class and said, "Well do I have a story for you!" We were enthusiastic to hear.

"The other night Andrew was dropped off at home right at supper time after a class field trip. He stormed in the door and said, 'I don't want to eat with you. You never have any food I like. I don't want to talk to you. I hate you'—Andrew at his best! I don't know whether it was because I had had the afternoon without him or because his ranting seemed so ridiculous, but I stayed perfectly calm. I didn't yell at him once! I said, 'We're eating now, so you'll have to go in the other room and draw or something if you don't want to join us and be civil.' He sputtered, 'I can't draw. I'm a terrible drawer,' but he did go in the living room. All during dinner I planned what I was going to say. You would have been proud of me. I even wrote it down. After dinner I went over to the table where he was and sat down next to him.

ME: It sounds like you're having a tough day. (Sally smirked at her skill!)

ANDREW: I am. It was just awful.

ME: Well, what was so bad about it?

ANDREW: The bus ride was noisy.

ME: Who did you sit with?

ANDREW: I was all by myself.

ME: On the way home or going to the Butterfly Park?

ANDREW: At the Butterfly Park. No one wanted to sit with me.

His face started to crumple.

ME: That sounds sad. Would you like to come sit on my lap?

He nodded his head yes, crawled onto my lap, and began to cry.

ME: It's sad when no one wants to sit with you, isn't it?

ANDREW: Yes, but that's not all. None of the butterflies landed on me. They landed on all my friends, but none landed on me.

We continued to talk about who they landed on and why, and we made a plan to go back when he had on a different color shirt. Now here's the interesting part.

"At this point I looked up for the first time and saw our reflection in the sliding glass door across the room. My stomach had begun to feel queasy when he said he sat alone, but when I saw the reflection of the two of us together I got really nauseous. I thought I was having a panic attack. I got dizzy and put my head in my hands. I finally asked Andrew to get up because I felt sick and had to go to my room. The dizziness didn't go away. Then I thought I was having a heart attack. It was overwhelming. I didn't feel dizzy the next morning, but I haven't felt really right since. It was the strangest sensation I've ever had."

The room was silent and spellbound. "Wow," was all anyone uttered.

"If I had reacted the old way, which would have been pretty bad considering how awful Andrew was when he came in, I would never have found out about him being alone or about the butterflies. I guess the butterflies went to my stomach!"

After some supportive comments from the group, during which time I gathered my thoughts together, I said, "I think what you saw in that reflection was a picture of what you have always longed for. You saw yourself holding and comforting Andrew—what you wanted someone to do for you." Sally stared at me, nodding silently, holding back her emotion. "I wonder if that longing was too painful for you to acknowledge, so your body reacted physically to keep you from feeling the emotional pain. It will be good to let that pain in little by little."

Sally's assumptions were that Andrew was *out to get her* and was *draining her of her life energy,* which caused her to feel resentful and enraged when he wouldn't do what she asked. Because of her belief that she was *responsible for everything* and *worth nothing,* she transferred it into her standard, which said, *Children should do what is expected of them with no complaints.* But her belief still led her to think that she was responsible for everything he did, so her resentment grew and grew. She didn't want to be responsible anymore, and Andrew seemed to be all that was holding her back.

We all encouraged Sally to keep up her empathic work with Andrew, saying that it would be her path to her own healing. She will probably feel pain along the way, but it will be better to have it out in the open where it can dissipate rather than fester inside to instigate her resentment. If she is able to give Andrew what she so deeply needed, she will feed that part of herself where the pain resides—her button. When she can hold Andrew with understanding and unconditional acceptance, not only will his resistant behavior lessen, but she will give herself what she is giving him.

PART THREE

SOMETHING NEW

CHAPTER EIGHTEEN

DEFUSING YOUR BUTTONS

The significant problems we face cannot be solved at the
same level of thinking we were at when we created them.
—ALBERT EINSTEIN

You have now learned why your buttons get pushed. You have had the opportunity to examine all the pieces that go into creating your buttons and why your child wants to push them. And you have seen how button pushing plays out in the stories of many different families. Now you are ready to start defusing *your* buttons.

Unfortunately there are no magic steps, much as we would like them, to change old patterns and cause us to react differently. There are many effective tools we can learn that will help us communicate with our children in ways that promote connection, cooperation, and responsible behavior. But when putting them in place is an obstacle in itself, much more needs to be learned.

Whenever your button is pushed, you react out of habit. In order to change the reaction you don't like, you need new habits.

The Nine Habits to Neutrality

The following habits are tools to help you defuse your buttons and achieve neutrality. You don't need to be strict about the order. You may need to work on some more than others.

1. Raise your awareness.
2. Breathe.
3. Name your feelings.
4. Identify your assumptions.
5. Don't take it personally.
6. Detach and witness.
7. Use affirmative self-talk.
8. Define your standards and beliefs.
9. Adjust your standards.

The temptation will be great to settle back into your old habits. Although some parents have reported that their new perception has changed their child's behavior almost immediately, you should anticipate that it will take time and perseverance.

To begin, reflect on these habits *after* a button-pushing incident has occurred. Don't expect to become aware of your thoughts and feelings in the middle of your next explosion. But do take time afterward to write them down, talk to yourself about how and why your button got pushed, and plan what you will try to become aware of next time. Eventually you will be able to respond differently *during* the incident, because you will have gained new habits.

1. Raise Your Awareness

Merely being aware of what you are doing is a big step. It does not guarantee a cure for ineffective parenting, but it does allow you a window into the subconscious messages that drive you. Being aware of the messages does not mean you will be free of them. But it does mean you will gain a new perspective of them, which diminishes their power.

The next time your button is pushed, become aware of your body. What is happening? Are your palms beginning to sweat? Is your stomach tied in knots? Is your chest tight? Is your heart rate speeding? One mother said it was "just that sinking feeling." Many kinds of physical responses accompany a rush of emotions. Take mental note when it happens so that you can see it as your cue to defuse.

AWARENESS MEANS

- noticing your physical and emotional state
- becoming aware of your child's reaction
- paying attention to how powerful your agenda is
- noticing that your child has a different, equally important agenda
- being aware of your assumptions
- taking responsibility for yourself and your emotions
- looking beneath the behavior to your child's emotions

---

2. Breathe

So many parents dismiss this very simple yet effective tool, thinking that breathing could never control the hugeness of their emotions. When we surge into an emotion or exert ourselves, we tend to hold our breath. When this happens, our minds and our bodies seem disconnected. Simply breathing deeply—focusing your mind and watching your breath, counting anywhere from three to twenty breaths—can ground you so that you can think clearly.

It takes discipline to focus the mind on the breath. We take breathing for granted. It happens involuntarily. But we can voluntarily control it and use it to calm us. "Becoming aware of the breath brings mind and body into the present moment with wakefulness and clarity of perception," state Jon and Myla Kabat-Zinn in their book *Everyday Blessings: The Inner Work of Mindful Parenting*. They offer extensive help on this breathing technique to "cultivate an awareness" and bring mindfulness into your parenting.

The next time you are in your car at a stoplight, try focusing on your breath and see if you can count up to twenty breaths, counting an inhale and an exhale as one breath. You may lose count quickly. Your thoughts will rush in and take over your focus on your breath. When you become aware of that happening, start counting again. This is an excellent practice to get yourself in the habit of breathing consciously so that you can use it at strategic moments to calm down.

3. Name Your Feelings

When your emotions start to take over, acknowledge them. You have a right to them. But *own* them. They are your responsibility, not your child's. Don't deny them. Don't dump them on your child with blame and criticism. Don't think you have to justify your feelings, just let yourself have them. It is very important that you do not blame yourself. Most of us will use any excuse possible to come down hard on ourselves: *If only I could . . . If only I didn't . . .* This is self-sabotage, and it keeps you from changing your behavior. Be kind to yourself. Honor yourself. You are not perfect, nor should you be. No one would want to live with you if you were.

After the incident is over, write your feelings down:

I'm feeling so angry, I want to run screaming from the house.
I feel like I'm about to explode.
I feel so guilty all of a sudden.
I feel sucked dry of everything.
Everything feels hopeless.

SOME WAYS YOU MIGHT FEEL

frustrated	exhausted	enraged	jealous
sad	betrayed	stepped on	invisible
taken for granted	explosive	hopeless	provoked
depressed	guilty	vengeful	placated
used	ignored	powerless	depleted
drained	hostile	resentful	pathetic
threatened	confronted	punished	abandoned
lost	out of control	defensive	trapped

It's like he's out to get me is a thought. Be clear about the distinction between your thoughts and your feelings. The feeling would be *attached*. It's usually easier to identify your feelings first, then the thoughts (assumptions) that provoked them.

You may want to tell your child how you are feeling. If you do, be sure to start with the word "I," so you are not tempted to say "You make me. . . ." Even though you are angry, "I feel really angry about what you just said" is a more responsible approach than "Don't you dare talk to me like that."

Your feelings need no reason or justification. You can, however, choose not to act on them. If you consciously name your feelings, you will raise your awareness and be better able to stop yourself from reacting. Remember you will gain nothing and teach nothing by reacting from your emotions.

You may have learned to "stuff" your emotions as a child. If so, your task will be to name them, let yourself have them, and talk about them.

4. Identify Your Assumptions

After you have named your emotions, try to identify the assumptions that were connected to them. Ask yourself what it was you must have been thinking to cause you to feel the way you did. These are the automatics that instantly course through your mind at lightning speed, so fast that they almost always go undetected. Write them down. Name what most embarrasses you. *I hate my kid.* Say what is hidden deep because you are ashamed of it. *I should never have become a mother.* Be brutally honest. You have a new opportunity to look at your assumptions and reevaluate them. Perhaps they will make you laugh!

One mother when I asked about her assumption said, "He's the devil!" She got red in the face and said with nervous laughter, "But that's ridiculous. I don't mean that." Her awareness helped her see that her assumption was inaccurate.

After you identify your assumption, try adding *"because . . ."* to the end of it to take it further. Then talk it out with yourself.

He's the devil because . . . *he hit his sister.*

That might help you change it to *He gets angry with his sister,* which is less apt to provoke rage than *He's the devil.*

As we discussed in chapter 4, check the accuracy of your assumptions by asking yourself the following: Is this true? Is this reasonable or unreasonable? *He's the devil* is an idea that was unreasonable. But right

away, this mother saw the effect that a thought like that, even unspoken, had on her emotions.

**CHANGING YOUR ASSUMPTIONS TO BE
MORE ACCURATE IS DETERMINED BY**

- how hard your button has been pushed
- your level of awareness of the assumptions
- how determined you are to change the dynamic between you and your
  child
- whether or not you realize it is your responsibility to make that change
- how much you believe your assumptions
- how important it is for you to hold on to your assumptions
- how justified you feel in keeping your assumptions
- how afraid you are to let go of your assumptions

If it is a perception that seems accurate, such as *She's going to be a
slob when she gets older,* go back and look at your reaction. Did you like
it? Was it effective? If not, backtrack. Your emotions can't be helped,
but they are generated by your assumptions. Therefore your assumptions, even if they seem correct, are getting in the way. Ask yourself if
there is a different perception you have not looked at—one that could
be more productive. If you are still stuck with, "What's wrong with
that?" get a second and third opinion. Does your spouse or a good
friend share your idea? If others agree with you but your reaction is still
not effective, it might be a good idea to seek help from a parenting professional.

Change your assumption to something more realistic yet still accurate. *She has such a hard time when she doesn't get what she wants* or *Her
sister can make her really mad* will more likely stimulate feelings of
compassion than *She's a spoiled brat.* Let this new thought take you to
How can I help her when she has such a hard time?

It will probably take a while before you can identify your automatic
assumptions at the time your button is being pushed. To begin, wait

until your emotions have cooled down before putting the pieces together. Hold on to the idea that your child is *having* a problem rather than *being* a problem.

5. Don't Take It Personally

Thinking that your child is just trying to annoy you when he flips the light switch off and on repeatedly is taking his behavior personally. Assuming that your daughter's attitude is a slap in your face is taking it personally.

When you get your button pushed, it's all about you—your agenda, your burdens, your anger. When you change your assumption to one that is productive, you can more objectively see your child's problem. Then, instead of screaming at your child about her rude behavior, which will not teach her to be polite, you will be able to either address what she is angry about or decide to leave her alone for a while until you are both calmer.

Remember, it's not about you. Even if your child's anger is directed at you, even if your child is calling you a name or telling you what a lousy parent you are, it's not about you. It's about how your child is feeling. Address the feelings. If you think it's about you, you will not be helpful.

When you know you are taking it personally, ask the following questions:

> *Why am I focusing on myself?*
> *Can I put my attention on my child's problem?*
> *What am I trying to protect by being defensive?*
> *Why am I ignoring my child?*

6. Detach and Witness

When you are able to name your feelings and assumptions, your awareness will begin to rise. You may find yourself watching or witnessing yourself. This disengagement is useful. If you are used to being sucked into the problem, detachment may make you feel cut off. But it is the detachment that will help you gain better perspective.

Detaching does not mean being cold and uncaring. It means having a mental and emotional objectivity so you can see the situation clearly and neutrally. Detachment enables connection. It means taking yourself—your worries, fears, and judgments—out of the picture so you can see the problem itself. From this vantage point, creative solutions you would never imagine possible pop into your mind, and the problem can become a stimulating learning experience for both you and your child rather than a draining, exhausting power struggle.

If it is hard to mentally detach, physically stepping out of the situation helps. Go into another room or outside. Walking away does not mean your child has won. It means that you have gained enough control to own your emotions and act responsibly. It is better to walk away than to react when your emotions are volatile enough to blame and shame your child.

One father told the group how he uses a mantra: "Detach, detach, detach." He can then walk away briefly until he has calmed down. A mother explained, "The first thing that happens is I get this tightness in my chest. If I leave right then, it's fine. I can go in the other room, breathe, and get my thoughts together; then I can come back in a more neutral state. But if I wait until I'm really upset and tell my son that I'm leaving, he follows me, yelling, 'No! Don't leave!' and I can't get away from him."

If you try to walk away after your control starts to slip, especially if your child is feeling blamed, he will likely react in a desperate attempt to be reassured that you are in control. Try quietly telling your child that you have to go to the bathroom and walk away. If that still doesn't work, stay with him and do something completely different until you can talk about the incident calmly.

Our children really do want us to remain in charge. They need our authority. Sometimes it *appears* as if they want the authority for themselves, but that is only because they are afraid and confused. **When you can detach, you can take your authority back with neutrality and respect.**

When you begin to see yourself detaching, you can ask yourself the important questions:

What is this behavior telling me?
What do I need to learn?
How can I help my child?

7. Use Affirmative Self-Talk

After you have identified your emotions and your assumptions, you may still feel upset. Here is where self-talk comes in. It's like analyzing yourself and the situation in your head. Talk it out with yourself—and breathe at the same time! Ask yourself the key questions stated above. Acknowledge your feelings and give yourself permission to have them. Remind yourself you are catastrophizing and not looking at reality in the present moment. Talk out how your reactions are affecting your child. Is he afraid? Angry? Parent-deaf? And why?

Affirmative self-talk is meant to counter your automatics—your negative self-talk. You need to put conscious focus on your thoughts and correct yourself when you are aware that you are spinning off in a negative direction. With breathing, when your mind has wandered, you bring focus back to your breath. With self-talk, you bring focus back to your thoughts.

SELF-TALK

You might use some of the following questions to get you started:

Why am I making that assumption?

Where did it come from? How long have I thought it?

How am I taking this issue personally?

Am I taking responsibility for something that is my child's responsibility?

What or who does my child remind me of?

What would have happened to me if I had behaved this way?

What incident in my childhood does it remind me of?

What are my expectations and are they realistic?

You will not necessarily emerge from self-talk with the answer to all your problems. But you will have raised your consciousness considerably. Your new awareness cannot help but affect your future reactions.

Another way of handling self-talk is to write it down when you are in a good state of mind. When you are feeling worried or distraught, you can pull it out and read it to remind yourself of a different perception. Your written self-talk should be a profile of all aspects of your child, using facts and accurate, realistic perceptions of him. Include descriptions of what your child does well with anecdotes of heartwarming situations you have experienced or witnessed with your child that will remind you that he in fact can function like a healthy human being.

8. Define Your Standards and Beliefs

Ask yourself what you expected in the button-pushing situation— *I expected him to get his homework in on time,* for example. Turn that expectation into a standard that you can use to identify many of your expectations: *Homework is a priority that must always come before enter-*

tainment to ensure its completion. It is helpful to use *always, never,* or *at all times* to understand how strongly your standards come across to your children. And don't try to be rational. State what you most want from your child in this situation. Your expectation of homework getting done on time may be perfectly appropriate, but your standard may show that you are projecting your own experience onto a child who needs to relax first. In other words, you may find that you are expecting your child to handle it the way you would and not allowing him to find his own way of meeting your expectations. Remember that your child has an agenda that is just as important to him as yours is to you, regardless of whether you can see any merit in it at the time.

Don't forget the standards you hold for yourself, as well. Ask yourself where they come from. There were expectations of you, spoken or unspoken, that you interpreted and acted on. Are you passing them on, compensating for them, or reacting to them?

When you define your standards, you may see right away that they need adjusting. Or you may want to hold on to them and make your child live up to them. If this is the case, dig deeper to look at the beliefs you hold about yourself. You will get there by looking first at what your child is reminding you of in yourself or what your parents would have done in a similar situation. You may see that you would never have dared behave this way. Why? What would have happened, or what would they have said? Here is where assumptions can *help.* Assume what you must have felt and thought about yourself.

9. Adjust Your Standards

Many parents fear that changing standards means being a slouch of a parent, letting their kids off the hook, allowing them to do whatever they want, or giving them all the control. The fear of swinging to the opposite extreme keeps us clinging to the way we know best. Adjusting your standards means finding a place in the middle, a balance where both you and your child are respected and understood. Flexibility makes success more likely. Rules can still be followed and expectations can still be high, but they are more appropriate to the specific needs of each individual.

THE GOALS OF *ADJUSTING*, NOT *LOWERING*, YOUR STANDARDS ARE

- to help you drop the rigidity and tone that inevitably accompany your messages to your child, so that she can hear what you intend.
- to take the pressure off both you and your child to live up to being someone you are not.
- to prevent you from projecting the standards from your childhood onto a different child living in a different family in the twenty-first century.
- to give yourself some breathing room so you can enjoy your parenting, and so your child can enjoy you.
- to help you see your child as an individual with individual needs requiring individual expectations.
- to prevent you from living out your own unfulfilled hopes and dreams through your children.
- to allow your children to have their own hopes and dreams.

Any child will resist unrealistic standards. Even a two-year-old will struggle to maintain her individuality and integrity. *I expect my children to listen to me most of the time* will provide more flexibility than *Children must listen to what they are told at all times.*

Unrealistic standards for ourselves can exhaust us mentally and physically. They come from the pressures and expectations we put on ourselves to be more than we are. *I must meet my child's needs all the time* is impossible to uphold. *I will do my best to meet my children's needs, knowing that I cannot possibly meet them all* is realistic, honest, and allows the flexibility to be human.

All this is *not* to say settle for what you have and aspire to nothing more. It *is* to say be realistic about what you can and cannot do, who you can and cannot be.

The Button Meter—What to Do

The more your button connects deeply to old wounds and beliefs, the more likely your emotions will soar into Zone 4 on your Button Meter. As you heighten your awareness, the needle will drop.

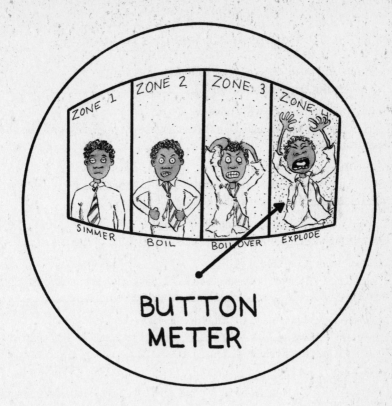

When your button is pushed, check out your zone and tell yourself the following:

Zone 1—Congratulations! You have learned to choose your battles, and this is definitely not one of them. You can see that your child has an agenda, too, and you are not taking the behavior personally. Let it go. Life is short!

Zone 2—Focus on the problem; do not blame your child. Acknowledge that your emotions are yours, take responsibility for them, and detach.

Zone 3—Walk away. Breathe deeply. Self-talk. When you have defused back to Zone 2, return to the situation.

Zone 4—Stop! Breathe very deeply. Wait. After you have calmed down, examine how you got there. Later, even days later, go over the situation with your child and talk about how it could have been handled differently by both of you.

● EXERCISE 10: **Putting It All Together (example)**

- Identify the behavior that pushes your button.
  She makes this horrible face at people   .

- Identify the assumptions you have about that behavior.
  She's being nasty, rude, ugly. She's inconsiderate of others. She's a brat. She won't stop when she's told to   .

- Describe the fears that come up about your child and about yourself.
  She'll never have any friends. No one will like her. I won't like her. I don't have any control over her. How have I raised her to be like this?

- Who/what does this behavior remind you of? Why?
  Me and my mother. She always told me to "wipe that smirk off my face."

- Name your fears based on that.
  That I'll keep telling her how awful she looks, and she'll resent me the way I resented my mother. We'll see each other as these ogres!

- Describe your parenting standard that is threatened by the behavior.
  It's my job to make sure that she grows up to be a nice person so she can do well in life and people will like her   .

- Describe what would have happened if you had behaved this way as a child.
  My mother would have yelled at me and called me a brat. My father would threaten never to take me in public again   .

- Identify the belief you had about yourself when that happened.
  That I could never be what my mother or father wanted me to be. I was never good enough. I always had to be sweet and polite to everyone   .

- How does this belief affect your parenting?
  If I had to be so perfect, I must expect my daughter to be perfect too. When she behaves rudely, I freak   .

- Describe what you can learn by uncovering this belief.
  Maybe I'm too hard on her because my standards are so unrealistic. If I'm supposed to be so perfect, I can't have an imperfect child. I don't want her to be rude, but maybe I'm sending the same message that she's not good enough for me, and this is how she's paying me back   .

- Write your new adjusted standard.
  I expect my child to be childish and not perfect. She will learn by example   .

● EXERCISE 10: **Putting It All Together**

- Identify the behavior that pushes your button.

  _____

  _____

  _____

- Identify the assumptions you have about that behavior.

  _____

  _____

  _____

- Describe the fears that come up about your child and about yourself.

  _____

  _____

  _____

- Who/what does this behavior remind you of? Why?

  _____

  _____

  _____

- Name your fears based on that.

  _____

  _____

  _____

- Describe your parenting standard that is threatened by the behavior.

  _____

  _____

  _____

● EXERCISE 10: **Putting It All Together (continued)**

- Describe what would have happened if you had behaved this way as a child.

  _____

  _____

  _____

- Identify the belief you had about yourself when that happened.

  _____

  _____

  _____

- How does this belief affect your parenting?

  _____

  _____

  _____

- Describe what you can learn by uncovering this belief.

  _____

  _____

  _____

- Write your new adjusted standard.

  _____

  _____

  _____

  _____

CHAPTER NINETEEN

JUST WHEN IT FEELS SO HOPELESS . . .

Estragon: "I can't go on like this."
Vladimir: "That's what you think."
—SAMUEL BECKETT, *Waiting for Godot*

After becoming aware of the origins of your buttons, how they play into your parenting, and what you need to do to defuse them, you may feel more frustrated than ever. What you want to do is not necessarily what you can do. You may feel encouraged and stimulated after understanding the process but then hopeless and defeated when you find that you are still falling back into old habits. Take heart and know that this is part of the process.

The Four Stages of Competency

William Howell's Four Stages of Competency are used in the field of education to illustrate the progress of raising one's consciousness in any area of learning. The stages begin with the ignorance before something is known to the automatic ease of new, learned behavior patterns. Learning to use a computer is a good example:

Stage One—Unconscious Incompetency. Life went on just fine before it entered my home.

Stage Two—Conscious Incompetency. I know it will make my life easier, but it makes no sense to me. The programs are indecipherable; the language is gibberish. I feel really incompetent, and I keep making mistakes.

233

> Stage Three—Conscious Competency. I've learned how to do what I need, but I am cautious and nervous when I am venturing around a new program.
>
> Stage Four—Unconscious Competency. I feel at ease with the programs and confident I could learn any new ones. I feel connected and at home with my computer and am reaping the benefits.

Applied to parenting, the Four Stages of Competency are as follows:

> Stage One—Unconscious Incompetency. I react automatically with no consideration for long-term consequences. I feel exhausted and resentful.
>
> Stage Two—Conscious Incompetency. I am aware of the effects of what I say and do. I have learned what I want to do differently, but when face-to-face with my combative child, I can't do it. I feel guilty, angry, and incompetent.
>
> Stage Three—Conscious Competency. With continued practice and support, I am focused on using new skills. I am effective most of the time. I feel hopeful.
>
> Stage Four—Unconscious Competency. I almost always respond automatically with effective communication. I feel successful, fulfilled, and have fun with my family.

We tend to drift back and forth between stages depending on what area of parenting we are dealing with at the moment. Reading bedtime stories to a preschooler may fall into stage four—easy, relaxed, connected communication—while setting limits with a teenager may fall into stage one, where automatic demands and reactions abound. The age of the child may determine what stage you are in. Many parents are more effective with infants and get more impatient with older children and vice versa.

Most parents who are looking for answers to parent differently find themselves hovering around stage two—conscious incompetency. This is a most discouraging stage—knowing what to do, but not yet able to do it. Some give up, claiming parent education is bunk, rationalizing their parenting as "good enough," and falling back on the old standbys. Others hang in through the pain and upheaval to reap the rewards. And hugely rewarding it is!

To be in stage one is to be unaware—to think your child doesn't know any better, to blame your child for how you feel and what you do, to demand that your child be who you want—to react automatically. Each time you question yourself and ask whether or not you are creating a gap, you are raising your consciousness to stage two. You are reaching stage three when you learn to take responsibility for yourself and your actions, when you become aware and stop your reactions, even some of the time.

The more you practice, the less often you slide back to stage one or two. The more conscious you become, you will find new and effective automatics slipping into your parenting. What was once hard and even painful to put in place becomes second nature. When you would never dream of saying the things to your child that used to slip out so automatically, you know you have arrived at stage four.

The Frustrations of Stage Two— Conscious Incompetency

Unless you have reached this point and learned all you need to change your patterns and defuse your buttons, you will probably find yourself in and out of stage two. You may feel angry at yourself and guilty that you are still overreacting. Take heart. This is normal. Do not give up.

Without discouragement and frustration over our failings, we would happily remain in stage one. Unconscious parents are not discouraged by their parenting. They find fault with their children, not themselves. Ignorance is bliss, as the saying goes. Without disruption, turmoil, upset, and conflict, change will not occur. There is no need for it. So the good news is that feeling incompetent and frustrated means progress is under way!

Consciousness comes in degrees. Think in terms of higher and lower consciousness as opposed to *being* conscious or *not being* conscious. Imagine a dimmer switch on your consciousness instead of an on-off switch. In *The Art of Living Consciously*, Nathaniel Branden says, ". . . [C]onsciousness can operate at higher and lower levels of intensity, and in any given situation, the question is not whether I am conscious . . . but whether I bring to the occasion the level of consciousness I require to be effective."

If you are questioning your reactions, intending to parent differently, looking at your ideas and emotions, and beginning to take responsibility for your actions, you are raising your consciousness, whether or not you are able to put it into practice yet. Let your feelings of incompetency give you a push toward change rather than an excuse to stay stuck in the ruts of your old patterns.

The Benefits of Failure

Thomas Moore, author of *Care of the Soul*, claims that we need to appreciate our failings and view them in a new and creative light. Instead of seeing failure as reason for defeat, Moore says that accepting our failings and limitations allows us to descend into the "mystery in failure [which] allows us to see through our inabilities and not overly identify with them."

Remember, our children could never have learned to walk without falling down again and again. If we weren't accepting of our failures, we would have little tolerance of others and no vision of a better way. We don't like our dark places. We tend to keep them closed off in our attic rooms and rarely share them with others.

One of the greatest benefits of parent education groups is that parents, often for the first time, share their dark side. To be able to describe a nightmarish scene with a child that a parent would never want anyone to know about and hear three other parents laugh and say, "I know just what you mean—that happens in my house all the time," is an uplifting experience. The laughter alone is healing. If we cannot allow ourselves mistakes and failures, how can we teach our children that making them is part of learning?

When Mistakes Equal Failure

Harold and Marjorie were concerned about their seven-year-old son, Coleman, who was pulling his hair out in clumps. He had gotten into the habit of rubbing it across his upper lip for self-comfort. Whenever he made a mistake, or was reprimanded, he would go for the hair. Sometimes he added, "I'm so stupid. What's wrong with me?" Harold confessed right away that he feared Coleman was learning it from him.

Harold's motto is "mistakes equal failure," and failure is unacceptable. It is his crusade to make sure his children learn to do everything the right way—his way. When Coleman spilled water in Harold's car by lifting the cup by its cap, Harold asked him how it happened. Coleman said, "I'm dumb." Trying hard not to put his son down, Harold said, "You're not dumb; you're just careless." Harold felt compelled to point out what Coleman had done wrong to cause the spill, how to pick up the cup properly, and that the car was going to smell of mildew. Harold could not let the mistake go by without "corrective" criticism. He had no faith that Coleman would learn on his own without careful instruction on proper cup lifting. Instead of learning how to correct a mistake, Coleman learned that he was inept.

I asked Harold what would have happened to him if he had spilled water when he was a child. "Oh," he exclaimed, "I spilled my milk once at the dinner table, and my mother upended the whole table. Everything went flying." I asked him what he had learned. He said, "Never to spill my milk again!"

Harold does not see that what he learned from his mother was intolerance of mistakes. He has not connected his past with his present standards. His pain remains protected, and so it is hard for Harold to see a different way to handle mistakes. The pain is triggered, and criticism erupts when anyone, including himself, makes a mistake.

"But there are ways of doing things correctly. Why shouldn't I teach him? I can't just let it go and let him think it doesn't matter," he argued. When I suggested saying nothing about the water spill, yet asking Coleman to blot up the water with paper towels and take responsibility for the spill without a lecture, Harold agreed that that would have been a good idea.

Harold was also able to see that Coleman's hair pulling was in reaction to the pressures he felt to get everything right. Coleman has a far more sensitive temperament than Harold, takes the criticism to heart, defines himself as stupid, and punishes himself by pulling out his hair. Strangely, he uses the hair for comfort, as well, to ease the pain of the self-punishment.

As Harold began to understand Coleman's hair-pulling habit, he stopped reprimanding him for doing it, and Coleman's hair has grown back. Harold still believes Coleman has to learn the right way to do things, but he is gaining better awareness of the pressure he puts on himself and others. Right now, he is struggling between stage one and stage two of conscious parenting.

The Uses of Guilt

There is bad guilt and good guilt. Bad guilt causes immobilization, stuckness, and together with self-judgment provides yet more excuses to give up and stay stuck. *Oh, I'll never get it right anyway. Who am I kidding?* is the voice of bad guilt. Good guilt can be a motivator, a shaker. *I feel so bad about the way I reacted. Why did I do that?* is the voice of good guilt. It can move you to change.

A workaholic parent who misses his children's sports events and music recitals, who rarely sees them during the week, and who doesn't have much of a relationship with them may react to his guilt by buying his children's love with lavish presents. This is bad guilt. Or he can pay attention to the guilt and use it to examine his priorities. This is good guilt. Listen to it. Guilt is essential for keeping our behavior in line with our values. Don't try to push it away, deny it, or get down on yourself for having it—you will only feel more guilty! Does it have something constructive to tell you?

Underneath feelings of bad guilt, resentment is often lurking—resentment toward people or events we perceive as causing us the guilt. If I feel like a failure as a parent, I will most likely feel resentful toward the child who is "making me" feel that way.

We criticize ourselves so often for feeling guilty that we compound the guilt by feeling guilty about feeling guilty! We never allow it just to

be. Our personal judge wreaks havoc—we are harder on ourselves than anyone else could ever be. Remember Angeles Arriens' advice to greet our demons and judges when they come knocking at our door, welcome them in, but lead them directly to the guest room so they do not destroy our house.

Often we blame ourselves for our child's misbehavior. The guilt can be immobilizing. *It's all my fault* leads a parent to claim responsibility for everything her child has done wrong. She readily ignores all other factors and variables, including the other parent, friends, school, temperament, and the child's emotional turmoil. By taking responsibility, she thereby releases her child from the responsibility that may be his. Her self-blame is internal, self-absorbed, and passive: *How have I managed to become such a failure? I meant to be such a good parent. I can't believe I've screwed up so badly.* This is not a parent who can easily decide to change old habits. The guilt most likely runs deep.

Change requires the belief *I'm worth it.*

Revisiting a Situation

You can always go back over a situation you feel guilty about, even days or weeks later. I often ask parents to remember an incident from their childhood that felt especially hurtful. Then, I have them imagine their mother or father coming to them today and saying, "Remember that time when I . . . I want you to know that I have never forgotten it. It was very hard for me to apologize at the time. But I was wrong. I made a mistake, and I'm sorry." Tears well up in their eyes even if the incident happened thirty years ago. It's never too late!

You are teaching your child a valuable lesson when you say, "I'm sorry I said what I did. It must have made you feel very bad. I'd like to talk about it again and come up with a different solution" or, "I've been thinking about what you said, and I've decided I was wrong." We want to teach our children to reevaluate what they say and do, and to apologize when they do something they are sorry for because it feels right inside, not because we tell them to. Shouldn't we do the same?

If we don't model the behavior we want our children to develop, we are in effect saying, "Do what I say, not what I do. I don't want to let on that I was wrong, but I want you to admit you were." If you do not set yourself up as always right, you have less far to fall when your child inevitably takes you down off that pedestal. You may even remain intact.

You do not need to apologize for your feelings. What you *do* with your feelings is another thing. If you are angry, no need to apologize for the anger. But if you react inappropriately in that anger, you can apologize for your reaction yet still acknowledge your anger.

Apologizing works wonders *unless* it happens too often. When you find yourself apologizing all day long, your bad guilt has gotten the better of you. You are using it rather than taking responsibility for your behavior. Your child is going to tune you out eventually. This is your cue to use that guilt as the kick it is meant to be.

Parents worry over lost authority when they admit a mistake and do not stick to their guns. Many parents think they must stand on principle and follow through even if they realize it was a mistake said in anger. When you do what feels right in your gut, regardless of what society or your mother-in-law thinks you should do, your strength and true authority will be seen in your integrity. Be honest with your children as well as yourself, and it will come across to your child as genuine authority. Holding your ground even when you wish you hadn't said what you did is false and dishonest authority. And your child will know it.

MOTHER-BLAME

So many parents in my groups talk about the tremendous pressure they feel from their own parents, in-laws, friends, the media, or the elusive "they" to parent in the ways they are struggling to leave behind. Parents feel scrutinized by the eyes of the world telling them they are either disciplining too much or not enough. If children misbehave in public, parents feel humiliated and blamed. It is no wonder we feel so responsible for our children and try desperately to control their behavior. So when parents work hard to change old patterns, there are countless outside forces pressuring them in the opposite direction. They feel caught between a rock and a hard place.

It's all my fault is a big button that especially plagues mothers, as we are still reeling from generations of "mother-blame." Mothers feel judging eyes at the supermarket, at student-teacher conferences, and in line at the bank. It's hard to shut out the stares, the comments, and the advice and to trust yourself to know what is best. It's difficult to stand firm in the midst of this stress and defend a new philosophy of parenting, especially when your child has yet to respond perfectly.

The impatience and self-blame mothers feel in this predicament easily translates to anger and rage, readily transferred to the children. It is imperative that we give ourselves a break, breathe deeply, and be mindful of the fact that we cannot be all things to all people. Mothers especially try to live up to standards of perfection—and it's so easy to fall short.

The Doubts

Hand in hand with guilt come the doubts—about everything. Am I saying and doing the right thing? Will I know what my child needs? Do I know what I need? Can I trust myself? Can I trust my child? How much do I push, and how much do I step back? Should I have done that or not?

The conscious parent—stages two, three, and four—is often filled with doubt. It comes with the territory. We will always be walking that line trying to find the balance when we are aware and parent consciously. Taking the time to question yourself, negotiate, and debate

the issues before you decide means that you are willing to be vulnerable, to make mistakes and be human. The unconscious parent—stage one—knows for sure, does not question, never doubts.

Then There's the Worry!

Worry, however, will take you to a stuck place. When we worry too much, we hang onto control. We overprotect and hold our children back from living their lives in order to protect ourselves from worry. Let the doubts come, step back, disengage from the worry, and ask what the doubts are telling you. They will be there. They are the mark of consciousness.

So many parents worry that they have already done harm. Give yourself a break. No one is perfect. You have parented in the best way you could given the knowledge and awareness you have had up until now. *Now* you know more. *Now* you have more information about yourself. *Now* is the time to take steps toward change. Even if you knew you wanted to parent differently, you were not ready until *now*.

● EXERCISE 11: **Awareness Exercise (example)**

If I become more aware of the feelings I have when my buttons are pushed, I will _be able to stop myself from immediately reacting_ .

If I know that I deserve to have the feelings I have, I will _feel less defensive when I get angry at my child and know that I have a right to feel that anger_ .

If I sit with the guilt I feel, I will _not try to make myself feel better by eating sweets. But I might cry and get to some deeper feelings—if I can let it be okay_ .

If I take responsibility for all my feelings, I will be able to _say what they are, at least to myself, and maybe it will help me stop blaming my child_ .

If I allow myself to make mistakes, I am afraid that _I'll really blow it and do irrevocable damage, and my husband will criticize me to no end_ .

If I change my assumptions, I am afraid that _I might be rationalizing and not looking at the picture realistically_ .

If I didn't feel guilty, I am afraid that _I would let myself do awful things and people would think I didn't care_ .

How I want my child to see me is _as someone who is human and able to make mistakes but then take responsibility for them. And as a caring and safe haven_ .

_____ .

● EXERCISE 11: Awareness Exercise

Please complete either or both of the exercises that follow.
A.

If I become more aware of the feelings I have when my buttons are pushed, I will ____

_____ .

If I know that I deserve to have the feelings I have, I will _____

_____ .

If I sit with the guilt I feel, I will _____

_____ .

If I take responsibility for all my feelings, I will be able to_____

_____ .

If I allow myself to make mistakes, I am afraid that _____

_____ .

If I change my assumptions, I am afraid that _____

_____ .

If I didn't feel guilty, I am afraid that _____

_____ .

How I want my child to see me is _____

_____

_____ .

_____

● EXERCISE 11: **Awareness Exercise (continued)**

B.

Describe what you do with your feelings when your buttons get pushed. Are you aware of what you are feeling before you react? Do you tend to stuff feelings, explode them, and/or blame them on your child for causing them?

How would the situation be different if you took responsibility for your feelings, both by naming them for yourself and owning them? How would it affect your reaction to your child?

Describe how you handle the mistakes you make. Do you try to hide them? Do you let your child know you make them?

Describe what kind of guilt you feel (if you do). Good guilt or bad guilt? What do you fear if you let the bad guilt go? Do you allow the good guilt to stimulate change?

CHAPTER TWENTY

TAKING RESPONSIBILITY FOR YOUR ANGER

Sometimes a scream is better than a thesis.
—RALPH WALDO EMERSON

A nger is the most common emotion resulting from a pushed button. As we've seen on the Button Meter, it bubbles up in many degrees, from frustration to rage. It is an emotion that humans don't like: don't like to have, don't like to see, don't like to deal with, and certainly don't like their children to have. Many of us grew up in a household where anger was unacceptable, let alone encouraged.

Because our anger in childhood was so often met with disapproval or denial, we learned that it was a bad emotion. We learned to either make up excuses for it, blame it on others, or suppress it. So most of us have no tools with which to deal with anger productively—either in ourselves or in our children. Our beliefs tell us it is wrong. So when we feel it, we often react as we did when we were children, either exploding it or imploding it.

If I had to back down when my parents told me what to do and never heard my side of the story, I'm probably going to react harshly when my child refuses to back down and doesn't do what I tell her. When we get into a power struggle, the fight is between my child and myself as a child. Neither of us knows how to take responsibility.

How Our Anger Plays Out

When we get angry at our children, we want them to pay. Punishment (anything that physically or emotionally puts down, hurts, or humiliates a child) is retaliatory manipulation for "making" us feel angry. We isolate them, we hit them, we yell at them, we deny them their privileges—all as means of appeasing our anger and chastising theirs. **Punishment does nothing to teach responsibility or accountability for one's behavior.** Instead it can shame or instill fear in the child, which sometimes stops the behavior, giving the parent the desired result. Mostly, it teaches children the six Rs of punishment: resentment, rebellion, retaliation, reduced self-esteem, repression, and revenge.

"My five-year-old has a request," a mother announced with a smile in our group one day. "He wants me to find out from my parenting group what else I could do besides sending him to his room when he does something wrong. He says that going to his room doesn't work at all, because it only makes him madder, and he doesn't learn anything!" We were amazed at the perception of this little boy. The mother said his exact words were, "You want me to think about what happened, but all I do is think about how mad I am!"

But when we get our buttons pushed, creative options are generally out of our reach. We get angry. And we punish. Then we get more angry when the punishment doesn't work, and the behavior happens again. Then we punish more. The cycle continues. We fear that if there is no blame, no punishment, we are letting our kids "get away with it."

Owning Your Anger

We do not have to be free of anger to be neutral, to focus on the problem and to stop blaming. **We have a right to our anger as much as our children have a right to theirs.** We need to honor our feelings, but we also need to take responsibility for them—to own them. We can do this by paying attention to how we speak to our children.

1. "You are such a slob. Just look at this mess. How many times do I have to tell you? I'm not cleaning up your garbage. You're not leaving this house until that kitchen is clean."
2. "I feel so angry when I see food left out in the kitchen. I should not have to clean up this mess. I want you to clean it up now, please. You can go to your friend's as soon as you are finished."

Which expression of anger is dumped on the child? Which is held responsibly? Which creates a gap? Which message is clear? Which child is left feeling ashamed? Which child is left feeling responsible? Which child can hear the request, and which becomes parent-deaf?

Even when spoken in anger, the message to the child can be heard when the anger is owned. In the first scenario, the father is in effect blaming his daughter for his anger and his reaction—"How many times do I *have to* tell you?" In the second, the response is honest and responsible, even though anger is expressed. The child knows her father is angry. She may feel guilty about leaving the kitchen a mess (good guilt), but she will probably not feel guilty about causing her father's anger (bad guilt). So it is easier for her to take responsibility and do as she is asked.

Julie came into class saying, "There is construction going on at my house. After weeks of dealing with the mess every day, I had a meltdown. I had already had a bad day, and I walked in the house to the familiar Sheetrock dust covering everything. In the middle of the mess was my eight-year-old son Cameron's Legos all over the place. It was the last straw. I lost it. I fled upstairs, screaming to Cameron, 'I have to go to my room, and I need you to leave me alone. When I come back I want those Legos picked up. I can't bear this house any longer!' A few minutes later, I heard a soft knock on my door. I called, 'Come in.' Cam slowly opened the door and peeked his head around. He said very quietly, 'I just wanted you to know that I understand how you feel, and I'll be downstairs if you want to talk about it.' Isn't that amazing!"

Julie had spent many years validating Cameron's feelings when he had his "nutties," as they fondly referred to his perpetual tantrums. It had paid off. Now she was able to have her own "nutties"—but without blaming Cameron. He saw how angry she felt, but he did not feel responsible for making it better. When she asked him to clean up his Legos, he did it without an argument. Her anger was powerful. He heard it, but he was free to empathize and cooperate rather than feel responsible for it or attacked by it.

You make me so mad is a common phrase that signifies the enormity of blame we place on others for our anger. We have heard it; we pass it on. It is time to stop the cycle and acknowledge instead, "I get so angry when . . ." The meaning, and hence the responsibility, shifts dramatically.

We generate our own anger. It's okay to be angry. But we must own it.

Don't Ask Your Children to Take Responsibility for You

Whenever Cheryl's six-year-old daughter, Nicole, balked at the clothes her mother had worked hard to buy, Cheryl felt like strangling her. Nicole complained that they were too puffy or too stupid. Cheryl's retort would go something like, "Do you have any idea how many hours it took me to make enough money to buy these clothes for you? You don't know how lucky you are. How can you say you hate them?" Nicole would fight back, and they inevitably ended up in a power struggle. Cheryl's reactions ranged from, "You will wear what I tell you to wear" to, "Fine, wear whatever you want and see if I care." Nicole was left in a puddle of blame either way.

Cheryl came from a very poor family. The few clothes the children had were hand-me-downs. Cheryl did not own any new clothing until she was a teenager and bought it herself. With ingenuity, Cheryl pulled herself out of the mire of her past. But she still tries desperately to hide it. Her daughter's many beautiful clothes are one of the signatures of her achievement. She could not understand why her daughter was not thankful for her abundance.

"Can you see that your anger is demanding that Nicole take responsibility for your shame?" I asked. Cheryl got it immediately.

In *Seat of the Soul,* author Gary Zukav states so well, "If you do not hold yourself accountable for what you experience, you will hold someone else accountable, and if you are not satisfied with what you experience, you will seek to change it by manipulating that person." Children should not bear the burden of our ups and downs. They should not have to ride the waves and wonder when things will calm down, or worse, think that they have to be good in order for us to be calm. They should not have to worry about what kind of a mood we are in and have no idea what to expect when we walk in the door.

You've given me a headache. Don't make me come after you. What will people think? Be good for Grandma. Now see what you made me do! You're going to put me in an early grave. These are all remarks that put the responsibility for the adult's well-being on the child. If your parents expected you to take responsibility for their feelings, it is logical that you would expect the same of your child.

Taking Responsibility Builds Good Boundaries

When we take responsibility for our own feelings, we will be better able to understand that our children are responsible for theirs as well. Giving them responsibility for their feelings and behavior enables us to remain detached and neutral. From this place we can support them and encourage them instead of fight with them or try to fix their feelings and problems. A healthy boundary allows them to figure out what to do and teaches them to take responsibility for themselves.

Jane had been coming to parenting classes since her now four-year-old Michael was a newborn. She had been through four tumultuous years with a very sensitive yet strong-willed child who expresses his persistent anger by screaming—long and loud and often. Jane has struggled with her own anger toward him, often feeling pummeled and punished by his behavior. She had resented his neediness and demands on her and had tried long and hard to make his anger go away. After her work on defusing her buttons, she understood that she was not the cause of, and therefore not responsible for, his anger. "What a burden it lifted off my shoulders," she said. She shared in class a story that would have driven the best of us into a rage.

One morning Michael was at the kitchen table for breakfast. Knowing how particular Michael is about how his toast is cut, she asked him if he would like to cut it himself. He said she could do it. She cut the toast, put it on a plate, and set it down for him. Suddenly he screamed that it was too far away from him. "I have to bend way over to get it!" In the past, his shrill whine would have provoked her to scream back at him and either resentfully do what he demanded or ignore him and incite a tantrum. Now she understood his temperament and knew that this was his problem, not hers.

Neutrally she said, "Oh, it's too far away from you?" (She acknowledged him.) "Then you can pull it closer to you." (She gave him ownership of his problem.)

"No, I can't reach it. You have to do it," Michael said, getting more hysterical.

Knowing how easily Michael escalates to the point of no return, she said, "Okay, but in a minute after I put this away." She knew he needed her help to get back in control, but she also let him know that she had needs as well. This time he was willing to wait. She moved the plate closer, but it was still not right.

"It's not turned the right way!" he screamed. This could have been anyone's breaking point. She wanted to yell, "Fine, I'll show you where I can turn it," and throw the toast in the garbage. Instead Jane detached. "You had a picture in your head of how you wanted the toast to be," she said compassionately, focusing on the problem, not Michael's stubbornness. "I didn't know what that picture was. It upset you when I put it down a different way. You can turn it just the way you want it."

She explained to him what had happened, so that he understood why he was upset (four-year-olds often don't know), validated his feelings so he knew he was okay, and taught him responsibility for his problem. Masterfully, Jane identified what was happening for him. Instead of perceiving his behavior as bratty and manipulative, she understood his perception and validated it without losing herself in a battle.

Michael immediately calmed down, the tension and stress visibly left his taut body, and he responded with, "Oh." He turned his plate the way he wanted it.

Jane empowered Michael to solve his own problem, because she gave him the right to his anger without denying it or disapproving of it. He was back to himself, and Jane had helped him get there by giving him what he needed, instead of what he asked for. Rather than feeling robbed of patience, energy, and control, she felt high, energized, and without a doubt that she had done the right thing for Michael and herself.

A boundary was drawn between Jane and Michael that allowed them to each be themselves. Jane said, "Now I know what it is. It's like a line that I can draw. He's on one side with his troubles, his problems, and I'm on my side with mine. He's in his world, his bubble, having his own little crisis. It has nothing to do with me. Now I can make a connection with him on his terms."

When Anger Is a Signal for Change

Confronting suppressed anger, which can manifest as depression, illness, or anxiety, is a fearful and uncomfortable undertaking. We experience the anxiety physically in our bodies. Our hearts race, our voice quivers, we may cry or feel ashamed. This is not fun.

By sweeping our anger under the carpet, we get to avoid feeling the discomfort of it, and we get approval from others for not expressing it. It appears we are doing ourselves a service. However, anger tends to leak out as sarcasm, criticism, resentment, guilt trips, even passive-aggressive behaviors such as chronic lateness. But when we least expect it, it explodes, and we have little control over it when it does. "I couldn't help it. I couldn't stop myself," laments a guilty parent who has just screamed at his child.

But what if you were to acknowledge the anger and accept it as a provoker of needed change? You don't need to make the change happen, just allow the anger. Many fear that this would unleash an untold amount of rage. Take the risk. Let it up a bit at a time. Just be sure to own it.

The Teapot Theory
If you put a pot of water with a lid on the stove, when the water boils, it will "blow its lid" by the strength of the steam, and the water will boil over. A teakettle, however, has an air valve to allow the steam to escape. Anger, emotions of any kind, is like that steam. If it doesn't have an outlet, it may cause a person to "blow his lid" or boil over into rage. But if it has an outlet, it can release to maintain equilibrium.

Opening Up: Stage Three—
Conscious Competency

Increased ability to access emotions increases consciousness and creativity. When you take responsibility for your thoughts and emotions, your perception changes. You have detached. It doesn't matter exactly what words or tools you use, because you will be coming from a place of understanding—your own "emotional intelligence." In stage three, we can no longer blame our anger on others. And when we become detached, we can see solutions—often for the first time.

After I had my heart-to-heart with my daughter Molly, the morning I changed my perspective of her behavior and acknowledged how hard mornings were for her, it was as if my attic had been cleaned out. Suddenly I was able to think clearly again. My mind wasn't cluttered anymore with anger and fear and impatience.

I found two tiny decorative jars with lids that we had in the house and asked Molly to pick which one she liked best. She loved them both but made her choice. I put them on the shelf over the bathroom sink. Then I got ten pennies and made a pile of them between the two jars. Each morning when we got dressed together in the bathroom, the first one dressed got to put a penny in her jar. We didn't make it a race; we just had a little incentive. Molly loved taking the little lid off her jar, dropping the penny in, and putting the lid back. When the pile was gone, we emptied out our jars, counted the pennies to see who had won, and piled them up again to start over. Some mornings Molly just couldn't get it together and didn't care about getting the penny. On those mornings, it was clear to me that she needed a little extra attention, so I helped her get dressed with no feelings of resentment. It was just not a problem for me anymore.

● EXERCISE 12: **Owning My Anger (example)**

When my child _speaks to me with rudeness and disrespect_ ,
(button-pushing behavior)

I feel angry because _I'm afraid I have failed to teach her proper respect_ .

I react to my anger by _shutting down, steaming inside, and walking away_ .

I believe that I feel angry and react this way because _my mother always got quiet_

when she was mad. She always kept it to herself, but I knew .
(what happened to you in the past)

I am placing responsibility for my anger on _my daughter_ , because _if she would_

speak to me respectfully I wouldn't feel this way .

If I take responsibility for it, I will have to _confront her_ .

I avoid responsibility by _keeping quiet and not dealing with it_ .

If I owned my anger in that situation, I would say _I don't like the tone you are us-_

ing. Please say again what you want to say with a different tone .

If I did that, I'm afraid my child would respond by _being sarcastic or ignoring_

_me_ .

I take responsibility for my child's feelings by _blaming myself and not holding her_

accountable by telling her how I feel .

If I give my child responsibility, I am afraid that _she would be mad at me and_

not talk to me ,

but if I do, I will teach him/her _to pay more attention to her words and her tone_

of voice .

● EXERCISE 12: **Owning My Anger**

Please complete either or both of the exercises that follow.
A.

When my child _____ ,
_(button-pushing behavior)

    I feel angry because _____ .

I react to my anger by _____ .

I believe that I feel angry and react this way because _____

_____ .
(what happened to you in the past)

I am placing responsibility for my anger on _____ ,

    because _____ .

If I take responsibility for it, I will have to _____ .

I avoid responsibility by _____ .

If I owned my anger in that situation, I would say _____

_____ .

If I did that, I'm afraid my child would respond by _____

_____ .

I take responsibility for my child's feelings by _____

_____ .

    If I give my child responsibility, I am afraid that _____ ,

    but if I do, I will teach him/her _____

_____ .

● EXERCISE 12: **Owning My Anger (continued)**

B.

Describe how your anger gets in the way of your child's feelings.

Describe how you feel—both positively and negatively—when you blame your child. Guilty, vindicated?

If you take responsibility for your anger and don't blame it on your child, what would your words sound like?

How do you think your child might react differently?

CHAPTER TWENTY-ONE

YOUR CHILD IS YOUR TEACHER

Grown-ups never understand anything for themselves, and it is tiresome for children to be always and forever explaining things to them.
—ANTOINE DE SAINT-EXUPÉRY, *The Little Prince*

Parenting is far less stressful and exhausting when we know it is not up to us to mold our children's characters, fix their problems, and be responsible for their pain. **When we know they are not extensions of ourselves, we can trust their individuality** and know that their wonder and mystery, which sometimes cause them fear, are healthy and appropriate. With this trust, we can learn as much from them as they learn from us.

By pushing our buttons, our children are exposing a problem we hold deep inside. We can look or we can turn away. If we look, healing can take place. Their behavior is signaling their need and at the same time pointing out—sometimes quite harshly—that perhaps the only way we can take care of that need is by taking care of our own first.

What we wanted most from our own parents is what we have the hardest time giving our children—even when we react by overcompensating for what we didn't get.

Martha's mother, Catherine, was a famous author and teacher who was narcissistic and unavailable. Martha was usually left alone with a nanny. When she did get to accompany her mother, she was left in the car with a book and some water, often for hours at a time. Her mother's students were given preferential treatment, and Martha was instructed never to interfere. Despite her mother's affluence, Martha was clothed in hand-me-downs and went on outings only when a friend's parent invited her. She was shipped off to boarding school her freshman year of high school and was allowed home only for Christmas and spring break.

Martha was determined to be the mother she never had. She was heartbroken when she found herself childless after five years of trying to get pregnant. She and her husband adopted a daughter. Martha pampered Carolyn, gave her everything she asked for and more. She never went out unless it was to take Carolyn somewhere. She anticipated her daughter's every desire.

Martha complained sheepishly in class one day that she was becoming aware of feelings that scared her. She confessed that a few days prior she had blurted out to Carolyn, now age nine, "You are selfish and ungrateful. You will stand here and say thank you to me, or you will have no dinner tonight." As she was saying the words, she horrified herself, but they kept on coming. She said she felt possessed.

"And to top it off, Carolyn refused to say thank you, so I sent her to her room without dinner. I had flashbacks of when my mother did the same to me."

"What did she have to say thank you for?" another mother in the group asked.

"I bought her the most adorable dress. She told me she hated it and would wear it over her dead body! Honest to God, I felt like smacking her. If I had been given a dress like that, I would have kissed my mother's feet. And she would have expected it too!"

"Was she with you when you bought the dress?" another parent asked.

"No. I just loved it and wanted to surprise her with it. She usually likes that."

"I wonder if she's becoming a bit more independent of what you want for her," I speculated.

"I guess so. She's not wearing anything I suggest anymore and is putting the weirdest combination of things together. The other morning I wouldn't let her go to school until she had changed. She looked like . . . well, awful." Martha was feeling vulnerable with her confessions. She had always boasted of her positive relationship with her daughter.

"It must feel confusing to you when Carolyn shows no gratitude for what you would have given your right arm for," I offered.

Her resentment began to surface. "How can she be so ungrateful? She just takes me for granted. Who does she think I am anyway?"

"Perhaps she knows you will do anything she wants, because that's what you have devoted your life to." Martha was intrigued and asked me to say more. "And so she hasn't had the chance to learn that you are not to be taken for granted. I imagine you wish you could have taken your mother for granted."

"Wow, what would that have felt like? So, I'm getting angry at her for being the way I wish I could have been? All I wanted was a thank-you. But that's what my mother always demanded of me. It never mattered what I thought. Am I telling Carolyn that what she likes doesn't matter?"

"Maybe," was all I needed to say.

Martha began putting the pieces together quickly. She realized that what she wanted her mother to be for her was not what Carolyn needed or wanted. She had no idea what Carolyn wanted. But she was beginning to see that Carolyn needed her opinions to be taken seriously.

Martha was thinking out loud. "I did everything I could think of for her, because I was so afraid of not being loved. I guess I needed to be loved so badly that I was blind to what Carolyn needed. I thought she would want what I had wished for, and if I gave it to her, she would love me forever." Martha laughed as she admitted this. It was out in the open.

Martha put a lot of work into creating the perfect childhood that she had always wanted. She projected her own wishes onto her daughter and then expected Carolyn to be grateful for everything she was given but didn't even want. Martha was beginning to see that Carolyn's refusal to say "thank you" was her attempt to get her mother to stop and pay attention to *her*.

Carolyn needs a mother who understands and accepts her for who she is, who doesn't ask her to satisfy her mother's frustrations. Exactly the kind of mother Martha needed. When Carolyn pushed her mother's buttons, she tapped into Martha's painful past and the beliefs she held about herself. Martha attempted to block the button pushing—to keep her attic door locked—with her resentment and resulting emotional outburst. So she could only see her daughter behaving selfishly and ungratefully.

In *Giving the Love That Heals,* Helen Hunt and Harville Hendrix say, "It can be a revelation and a relief to understand that what a parent dislikes in her child can exist as a potential for her own further growth. . . . When parents promote the wholeness of their children, their actions are healing for them as well."

Are you willing to allow your children to point the way? Can you acknowledge that the buttons they push are the sore spots that require your attention and care? Can you see that their behavior, frustrating as it may be, is a clue to your need as well as theirs?

To Trust Ourselves

To trust our children, we need to trust ourselves.

Antonio was ten when his father and mother separated. The night before his father left, he raged at Antonio for leaving his tool kit out on the dining room table, where Antonio had been making a project for school. "Whose house do you think this is anyway?" Antonio remembers his father yelling. "You leave your stuff everywhere and never think about anyone else. Nobody likes a selfish, thoughtless person." He then swiped the table clean with one swing of his arm and screamed at Antonio to get to his room.

No reassurance from his mother could convince Antonio that it was not his selfishness and thoughtlessness that had caused his father to leave. He stopped trusting himself. He never looks forward to anything, because he knows he will be disappointed. He doesn't make plans, because he is afraid they won't turn out right, and he will be to blame. Yet fears of the future abound. He envisions catastrophe. He overprotects his children for fear that harm will come to them if he is not near. He is adamant about making sure that they know he will never leave, so he works from home. He refuses to hire a baby sitter or allow his children to spend the night at a friend's. So far they have not been allowed to go on school field trips. Antonio is in danger of passing on his distrust to his children, who might either accept it or resist it with risky behavior.

Antonio knows now that his father did not base his departure on his argument with his son. But still lurking in his attic are the beliefs that his selfishness can cause great harm if he is not vigilant, and that people are not to be trusted. If Antonio can examine, identify, and keep naming the source of his fears and distrust, he will be able to own his fears rather than project them as "the truth." Then when his children want to go to a friend's, he can acknowledge his concern without denying it; he can own it, rather than forcing his children to adopt his beliefs. When he can forgive himself his childish fears, he can have compassion for that little boy hiding in the attic, rather than blame him. Little by little, he will be able to leave his distrust in the past where it belongs.

To not trust ourselves is something we learn. How often did your parents let you decide when you were hungry or full without telling you to eat or not to eat? Was it ever up to you whether you needed a coat or not? Was your opinion ever asked for in family discussions? Did your concerns about school, sports, friends matter? Did you ever win an argument with your parents? How early were you able to decide about events in your life and experience the consequences of those decisions without someone either bailing you out or blaming you?

For many of us, our childish sense of wonder and awe was more often squelched than encouraged, our mysteries and fears overprotected, and our fantasies reined in. We were told to act like a grown-up, not to be silly, and to stop making so much noise. We were given messages that our laughter, play, spontaneity, and babble were annoying or inconvenient. Our taste in music and clothing was looked on with disdain. More often than not we felt a nuisance or a burden to our parents. Our play soon turned to work; our fantasies died with childhood; our spontaneity became organized; our curiosity turned to skepticism.

It's hard to trust ourselves when we never learned how.

Thomas Moore states in *The Re-Enchantment of Everyday Life,* "We have little or no trust that a child's knowledge is real knowledge, that their play is important work, or that the animated world they inhabit is as true as the Newtonian world we prefer. We believe firmly that we have to teach them and that we have nothing to learn from them. In an enchanted world, it would make sense to let children do some of the teaching and to give lessons in what they know best—play, animism, and charm, the very things our culture lacks."

DO I TRUST MYSELF?

- How often am I able to confidently take action or change course in my life to do what I really want?
- Am I clear about what I need to do in order to get what I want? Or if I'm not sure, do I trust that the way will be made clear at the right time?
- Do I feel confident in my decision making?
- Do I feel confident in my parenting?

or

- Do I find myself shying away from doing what I always wanted to do, staying where it feels safe?
- Do I even know what I want in my life? Am I afraid if I don't know, nothing will ever happen?
- Do I shirk from making decisions when I question the outcome?
- Am I chronically afraid that I'm doing the wrong thing?

To Trust Our Children

To trust ourselves, we need to trust our children. Watching what our children can do, perhaps with the courage and expressiveness we were never allowed, we can learn. **To raise our children with the ability to trust themselves is the greatest gift a parent can give.** As respect is learned by being respected, trust is learned by being trusted.

Right away we teach our children to listen to us for the answers, believing that they can't possibly know. But do *we* really know? We don't answer their cries, because we have been told that indulging them leads to habits that will inconvenience our lives and make us miserable. When we tell them what to do, when to do it, and how to do it, we don't allow them to learn from their own mistakes. We fix, nag, do their homework, and make their projects. We sign them up for things they don't want. We tell them what to say and do. And all of it is to make us feel better.

Can we set our standards not by how we think our children should measure up, but by how our standards can measure up to our children's potential? That way our standards provide the guidelines and structure they need to feel secure while giving them the freedom to find their own path and not to follow ours.

Do we ever turn the tables and listen to what they have to tell us? We rarely trust their remarkable capacity for solving their own problems, handling their own feelings, asking for help when they need it, and pointing things out to us that we have missed. Shouldn't we trust that they actually do have their own best interests in mind?

We need to trust their integrity, and that their button-pushing behavior is a struggle to preserve that integrity. When their cue goes unanswered or is misinterpreted, their integrity goes into fight mode. Their behavior has to get more and more dramatic in further attempts to make us see, to grab our attention, to let us know they are floundering. We must trust these cues. When we do, our children will learn to trust themselves.

Molly Teaches Me Again

My daughter, Molly, continues to teach me even when I think my active parenting is done. It still isn't easy to have her tell me with her words or her silence that I need to change what I'm doing.

The summer before she left for college, the new lesson she had to teach was how to let go. I thought I was doing a perfectly fine job of it, even though it was hard.

She had always needed home-alone time, but she used to hang out downstairs. That summer, she had a different agenda. Whenever she wasn't working or with her friends, she was alone in her room. Conversations ended. She became more impatient with her father and me, and her rude comments and attitude pushed our buttons. After a number of unpleasant interchanges, I lost it. My button flew into Zone 4 on the Button Meter. We were at an impasse, and communication stopped entirely for a couple of weeks. I tried to get through to her, but to no avail. I was hurt and at a loss.

After much self-talk and deliberation, I slowly came to realize that she needed a clean break in order to separate and begin her new life at college. We had always been extremely close. Now she needed her independence. And the only way she knew how to get it, while still living at home, was to shut down.

She had been home all summer working hard with little time for herself. A family friend three thousand miles away suggested we send her out. I said it was impossible. A voice yelled inside my head, "Why should I give her anything? She's rude and unappreciative. Shouldn't she be held accountable?" But it finally occurred to me that this might be an opportunity for her to get what she *needed*. My husband agreed.

I presented the idea of the trip to her. She jumped at the chance, and we agreed to split the cost. She had many complicated connections to make, switching planes, getting a bus, catching a ferry—plenty of occasions to test her wings.

Some might see this as a reward for hurtful behavior. But we took the chance. I put the voice that told me she was "getting away with it" in the guest room and let her go. She came back, not only from the trip but into our relationship. But it is a different relationship. Now we are struggling to be two independent adults together. When I honor her independence first, she can honor me.

What Molly taught me was that I needed to separate in *her* way, not in *my* way. She's an introvert; I'm an extrovert. We process things very differently. My job as her mother is to help her find *her* way, not do it *my* way.

Molly continues to demand that I understand her needs. She has never been one to acquiesce. Her will has taught me to let her travel her own journey. I get tremendous satisfaction and fulfillment from supporting that journey and watching it unfold, even though the pain of letting go is very real.

The belief that I held from my childhood—*I don't count*—has made it hard at times to empathize and understand her need when that old belief gets triggered by her behavior. It seems that she's saying to me *You don't count*. But I have learned that I *do* count, that my needs *are* important; so when I stop and think, I can see her behavior differently. When I trust myself, I can trust her as well. So far, trusting her has paid off.

Reparenting Ourselves: Learning from the Past

It wasn't until I had Molly that I saw what was missing from my own childhood. She was screaming no in situations where I, as a child, would have conceded. I resented letting her get away with something I never could. But when I understood where my resentment came from, I could see that I had a right to say no too. I could then give her what I had never had. In the giving, I have gained in self-confidence and self-trust.

Put yourself back into the shoes of the child you once were. Look at what that child wished for. It may be painful if she was ignored, denied, abused, or used. You may have shoved her into the back corner of that attic if the shame was great. You may not want to remember, because it's possible that she blamed herself for whatever happened and still feels the blame. But reach in to her. She needs your hand.

When we can give what we did not get, our giving comes back to us. But if we protect our buttons and keep our wounds hidden, we pass the hurt on to our children and stay attached to our past. **We cannot use our children to fix our problems, but we can use our children to help us heal.**

All it takes to begin is awareness.

● EXERCISE 13: **Myself as Teacher (example)**

When my child ___*wants to do something I think he is too young for*___ ,
(behavior or event)

　　I react by ___*telling him he can't and keeping him at home*___ .

This reminds me of when I was a child and ___*I got to do anything I wanted and*___

　　my parents didn't seem to care. I wanted them to tell me I couldn't do some-
(state what happened or what feelings came up)

　　thing .

I reacted by ___*sometimes getting into trouble to try to get a reaction out of them*___ .
(childhood behavior you did in reaction to what happened)

What I was trying to tell my parent was ___*that I count and I wanted them to get in-*___

　　volved with my life and school stuff—to know who my friends were .
(what you wished you could have said about what you did)

If my parent had heard that, s/he might have ___*started paying more attention to what*___

　　I was doing and realized that I needed a parent to watch out for me .

What I wish s/he had learned from me is ___*that my getting into trouble was a call for*___

　　attention instead of being disrespectful and bad .

If that had happened ___*I probably wouldn't have gotten into trouble*___

　　_____ .

And I would have learned that ___*I was cared about and important*___

　　_____

　　_____

　　_____

　　_____

● EXERCISE 13: **Myself as Teacher**

Please complete either or both of the exercises that follow.
A.

When my child _____ ,

(behavior or event)

   I react by _____ .

This reminds me of when I was a child and _____

_____

(state what happened or what feelings came up)

_____ .

I reacted by _____ .

(childhood behavior you did in reaction to what happened)

What I was trying to tell my parent was _____

_____

(what you wished you could have said about what you did)

If my parent had heard that, s/he might have _____

_____ .

What I wish s/he had learned from me is_____

_____ .

If that had happened _____

_____ .

And I would have learned that _____

_____

_____

_____ .

● EXERCISE 13: **Myself as Teacher (continued)**

B.

Describe an incident from your childhood that your child's behavior may remind you of.

What were you trying to tell your parent/s with your behavior?

If your parent/s had known that, how would you have hoped they would respond?

How do you think you might respond differently today if that had happened?

● EXERCISE 14: My Child as Teacher (example)

I have set up barriers with my child that have prevented good communication by

telling him what he should do and expecting him to do what I say

_____ .

My child has reacted to those barriers by *not doing what I tell him, being defiant,*

and always insisting he doesn't need any help—and then messing up .

If I were a child now, I probably would react to me by *either doing it to be a good*

girl or, if I had been allowed to be myself, probably exactly what he is doing .

What my child is teaching me is *I am being too overpowering. He needs to make*

his own mistakes, and I need to let go .

I can listen better now because I understand that *his resistance to me is not*

necessarily to make me mad but to tell me what he needs .

What I need to learn from my child is *that he needs to have more independence*

and make some of his own decisions ,

because *if I don't, I'm going to get more and more resistance until he can*

walk out the door and not come back .

So, from now on, instead of *telling him what to do, which would be my way* ,

I will *first ask him what he thinks would be the best way, even if I don't think*

it's very smart, I will let him do it anyway and learn from his own mistakes

_____ .

● EXERCISE 14: **My Child as Teacher**

Please complete either or both of the exercises that follow.
A.

I have set up barriers with my child that have prevented good communication by

_____

_____ .

My child has reacted to those barriers by _____

_____ .

If I were a child now, I probably would react to me by _____

_____ .

What my child is teaching me is _____

_____ .

I can listen better now because I understand that _____

_____ .

What I need to learn from my child is _____ ,

because _____

_____ .

So, from now on, instead of _____ ,

I will _____

_____

_____ .

● EXERCISE 14: **My Child as Teacher (continued)**

B.

What barriers do you recognize that you have set up between you and your child? And how does your child react to them?

How do you think you would react to them if you were in your child's shoes?

What do you think your child is trying to tell you with the behavior that pushes your buttons?

If you listened to that, how do you think you would respond differently?

What is it you think you need to learn from your child?

CHAPTER TWENTY-TWO

THE LIGHT AT THE END OF THE TUNNEL

*Obstacles are those frightful things you see
when you take your eyes off your goal.*
—HENRY FORD

The goal of defusing your button is to disengage from the situation enough so that you will become neutral. Being neutral means that you won't *react*. Being neutral means that you will *respond* in a way that can be heard by your children. Being neutral means that you won't take their behavior personally. You will have more appropriate perceptions of your children that will not generate the emotions you hate. You will get your message across as it was intended. You will be able to step into your child's shoes, see his problem, understand his agenda, and empathize with his point of view. You will be able to set clear limits and establish strong boundaries. Your respectful response will elicit cooperation and listening more often than not.

Putting parenting skills into practice effectively requires both neutrality and compassion. Neutrality allows an objective perspective so that creative solutions are available. Compassion allows you to be able to say, *My child has a problem. How can I help?* instead of *How can he be such a problem?* It means you can reach across the gap and look at what your child needs rather than being stuck in your own head focused on yourself. Compassion grants you the perspective of your child as a whole, important individual rather than as an unruly problem needing to be molded and tamed.

There are no "5 easy steps" to change the way you react when your buttons get pushed. But here are some reminders of what to do. Review chapter 18 for more help. Use the easy times to practice. If you are in Zone 1 or 2 on the Button Meter—annoyed or frustrated rather than enraged—practice defusing. Don't let a minor button go by and wait for a major explosion to begin work on your new habits. It will be much easier to deal with harder times when you have some small successes under your belt.

WHAT TO DO WHEN YOUR BUTTON GETS PUSHED

- **Stop. Breathe.** Walk away if you need to
- **Detach! Detach! Detach!**
- Notice your **agenda**
- Acknowledge your **feelings**
- Identify your **assumptions**
- Don't take it personally—**it's not about you!**
- Change your **perspective**—think differently
- Use affirmative **self-talk**
  - —Check **accuracy** of assumptions
  - —Are your assumptions **productive**?
  - —Add "**because**" to your assumption
- Look at the **behavior** as your **cue**
  - —*What is this behavior trying to tell me?*
  - —*What do I need to learn?*
- Reach across the gap and **connect**

Later:
- Identify your **standards** and **beliefs**
- **Adjust** your standards

When you get your button pushed, you can punish your child for pushing it, or you can listen to what the button has to tell you, take responsibility for it, and discipline more effectively. "Because I'm the boss, and I say so" or, "Whatever you want, sweetie" are the two extremes that come easily, but they don't work in raising responsible, respectful people.

Reactive parenting is no fun. It is what turns us into the screaming maniacs we hate and what causes us to fall into bed at night exhausted, drained, and worried. What standards you are willing to let go of, what you hang onto with fierce conviction, and what you are willing to negotiate strongly affect whether your children cooperate or rebel.

Choose the journey toward parenting that is mindful and aware. Finding what works for both you and your child takes much more effort but is far more rewarding in the end.

Allow for regression and failures. You cannot learn new habits without them. Don't expect years of old patterns to disappear quickly. Self-discovery is a peeling-away process—one layer at a time. Think of peeling the leaves of an artichoke one leaf at a time, slowly but surely exposing the heart.

Blocked emotions are based on fear. Channel your fears into courage. Courage to feel without blame or defense, to take action, to change old patterns. Courage requires vulnerability. Courage means having the guts to be yourself and accept everything that comes with you.

Connection with your child is the goal. It is the moments of connection your child will remember. Connection makes a lifetime of difference.

APPENDIX

A t the end of my "Buttons" course, I give parents the assignment of writing a mission statement for their parenting based on their new understanding. Most parents are daunted by the assignment but are grateful after they complete it. Many consider it the most valuable part of the class.

I encourage you to do the same. Think of this as a new job description for your parenting. Use whatever form of writing you feel most comfortable with: bullet points, before-and-after lists, journal writing—there is no right or wrong way to do it. You are creating new standards for you and your child to live by. Do not be concerned if you are not presently parenting in the way your mission statement describes. This is your goal, your intention from now on. Write in the present tense, using "I" as the pronoun. And write as if you are parenting this way 100 percent of the time. Then aim for over 50 percent to start. When it is written as the truth, it has a way of becoming the truth—a new self-fulfilling prophecy.

With their permission, I am including a few mission statements from parents in my groups to stimulate and encourage you to write your own. Listen to the new standards they are establishing. Each time a parent reads his or hers in the last class, it is never less than inspiring.

When my child isn't listening to me or cooperating, I know that I can step back rather than immediately react. By stepping back, I can see our surroundings more fully and how I might plug into or connect with him. Instead of setting up corners of silence or walls of belligerent resistance, I give my child and myself permission to be ourselves, to fully express ourselves. I allow enough room for all emotions and responses, which elicits more creative solutions than I ever thought were available.

I used to believe it was my job to maintain the household by keeping everyone happy. I used to believe that children were to be presented in public with a neat appearance and good, respectful behavior in an on-time manner and in good health and to make myself and others happy.

I now believe that it's okay to have a noisy house until the children go to bed, and that I don't have to run the whole house by myself. The belief I hold closest to my heart today is that children need to be and feel respected. I now know that if they feel respected, they will return the feeling with actions and words. I understand that we all have our good days and our bad days, which makes getting through the bad days much easier. Being on time isn't worth the negative feelings and actions that it takes with children sometimes. Forcing children to dress, behave, eat, or speak in a specific way is not a realistic, respectful, or productive way of parenting.

Old Standard:

"Giving in" to my child means she will become spoiled, and it will feel like she is controlling me.

New Standard:

I now believe that "giving in" usually means I am able to adapt my ideas about a situation so that I can say yes to her. It also means more of my time and understanding, which is a *good* thing for her. I will think about what she is asking me to do and think about the consequences. Are they so bad that I cannot say yes? If she wants to put water on her cereal, I'll say yes (she'll probably never try it again). If she wants to make her own cereal, I'll say yes. It only means a few extra minutes than if I did it myself.

Commandments I will live by as I parent my children:
  I will guide rather than control.
  I will trust rather than mistrust.
  I will listen rather than react.
  I will celebrate rather than judge the differences among us.
  I will be honest with and honor my feelings as well as those
    of others.
  I will feel adequate rather than guilty.
  I will find a way to express anger without hurting others.
  I will be grateful for and appreciate the gifts we each bring.
  I will take time to consider, review, and reflect before deciding
    on a course of action in an unwanted situation.
  I will parent from my heart rather than my head.
  I will find the courage to honor these commandments.

1. I am learning that it is OK for my children to whine and have temper tantrums. They need to express their feelings. I need to remember that it is age-appropriate and that they are more important to me than others' expectations of me.
2. When my children fight or struggle, it is not my job to make them stop or fix it but to listen and affirm their emotions. I will strive to trust them to work out their own problems and will endeavor to teach them the problem-solving skills that will help equip them for the many problems they will face in life.
3. When I reach my own toleration limit, I need to respect myself as well as my children and allow myself the right to feel angry or hurt or whatever emotion surfaces. I have a right to be respected and listened to, and so do my children. Often I need to readjust my expectations so that they are realistic.

4. I need to own my feelings and convey them honestly to my children, modeling that it is OK to be hurt or sad or angry but not to hit or blame or make another responsible for my emotions. I need to trust them and let go of my need to control them. I must believe that they will learn and grow and develop a sense of ethics without telling them what to do and believe. I have to trust their inner goodness, respect them as individuals, and love them for who they are.

Old: "A good mother should feel secure in all her decisions surrounding boundaries and discipline issues with her children."

New: "I accept that I do not have all the answers but continue to learn from and listen to my child while respecting my boundaries and the boundaries of others."

Old: "Children should listen and want to do whatever I ask without disagreement. My agenda should be my children's agenda."

New: "I consider my children's age-appropriate behavior and honor their agenda, hoping to develop a spirit of cooperation."

Old: "A mother's job is to instill a sense of order in her children's lives."

New: "It is important to model a sense of order for my children but not to impose my order on them."

Old: "My child's behavior is a direct reflection of my competency."

New: "Each of my children have their own temperament and personality. Therefore their behavior and decisions are not a reflection of my competency."

Old: "If I am a good mother, my children will love me at all times."

New: "I am able to allow my children to express feelings and disagreements without it being a reflection of their love for me."

1. My children deserve love, respect, and clear communication at all times.

2. When I am stressed, and my children stimulate the feelings that

are simmering below my surface, I will remember to step away emotionally and find a rational way to defuse the situation.

3. I will find three effective ways to reduce my stress, so that the great dad I am will be available.

4. When I think my daughter has erected a stone wall, I will remind myself it is only a stone, and there is always a way around it.

5. Rather than punish negative behavior, I will wait until I can offer a consequence that makes sense or let a consequence come from the real world.

The power of writing is not to be underestimated. How often do we actually take the time to put our goals for our most important job in writing and then make a conscious commitment to them? Isn't it worth it? Is there any better way to spend your next half hour?

MY MISSION STATEMENT

_____
_____
_____
_____
_____
_____
_____
_____
_____
_____
_____
_____
_____
_____
_____
_____
_____
_____
_____
_____
_____
_____
_____

SUGGESTED READING

Arriens, Angeles. *The Four Fold Way: Walking the Paths of the Warrior, Teacher, Healer and Visionary.* HarperSanFrancisco, 1993.

Bennett-Goleman, Tara. *Emotional Alchemy: How the Mind Can Heal the Heart.* New York: Harmony Books, 2001.

Branden, Nathaniel. *The Art of Living Consciously: The Power of Awareness to Transform Everyday Life.* New York: Fireside, 1997.

Fishel, Elizabeth. *Family Mirrors: What Our Children's Lives Reveal about Ourselves.* Boston: Houghton Mifflin, 1991.

Goleman, Daniel. *Emotional Intelligence: Why It Can Matter More Than IQ.* New York: Bantam Books, 1995.

Hendrix, Harville, and Helen Hunt. *Giving the Love That Heals: A Guide for Parents.* New York: Pocket Books, 1997.

Hillman, James. *The Soul's Code: In Search of Character and Calling.* New York: Warner Books, 1996.

Kabat-Zinn, Jon and Myla. *Everyday Blessings: The Inner Work of Mindful Parenting.* New York: Hyperion, 1997.

Kurcinka, Mary Sheedy. *Kids, Parents and Power Struggles.* New York: HarperCollins, 2000.

———. *Raising Your Spirited Child.* New York: HarperCollins, 1991.

Lerner, Harriet. *The Dance of Anger.* New York: Harper and Row, Publishers, 1985.

———. *The Mother Dance.* New York: HarperCollins, 1998.

Liedloff, Jean. *The Continuum Concept: Allowing Human Nature to Work Successfully.* Addison-Wesley Publishing Company, 1977.

————. *The Dance of Connection*. New York: HarperCollins, 2001.

Miller, Alice. *For Your Own Good: Hidden Cruelty in Child-Rearing and the Roots of Violence*. New York: Farrar, Straus, Giroux, 1984.

————. *The Drama of the Gifted Child*. New York: Basic Books, 1981.

Moore, Thomas. *Care of the Soul: A Guide for Cultivating Depth and Sacredness in Everyday Life*. New York: HarperCollins, 1992.

————. *The Re-Enchantment of Everyday Life*. New York: HarperCollins, 1996.

Ruiz, Don Miguel. *The Four Agreements*. San Rafael, California: Amber-Allen Publishing, 1997.

Samalin, Nancy. *Love and Anger: The Parental Dilemma*. Penguin Books, 1991.

Seligman, Martin E. P., et al. *The Optimistic Child*. New York: Harper Perennial, 1995.

Tannen, Deborah. *I Only Say This Because I Love You*. New York: Ballantine Books, 2001.

Zukav, Gary. *The Seat of the Soul*. New York: Fireside, 1990.

INDEX

Index

ABOUT THE AUTHOR

BONNIE HARRIS, M.S.ED., has worked with thousands of parents in her parent education classes and lectures over the past fifteen years. She founded The Parent Guidance Center in Peterborough, NH, where she developed The Effective Parenting Workshop, a twelve-week program and curriculum guide. Bonnie has designed and taught a variety of courses for parents of infants through teens and has trained parent educators and professionals who work with children and families. She has a newspaper column, and a counseling practice for parents and families. She received her masters degree in Early Childhood Education from Bank St. College of Education in New York City with a specialization in Infant and Parent Development. In her previous life, she was a professional actress in New York City. Her most important learning has come from mothering her son Casey, who is grown and launched, and daughter, Molly, who is only a few steps behind. She lives with her husband, Baxter, and their dog, Tucker, on a beautiful hill in New Hampshire.

Her website is www.bonnieharris.com.